When I first met Glenn Gregory, there were numerous small operators in the Interior of Alaska. Glenn's Tanana Air Service was one of the very few that I would say was successful. His was a far cry from the typical operation. He proved himself to be a professional as an airman and as a businessman.

When Glenn brought his aircraft to Bachners Aircraft for maintenance, we knew exactly what he expected. That was a piece of equipment that was properly serviced, safe, and trouble-free until the next scheduled maintenance.

There were hitches however. The one that still burns in my memory is the time Glenn's senses caught the first sign of engine trouble and he turned back to town. He ended up making a very successful off-airport landing with a plane full of people. No damage, no injuries. I'm still very thankful that Glenn was at the controls.

We all had a lot of respect for Glenn. He was a valued customer, but better than that, a valued friend.

-- Ed Keith
(Bachner's Aircraft)

To Howard,

A successful Bush Pilot learned, early on, that a good mechanic should be among his circle of friends.

Glenn R Gregory

Some books are written about famous people who were legends, and others were said to be heroes, but these are not required for a good life.

Glenn Gregory was born before the big depression, which was a time of no money, little food, some clothing and self education was a must. This education was composed of imagination, honesty, truthfulness, cleanliness, but plenty of hard work and helping your fellow man. The author, over the years, has fulfilled his education by following these guidelines. The stories told herein are how these guidelines were directed.

In 1951, Glenn married Lena Laraux, of Akiak, Alaska, a wonderful girl and over the years raised eight children, seven girls and one boy. For a number of years, Glenn was busy making a living and educating their children as he was educated.

The life on this planet is a strange thing. By living a life-style as told in this publication, the later years of life will always be rewarding. You don't have to be a legend or a hero; however, by living a good and wholesome life, you may become both and not realize what has happened to you.

-- Randy Acord

Stretching between the lifesaving efforts of the health aides in Rampart and St. Joseph's hospital in Fairbanks, were eighty-five miles of night, flying over mountainous country. None of us, including the badly burned patient, doubted that Glenn could do it; it was a long night.

--Valerie Matthew

Never Too Late
to be a
HERO

Glenn R. Gregory

PEANUT BUTTER
PUBLISHING

Seattle, Washington
Portland, Oregon

LOC 95-069876
ISBN 0-89716-571-3
12.0036
Cover design: David Marty
Editing & Production: Elizabeth Lake

First Printing November 1995
Second printing March 1996
10 9 8 7 6 5 4 3

Peanut Butter Publishing
226 2nd Avenue West • Seattle, WA 98119
Old Post Office Bldg. • 510 S.W. 3rd • Portland, OR 97201
Cherry Creek • 50 S. Steele • Suite 850 • Denver, CO 80209
Su. 230 1333 Johnston St. Pier 32 Granville Isl., Vancouver, B.C. V6H 3R9
e mail: P NUT PUB@aol.com
http://www.pbpublishing.com

Printed in the United States of America

Dedication

To the colorful old timers who awakened the "Spirit of the North" in my soul.

      Names like Billy Melvin, Paddy Daugherty, Harvey Van Hook, "Moose John," Harry Badger, "Papa & Mamma" Raats, Eddie McKinzie, George Harris, Joe Ferris, Billy Goldbraugh, Frank Costa, Walter "Blank" Blankenship, John Sommer, John Hajdukovich, "Rika" Wallen, "Old" Stockman, "Old Butch," Frank Glazer, Dick Jensen, and my father-in-law, Arthur Laraux, come to mind—and many other faces that I can see by just closing my eyes but to which I fail to be able to attach a name. Some told the typical stories that still enthrall the listener, others revealed more of their nature and experience just in their casual conversation, but all shone with that aura of zest for living and freedom of spirit they all cherished above all else. To the man, they cherished their freedom and independence from a life regimented by laws and restrictions. They allowed others the privilege to exercise their own personal opinions and idiosyncrasies. Just to be in the atmosphere created by those old timers gave me the drive and desire to live many of the experiences they described. I have enjoyed a life of tranquility I would trade for nothing.

Table of Contents

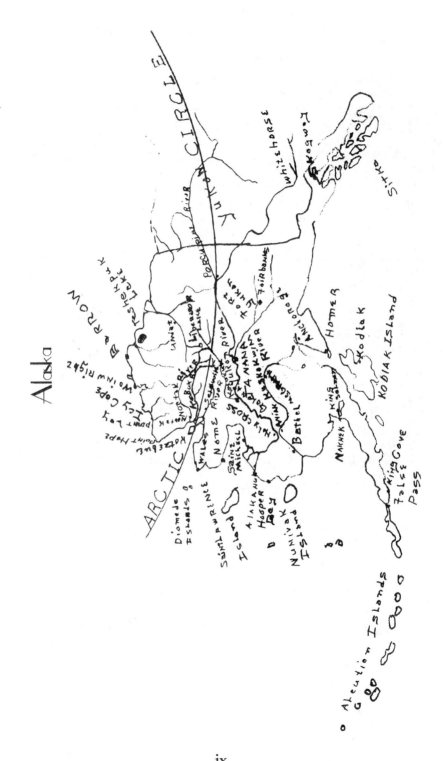

Forward

This autobiographical collection of short stories is full of entertaining characters and interesting places. It chronicles many of the excursions made by this adventurous, resourceful bush pilot. The reader gets a real feel for Alaska's many different facets. He can be an armchair explorer, sharing some incredible experiences about the trials and tribulations of living and flying in and about the Alaskan bush.

-- Elizabeth Lake

Acknowledgments

The original manuscript for this work was written to pay tribute to all those wonderful friends and acquaintances who contributed to my education, knowledge of life, and this great land of the north. Glowing descriptions and spellbinding tales were set down on paper to enthrall the reader. After submitting that material to writers with much more knowledge and experience than I, it was necessary to descend the stairway back to Earth and employ a cleaver and rendering kettle.

Jim Rearden assured me he had actually read every chapter submitted, which was to me, a compliment in itself. He impressed upon me that he knew what he was saying was not what I wanted to hear but, conversely, he was only half correct. I wanted to hear the pure, unadulterated truth. If repairs were to be made I needed expert guidance in finding the starting place. Once an error is identified it can be corrected. I also realized that he could not teach me in one letter what he had spent forty years learning. Naturally, I would have been enthralled had he told me the manuscript needed nothing that he could add, but realistically that was not even remotely in the realm of possibility. For his honest critique, I am deeply grateful.

Lael Morgan also paid me the compliment of reading the entire manuscript. It will give the readers a chuckle, and an appreciation of those two professionals, just to know that I was so naive as to submit to both a printout single-spaced in size ten type. I am amazed that either more than opened the envelope, much less read the entire manuscript. To both I extend my most heartfelt apology. Lael Morgan also suggested it might be wise to start all over by just shelving the entire manuscript and using it as a treasure trove for future reference. That was done. The maddening lack of chronology was rectified.

Jim Rearden advised that I could probably use all the original anecdotes.

When my own life experiences were inserted to provide the common thread and chronology necessary the result would have been so voluminous it would have put James Michener to shame.

Dermot Cole took the time from his hectic schedule to read and analyze the product of my pen. His critique and encouragement was articulated in such a way that it brought all the suggestions and critiques of the previous reviewers into a much clearer focus. To him I extend my gratitude.

In the parlance of dog mushing circles, one often hears that races are won, not so much by the dogs in the team, but by the judicious selection of the ones to be left behind. It is hoped that the trimming and elimination process has resulted in the dogs necessary to produce a winning team.

Mention was made of many of those with whom I worked in the early years of my learning process; due to the trimming, rendering, sluicing, and arbitrary selection of the 'dogs' to be dropped, many of my friends may, to their great relief, search in vain for mention of their name in some anecdote in which they actually played a part. Lest they become too smug, those stories still exist in the aforementioned treasure trove and may yet surface to embarrass them in some future race.

This work was assembled strictly from memory, a faculty of which I have always been justly proud. My ability to recall incidents and category them chronologically is exceeded only by that of my wife of over forty years. I boast no detailed diary with which I can prove the finest of points nor have I kept the famous, meticulous log book to the last minute. I have always been able to substantiate, when necessary, times or happenings from the flight records—the keeping of which is mandatory. As a consequence of not having such written records for reference at my fingertips at all times, anecdotes are produced from memory to the best of my ability to be correct and honest. There will be no quarrel, on my part, with anyone who was a player, on the scene at any time, who remembers things differently than I do. I sincerely hope I have embarrassed no one by simply telling the truth as I saw it.

My thanks goes to Bob Zwilling for being my friend for over fifty years, during which time he has influenced and encouraged me on many occasions. His knowledgeable suggestions and critiques have been helpful. He steered me into a text book that greatly improved my ability to properly utilize the King's English.

I am grateful to my daughter, Vicky Phipps, for her reading and correcting grammar and spelling. I appreciate the consideration, patience and encouragement received from all my family, especially my little neglected wife.

I would certainly be derelict if I failed to mention that people have been telling me for fifty years, "You should write a book." I have thought about it and even started to assemble the material only to launch some other project that took precedence over the book. It was Marian Acord who finally pushed the button that actually engaged the mechanism which sat me down to the typewriter. There have been a number of times that I was not sure whether to thank her or cast a hex upon her future, but after all is said and done, writing this has been an extreme pleasure. For one thing it has left my conscience clear from the guilt of feeling there was some task yet unaccomplished.

My sincere thanks to Randy Acord for his suggestions and encouragement, verification of facts relating to dates, instrument procedures, types of equipment etc., with which I was less familiar than he.

I would be remiss if I failed to acknowledge the hand of Brian Thompson, one of our former pilots and a longtime friend. It is hereby appropriate to offer him thanks for sending me a little book detailing procedures for publishing which has made it possible to avoid errors and wasted time. His constant encouragement has also been appreciated.

Last, but not least, my thanks to Elizabeth Lake for her editing and suggestions which helped polish this work for presentation as a work to be enjoyed.

The Dream

Once upon a midnight dreary, as I stumbled weak and weary
O'er many fallen logs along the mighty Yukon shore.
The rising moon inspiring, my dog team slowly tiring
As I drew nearer to my lonely cabin door.

The northern lights were glowing and the wind was gently blowing
O'er a great and glorious land of gold and lore.
As the stars began to twinkle, you could almost hear them tinkle
As I drew nearer to my lonely cabin door.

I was through my frozen lashes peering as the cabin I was nearing
When I heard that mournful, eerie, lonely howl!
The moan was deeply thrilling, the thought was so blood-chilling,
That now I knew some wily wolves were on the prowl.

I drew safety from the fire as the glowing flames grew higher
In my cabin on the lonely Yukon shore.
With the huskies in their bedding, from a long, full day of sledding,
I wanted rest, food and warmth, and nothing more.

As the coals continued glowing and my thoughts commenced their flowing,
My deep slumber turned to happy, vivid dreams.
With age and time retarded and all aches and pains discarded,
In my youth, I was back panning in the streams.

Though I'd tramped for many miles the bright gold seemed there in piles—
It made the panning, sluicing, cooking, just a chore.
Many happy days I'd spent, in the cabin or the tent
On rocky streams along the lonely Yukon shore.

The summertime did wane; the ducks, and geese, and crane
Headed south for lakes with warmer, friendly shore.
And where I'd spend my find? A thought foreign to my mind
For say I, "Leave the Yukon?—Nevermore!"

As snowflakes began descending, their weight the branches bending,
The rivers, creeks, and lakes were frozen o'er.
With trails and lines extended to catch the fur intended
For damsels on a distant, foreign shore.

Many storms would soon be brewing in the days that were ensuing
As nights and shadows longer grew.
New life began its glowing as spring melt began its flowing;
Ducks and geese and cranes all northward flew.

In my chair I am still shifting as back to sleep I'm drifting
As my sweet dreams I harbor just once more.
Almost time to stop my wishing and begin my summer fishing
From my cabin on the lonely Yukon shore.

Like the river in it's bending, 'tis a life that's never ending,
For alas, it has gone full circle just once more.
Though I've spent the night in dreaming-'tis a life that's ever gleaming
In my cabin on the lonely Yukon shore.

There are lovely spots I reckon, and at times I'm sure they'll beckon
From some southern city, plain, or shore.
And though I may search for El Dorado in Mt. McKinley's shadow
Shall I leave it? Will I leave it? Nevermore!

-- Glenn R. Gregory
Copyright © 1984

Preface

At the end of World War II, stepping out of the military uniform and into woolen shirt, long handled underwear, socks, scarf, and a pair of Eskimo mukluks, was, for me, not a difficult transition. In doing so I was entering an atmosphere relatively unspoiled by modern man.

Never one to feel comfortable in crowds, conversely, I felt very comfortable on my stomach on top of a gravel knoll, overlooking a large valley, watching a huge bull moose move closer to my position in response to my calls. In every direction was God's handiwork—unspoiled and beautiful. A person enthralled by such an experience feels extremely inadequate describing those feelings to others.

A saying that originated during the Dawson gold rush days stated there were nothing but *MEN* in the Yukon—the cowards had never started the tedious trek over the treacherous Chilkoot Pass and the weak had all died on the way!

I am proud to be able to say I personally knew a number of the men and women who climbed that mountain, crossed Lake Bennett, then rafted or poled a boat down the Yukon past the Whitehorse Rapids to Dawson. To them it was no big accomplishment because everyone else in Dawson had arrived in like manner.

One of the character traits common among all the Sourdoughs it was my privilege to meet was their willingness to accept a person at face value. If a person later proved unworthy of that trust, that was a different matter.

Law and order, to a very high degree, was maintained simply through the medium of respect and ridicule. No one wished to be the subject of ridicule so most people conducted themselves so it would never happen. However, if one did find himself the butt of the joke, those old miners could pull it off with a wit and humor to which no man could take offense and retain any degree of dignity and self-respect. I later learned the Eskimos were masters at the same game. That was probably the origin.

On becoming acquainted with the extreme cold of winter and the bountiful offerings of summer, the incomprehensible power of the Mighty Yukon River at breakup time and the smooth, placid waters of summer lakes and streams, the tortuous fields of muskeg on the level and the magnificent mountain backdrops, I learned an admiration and respect for those old Sourdoughs which taxes my ability to adequately describe. Just being accepted and respected by that caliber of friends left me with a feeling of obligation to provide a service to them that would return to me a livelihood. In doing so, I was constantly privileged to associate with them and revel in the atmosphere provided by this magnificent country.

Referring to society in general, few people ever know the thrill of mushing a team of dogs. Observers unfamiliar with a dog team may feel dogs are driven, but in reality, allowing them the privilege of being a member of a team is the ultimate reward. In their desire to be off, even on a freight run, they will set up a howl of intensity that is unmatched by any draft animal that has ever come to my attention. That enthusiasm penetrates the senses of the driver, leaving him with a feeling of awe for such a faithful, willing companion. A good driver becomes one of the team.

One becomes awe stricken by the observance of northern lights which appear across the sky in a set of colorful bars that appear as shafts of light piercing a layer of clouds. On occasions the lights are shimmering colors, like a flag waving in a light breeze. At other times they are bars, then they change from one to the other. When questioners ask how I tolerate the extremes of Alaska, I can only pity them for their lack of ability to comprehend and appreciate the handiwork of our Maker.

Those old Sourdoughs were all rugged individualists— doing things their own way and by themselves most of the time. Villages seldom contained a group of old timers who found it even important to get together and cooperate doing things— until one of their own fell upon hard times. If a cabin burned down, no meeting was ever necessary, they just did what had to be done to get the unfortunate ones back into a home and into business.

By following a commercial flying career for over thirty years, I was constantly able to maintain contact with the people of the bush: solid, unspoiled people who understood nature as God created it. I was their solid contact with civilization. I was often their salvation in times of emergency.

In telling some of the story of a lifetime spent in the greatest country I have ever known, I have presented some wit and humor that should offend no one. My ability to tell a story as it happened has been adequate to bring pleasure to many who were not as fortunate as I have been. It is hoped the reader can join those ranks.

On occasion, descriptions seem redundant, but it is only because of a sincere desire to describe God's creations so the reader can visualize them as they are. It is seldom possible to paint the word picture with perfection.

In learning the art of flying an aircraft by instruments, navigating by using sophisticated equipment and locating devices, or building vast dams, bridges, and buildings, man is not overcoming nature, but learning to work with it.

The knowledge that the Creator placed all of these wonderful possibilities here for us, if we can but comprehend and use them, should tend to keep us all humble. An attempt to bring some of this knowledge to the surface has been followed throughout this book.

North

Our wood yard was across a narrow creek, so located that it made a very nice roadbed for about three hundred yards. We had crossed the same creek several times with a large truck hauling ten cords of wood. We used that route daily on foot. Once each day I would drive my pickup over it to take a cord of wood to a customer in Fairbanks. This stand of trees we had saved from the ravages of fire a couple years before.

On one particular trip, Carl came out to check some marten traps. Just as we were beginning to turn off the ice, walking up the bank in the same tracks where we always drove, I dropped straight through the ice clear up to my armpits. "Stay right there, stay right there," Carl said.

It was forty below. I thought he must have lost his reason, but I realized the water did feel warm and Carl had a lifetime of experience in the far north. Soon Carl had two huge fires blazing and called to me to come on out of the water. He hustled me between those two fires and started taking off my clothes. I was really surprised at how fast my clothes froze. I would never have been able to build my own fires or get my own clothes removed before stiff clothing and fingers would have made it impossible.

As I stood there on a six-inch mat of green spruce boughs, between two blazing fires, in my black-handled underwear, turning like a leg of lamb on a perpendicular rotisserie while a fog of steam was rising as the underwear dried, I couldn't help wondering what had brought me to this point in life. Did I orchestrate this, or did it just happen?

1

I was born in Dolores, Colorado in 1925. Economically, those were good times. The great depression was still four years away. My father, a cattleman, was in his youth and vigor. My mother, who knew cattle and horses as well as any range hand, was twenty-one years of age, healthy, and could ride anything you could saddle. Having been born healthy, I was off to a good start.

My earliest memories were the winter of 1927 and '28. We wintered the cows in the area of Bluff, Utah. Upon returning to the high mountain country of Colorado, deterioration of the marriage of my parents began. By the next winter, I became a guest in many different homes — but that is a story in itself.

My education began in the usual one-room school houses so common in rural areas during the twenties and thirties. For the first seven grades, my schooling was totally in one-room schools. My eighth year, my stepmother, younger sister Janice, older sister Grace, and I, moved to the town of Cortez, Colorado so Grace could enter high school. Janice and I both graduated from the same high school.

Even after two years of playing high school football, reading vast volumes of literature for book reports, as well as my own pleasure, I still felt like a kid from the sticks. I was not interested in the big cities, but like my pioneer ancestors, still wanted to see what was beyond the horizon.

A few writers and a few acquaintances piqued my curiosity and interest in the vast Arctic Wasteland. I knew I'd have to experience it to understand it. Reading, searching reference books, and listening to hair-raising stories would not satisfy my tremendous hunger for the vastness described by Robert Service, James Oliver Curwood, and Jack London. For my young mind, visualizing the loneliness, vastness, beauty, and spell it cast on men, was totally beyond my comprehension.

To me the Far North translated to Alaska. I knew I must feel, experience, absorb, work, and grow with it. Doing all those things for the past forty-five years still hasn't completely filled my great curiosity with answers, but conversely, has opened up continued horizons to explore.

Those writers caused me to think seriously of visiting that great land—someday. Someday was to be immediately after graduation from high school, but in 1941 Admiral Yamamoto accomplished a goal changing the lives and plans of many young people.

On my eighteenth birthday, I volunteered for the U.S. Army and was called to active service immediately after high school graduation. After brief assignments at various training camps my group was sent overseas within six months.

Some of the shoals and beaches that came into my view were Oahu and Maui in the Territory of Hawaii. Such places as Kwajalein, Eniwetok, and Saipan, were brief stopping places. Guam became a permanent place of residence for about eighteen months.

Twenty-six army "experts" were assigned to help an old Marine Corps Colonel, with thirty-two years active duty in the Marine Corps, set up and run the Fifth Field Depot. Of all the officers with whom I was affiliated, I admired him the most. That was some of the best duty of my entire tour. You can be sure we contributed vastly to his education and ability as an officer.

We loaded out the ships that supported the campaign at Iwo Jima and Okinawa. We were loading ships that were poised to go to Japan, had that invasion not been canceled. Two atomic bombs hastened the decision for the Japanese surrender. I am sure there will never be agreement concerning whether or not dropping them was wise. I do know we had ships anchored as close as they safely could

Author just before leaving Guam in 1945.

be, for as far as a person could see and in every direction. Later I was told the same situation prevailed at Saipan.

My enlistment was for the duration of the war plus six months. Five months after the Japanese armistice I was back in Colorado preparing to continue the rest of my life.

Uncle Bob Holmes did not persuade me but his conversation did influence me. Just having someone I knew go with me and help guide me to do what I wanted was a tremendous influence upon my decision to go north. When Uncle Bob was ready to return to his job in Alaska, I asked him if I could accompany him. He was agreeable, but did lay down some ground rules: I was strictly on my own. He would coach me where he could and introduce me to the people of influence that he knew but the rest was up to me. I wouldn't have wanted it any other way.

Uncle Bob liked to smoke a pipe, wore glasses and a small, felt hat for shade from the sun. He was a very hard worker. He had also grown up in the Colorado country and suffered the depression so familiar to us all. He was a very conservative person who always felt an obligation to his employer. His sense of humor was close to the surface, but his overriding serious nature predominated his personality.

My maiden voyage to Alaska started three months after returning from Guam. After spending three days in Edmonton, Alberta, due to the scheduling of flights at the time, we departed for Fairbanks, Alaska. During the flight from Edmonton to Whitehorse, I observed my first tundra. We arrived in Fairbanks about one o'clock in the morning and engaged a room at the Nordale Hotel[1].

Early the next morning, after a good breakfast, we went about the business of seeking gainful employment. We went to the brand new employment office where I was dispatched for a job as a truck driver for the Alaska Road Commission (ARC). Bob had worked for them for several years, so all he had to do was sign a couple papers at the office of Frank Nash, the superintendent of the Fairbanks district.

---

[1] The Nordale Hotel burned to the ground 22 Feb. 1972, with two lives lost.

That very morning I met and was visiting with Frances Young, a cook for the ARC, who asked me how I liked Alaska. I told her it was yet a little premature to say, but I'd be more apt to have an opinion by fall. She then told me there was something about Alaska which seemed to get into a man's blood, especially a young man -- he would come, look, and stay. I told her I had only come up for the summer to see what it was like. With an all knowing look she said, "We'll see."

That was in May 1946. I did not return to Colorado for eighteen months. When I did, I had a homestead filed and a cabin built, waiting for my return. Within five months I was back in Alaska. I have stayed over forty-five years, with the exception of about five winters, and have never missed a shift or a meal, unless it was due to my own actions.

Many times I have been asked to relate to a social gathering or a class of students, some of my Alaskan adventures. I always shy away from that terminology. To me, an adventure is the act of finding yourself in a situation in which you would have never been, had you known what you were doing in the first place. During my entire life, no matter what my project happened to be, the prime objective has been to enter the project well prepared and bring it to the most dignified conclusion my capabilities would allow.

It has come to my attention that the farsighted people seem to live the longest. I'm not speaking of just pilots. Any profession seems to add longevity to the farsighted, groundbreaking type of individual. Those who seem to be slightly slower in making decisions about important situations, but are decisive once that decision has been made, seem to endure.

In the following pages, many such individuals will surface.

Starting to Fly

✈

The first season I worked in Alaska was a learning experience. I was fortunate enough to work with Harold Southerland, a certified Caterpillar mechanic, who showed me many things I was able to use for the rest of my life. Casey Compton, Don Raats, Fred Lorz, Grove Kunz, Al Sherlock, and several I'm probably overlooking, helped me learn enough about dirt moving to be able to hold onto my next job working for Birch, Johnson, & Lytle on the Twenty-Six-Mile airport, later named Eielson Air Force Base.

During the summer of 1947 I worked with Hanz Rutzebeck, a cat skinner, who flew. His conversation about flying dominated every gathering of dirt movers when he was present. It seemed if you wanted to go anyplace, or really see Alaska, you had to fly. A number of the fellows talked constantly about their boats. I finally decided both were quite important as means of transportation.

At the end of the season Paul Bush, "Curly" Justus, and I drove my newly acquired International pickup down the "Alcan," now known as the Alaska Highway, back to Colorado. At the time, that was a feat which received a degree of admiration from the locals. It was not a difficult undertaking if a person was well-prepared but could be quite devastating if one was not. The Canadian government immigration officers at the border were insistent that certain spare parts, chains, and adequate money be displayed before vehicles were cleared to travel through Canada.

Paul was also a veteran who had spent the war years in the Navy. He and I had worked together for the ARC the summer before. He was a grader operator. "Curly" was a fairly new acquaintance we had met on the present job. He was also an operator. He had been running a Tournapull scraper, or car-ryall.

Upon arriving in Colorado, I heard there was a flying school right in the town of Cortez. I checked into it.

It seems when good things start to happen they descend like a covey of quail into a grain field. Grady Thompson, a former high school classmate, came to me and wanted me to work for him as a sheet metal worker and installer. I agreed, providing I could take time off for flying lessons.

I dislike designating any certain time or place that I learned to fly. I feel many situations have contributed substan-tially to my knowledge and ability. I also feel I am still learn-ing. My first training was a locality with which I became quite well-acquainted in my youth; the Four Corners area in South-western United States. It is the only place in the U.S. where four state corners share a common point, or surveyors' hub. Colorado, New Mexico, Arizona, and Utah make such a meet-ing at a location slightly over thirty miles south-southwest of Cortez. The town boasted of a nice little dirt airport, complete with approved flying school and repair station.

The airport was owned and operated by Rolin Usher and his wife, Polly. Rolin owned the bank and had flown since his youth. He owned a new Stinson Voyager, but really didn't fly it much. Polly was an excellent pilot and was a designated flight inspector. She always impressed me with the very pre-cise smoothness with which she accomplished maneuvers.

I had known them before the war, but not well. Few high school football players become well acquainted with the bank president. In their employ was Frank Brgoch, an instruc-tor who had flown B-25's in the Pacific during WW II. Frank was a small man who possessed a degree of self-confidence that made it easy for him to transmit his knowledge and ideas to others. His sense of humor made it easy for him to teach by telling stories of what he had seen in like circumstances. He guided me through the first essential period during which I learned the joys and responsibilities of flying and earned my private pilot license. Polly gave me the flight check and approval for the license.

The Southwest was an ideal place to learn the basics of flying. Weather was so accommodating. I cannot remember a time when we had to cancel a flight due to weather. We were always able to start an engine. Wind was seldom a problem. At some of the surrounding airports to which we flew for cross-country training there was enough of a problem, at times, to acquaint us with the necessity of being on guard. The flat topped mountains with sheer drops on all sides to a valley floor several hundred feet below were an ideal setup for down drafts.

I knew, since I couldn't see wind, I must devise a method of visualizing it in order to keep the airplane within an area from which it could be maneuvered to safety at all times. My method, which I still use, was to imagine the air filled with smoke, thus making it mentally visible. I would then determine which way the wind was blowing and the down, or updrafts, could be visualized. Smoke flowing over a bluff would appear much as water flowing over rocks in a stream, and after all, who would be so indiscreet as to try to run a motor-boat up a waterfall? Who would try to fly up a downdraft?

The elevation of the airport was just under five thousand feet. All the mountains in any direction were high enough that great care and attention to details was necessary to insure safety, especially on cross country flights. The flight characteristics of small airplanes are considerably diminished by altitude.

Landmarks were so prominent, one could orient himself easily when coming home if he just kept in mind all of them would look somewhat different from another angle. The Sleeping Ute, a mountain west of town, looked surprisingly like an Indian reclining on his back with his arms folded across his chest, wearing a full headdress. It was a landmark recognizable for many miles, from many directions. To the east was the high promontory on the northwest corner of Mesa Verde National Park. South was the famous landmark known as Shiprock, just over the line into New Mexico. To the north was irrigated farmland which was easy to identify from the air.

It was so green in contrast to all the sagebrush and rocky soil not so watered. A pilot could get lost, but he would have to work at it.

There were no radio aids to navigation and no airport traffic control. Sometimes I feel the new crop of pilots are cheated somewhat by not having to learn those basics that never fail, even if all the lights, radio stations, or other navigational aids are completely unavailable. I never used a radio until I owned my first airplane.

My first cross country flight was to the famous Monument Valley of Utah, to the west. We flew right over the home of Norm Nevils, well-known white water boatman of the Colorado River. He was, at one time, known as America's foremost white water rafter. Frank, my instructor, also gave Norm his introduction to flying. Norm was later killed in an aircraft accident.

I realized early in my flying career that horse play and funerals were practically synonymous. During the war I saw a number of needless tragedies that were strictly a result of, as some like to call it, a practical joke. Just a couple of weeks before leaving the job at Eielson, there were a few operators hauling gravel with tournapulls, a large scraper invented by R.G. LeTourneau. They thought it great sport to race from the gravel pit to and from the runway area. We had two roads, one from the pit to the runway, another for the return, making it one way traffic each way. No passing in opposite directions was necessary. One fellow thought he had a slight edge, but was going to insure he returned to the pit first by returning via the haul road instead of the return road. Naturally that put him going the wrong way in one way traffic in the dark, but he got away with it, almost. He knew where the other tournapulls were, but when a grader appeared out of the dark right in the middle of the road on a turn, everything he did from then on was wrong. In leaving the road the bottom of his scraper caught the shoulder of the road and momentarily stopped the forward motion, but it also bounced. As the forward motion stopped, the operator was thrown from the seat and landed on his back in front of the drive wheel. The entire machine bounced enough to move forward a few feet and rolled over him. He lived about five minutes. Paul Bush was the grader operator who witnessed the scene. *Don't horse around.*

The first published embarrassment of my flying career was during my basic flight training. After I soloed, I was free to take an airplane and go practice. I reasoned practice was meant to sharpen all maneuvers taught by the instructor, so I found a likely looking place to practice forced landings.

The location was a hay field that had been put into pasture after the last hay crop of the season had been harvested. Stock in the pasture wasn't a problem as they were all laying down near one corner of the pasture. The field lay along the main highway with a fence and a power line running between pasture and road. About four hundred yards from the road was a sloping ridge on top of which was another power line, parallel to the road. I saw no poles crossing the pasture from the ridge to the road. I must admit my experience was so meager at the time, I really didn't look for poles though I would have noticed them had they been there. Of course poles translate to power or telephone lines. Even if you cannot see the wires from a few hundred yards the poles tell you they are there.

About a quarter of a mile from where I planned to make my pretended landing, an aqueduct crossed the road. It formed a border at the end of the pasture. Due to a light breeze I set up my approach to pass over the aqueduct then used a slip technique.

A slip is a maneuver where the pilot uses crossed controls to cause excess drag which causes an airplane to lose altitude faster. It is employed when an obstacle has been cleared, but more altitude should be shed to insure touching down onto the airport closer to the approach end. This allows more braking room to stop forward motion. A pilot cannot use brakes on the runway he allows to escape behind him. The slip was used frequently on aircraft manufactured prior to the popularity of flaps, which perform the same function, but in a much more coordinated manner. I was proud of my ability to slip. I could do it so well, at least Frank had ceased to criticize it.

Suddenly there were two wires directly in front of me. After years of experience I would now go under instead of over them, thus missing the wires and salvaging airspeed. I tried to go over the wires, but instead I went between them.

When the wire broke, it left the ripple full length of the left wing and there was such a loud *bang,* I was sure I had just passed low over a hunter's duck blind. The wire catching the top of the landing gear felt as though it was made of bungee cord. Fortunately, after stretching an unbelievable amount, that wire also broke at almost exactly the same distance and at exactly the same time, on either side of the airplane. There was a considerable length of wire trailing down both sides. It would drag across and short lead-in wires to various homes. It plunged numerous houses into darkness as I staggered around over the countryside trying to assure myself the airplane was going to continue to fly. Those shorting wires made a sound that I do not care to hear again. Needless to say, there were a number of people who came home from church to find their roast not quite done. I heard about some of them.

I managed to keep the airspeed above a stall long enough to get headed back toward the airport, gain a little altitude, and reestablish something on the order of cruising speed. There were about fifteen minutes to think about the best approach and landing procedure to employ. Bear in mind a power line ran directly across the end of our home field. I was determined to not listen to any more shorting wires if I could help it. Since our runway was quite long, I came in high. Settling onto the airport I could hear and feel the drag of those wires. Adding power kept the airplane from nosing over after the good job of getting it that far. I'm not sure if adding power helped or hindered, but we didn't have to change the prop so I was satisfied with the result. With full power I could not pull the wire, so I had to stop the engine and push the airplane backward, off the wire.

Johnnie Gudschinsky, airport handyman, came down with the Jeep and pulled four hundred sixteen feet of number nine wire back to the hangar area. I slipped into the office to quietly peek around the corner and determine if people were laughing. They were not. It appeared I could safely tell my story first.

Frank didn't say much. He just told me I would have to go talk to Usher.

The Ushers lived in a new house near the airport and being Sunday, he was home. After hearing me out he said very little—just asked how much damage there was to the airplane. I told him hardly any, but I could tell by the expression on his face he had heard that before only to later find substantial damage. Actually he was pleased when he saw the airplane. Mr. Usher asked me if Frank hadn't instructed me to not practice forced landings without an instructor aboard. I thought, "Oh, oh, now I have caused Frank some trouble," so I told Rolin he had probably told me but I didn't remember it. Frank said he hadn't told me.

The power company sent me a bill for one hundred sixteen dollars and forty-two cents. That was a lot of money in 1948, but the real embarrassment was being accused of buzzing. The only people I could actually convince I wasn't buzzing, were Frank and Mr. Usher. Actually they were the only ones who really mattered, but I disliked the constant razzing about buzzing with an airplane. To me, buzzing has been anathema ever since. There also wasn't a great deal I could do about the headlines in the newspaper Monday morning. *Don't horse around!!*

Immediately after completing my flight training, taking the check ride and receiving my pilot's license, I started making arrangements to head back north. Of course before leaving Cortez, I took my boss, Grady Thompson, for his first ride and spin.

My cousin, Jess West, decided to head north with me. The trip up was uneventful, but we were too early to find work soon after arriving. After about a month Jess returned to Colorado with a lot of fond memories but little money.

I worked for Morrison-Knudsen (MK) Co. building the new railroad roundhouse, associated track and yard. At the end of the season, wondering what I had done with those fabulous wages everyone knew we construction workers made, I began thinking of all the fire-killed spruce trees near Eielson which, the summer before, we had encircled with bulldozers to prevent the fire from spreading further. I went to the Bureau of Land Management, obtained a firewood cutting permit, and became a professional woodcutter.

A Woodcutter Turns Mechanic

C arl Carlson was my mentor during the first couple of cold winters when I gained my livelihood cutting wood. He helped me some on the woodpile but mostly he cooked, kept the cabin warm, and always had a meal ready when I came in after a hard day cutting wood.

Since the daylight hours were so short, we had long evenings after dinner. We would read, but I was fascinated by the stories Carl would tell if I could get him to talking about days of yore. Carlson was not his real name. He had, in his youth, been a purser on a Swedish ship. He told me the stories the returning gold miners would tell. Remember, he saw only the successful miners on those return trips. They would tell him stories about how they could find gold nuggets the size of horse biscuits at the grass roots. In his words, "It would drive a young man crazy."

Carl jumped ship, changed his name, and got lost in Alaska. A feat easily accomplished in the days of slow transportation and lack of communication. I met him my first summer working for the ARC. We called him the old Swede. He rather liked that as he was really a Finlander, but being called Swede somewhat distanced his identity more than just a name change. He was my nearest neighbor at the cabin I had built on the Salcha River, forty miles east of Fairbanks on the Richardson Highway.

Carl was a small man with a fiercely independent nature. His eyes were blue and his hair was all gray by the time I met him. He must have been close to sixty years old, but still quite capable and hard working in the woods. He liked me and I flew him to different locations and performed little favors for him. He liked to drink. When drinking he would lose all control of his money. It just disappeared. Several times when I saw him drinking, I would steal most of his money so he would have some the next day when he again became sober. He appreciated that.

Carl ran a short trap line, taught me how to trap marten, skin and stretch the catch, and keep my feet warm. He also produced a good number of the huge Arctic hare for the table during the winter. In fact we ate half of one for our Christmas dinner. For some reason the apple pie I made for the holidays caused him embarrassment simply because we were on the trapline. He did however, condescend to eat a second piece.

I'm glad he happened to be with me the day I fell through the ice at forty below. Had he not been there my career as a story teller would have been short. We later determined there were warm springs in the bottom of the creek bed. That brilliant discovery was made soon after we dropped the pickup through with a load of wood at another location about one hundred yards further down the creek.

Little errors of that nature really contribute to the education of an aspiring outdoorsman if he will swallow his pride and acknowledge that a little more forethought and less haste could have prevented the problem. For instance, just a few days before, I had been out in thick, tall spruce trees, looking for likely places to make some sets for marten and snowshoe hare. The timber and brush were so thick it was impossible to walk a straight line. I was careful to walk as straight as the thick brush would allow. I really do not believe a person who has not experienced such an occurrence can relate to the feeling of disbelief which came over me when I crossed a fresh snowshoe trail—I knew Carl and I were the only human beings for miles.

My first thought was, "Who in the world could possibly be way out here without my knowledge?" That was a new trail, made that day. I was certain I was the only person in the area, other than Carl, and I knew he had not made the tracks. I had been so careful to not circle and felt if I had deviated at all, it was to the right. I was convinced there was no other person who could have possibly made that trail. I finally had to admit it was my own, then backtrack to the cabin, even though it seemed all wrong. That is the only time I have ever been completely disoriented, but it served to teach me it could happen, even to me.

Little did I know then how valuable those learning experiences would be in guiding my future as a pilot. It seems most of my experiences were guiding me to a better understanding of situations that would later affect my future in flying.

I became poverty stricken when the snow became so deep I could no longer get into my winter wood yard. I had a dandy stand of fire-killed spruce but the deepening snow and warm springs in the creek made life less than tranquil after December. I couldn't seriously consider opening the road with a bulldozer. I knew the ice would not support one. I maintained a room in Fairbanks but spent most of my time at the cabin at the wood yard. When I got snowed out, my Fairbanks roommate, Dick Goff, who worked for Wien Alaska Airlines, suggested I contact Fritz Wien about a job. Wien had a Douglas DC-3 on which they were conducting a ten thousand hour inspection. They needed help, not necessarily educated help.

Fritz hired me and sent an Eskimo fellow with me over to the old Pan American hangar, on Weeks Field, to work under the direction of Harold Herning. That was my first encounter with a dirty, neglected aircraft. I'll not bore the reader by describing the filth that had worked through the cracks in the floor but to this day my hands hurt just thinking about the gallons of solvent in which we soaked our hands in the cleaning process. From that obscure beginning I evolved into a full fledged aircraft and engine mechanic.

At the time I realized how fortunate I was to be working, but not how fortunate I was to be working with that particular crew. As mentioned, Harold Herning was the shop foreman for Northern Consolidated Airlines, performing the inspection for Wien. The Wien hangar had burned in September, leaving them without hangar facilities for such a large airplane.

Harold is a small man with an infectious smile and an amazing amount of energy. When he took the helm, things began to happen. He loves Alaska as few men do, and was on friendly terms with many of the old timers like "Rika" Wallen,

Fred Purdy, Slim Moore, Frank Glaser, and others who occasionally cropped up in our conversation. He always sees the bright side and the possibilities that lie ahead. He could always get the best out of his men and assembled a crew of which he could be justly proud.

Among that crew were some of the best craftsmen in the business. Paul Berg had been working for Wien before the fire. He was a superb aircraft and engine mechanic. He explained to me many things, as we were working side by side, that kept me out of trouble when I was working alone in the future. He had been in the Air Force and was intimately familiar with the Douglas DC-3.

There was Jennings Johnson who also had worked for Wien before the fire. He was a top-of-the-line mechanic at any position. Jennings liked to play his guitar and sing. He liked jokes, but was a serious worker. He was also an accomplished cartoonist. He had worked in construction trade and was not at all limited to working on airplanes where he excelled.

Dick Johnson had worked for Consolidated in Anchorage and was working at Fairbanks when I arrived upon the scene. As his name implies, he was very tall and blond. He owned and rebuilt an old Fleet bi-plane with a Kinner, five cylinder engine. The only one I ever saw.

Warren "Tilly" Tilman was "king of the welding shop" and a master at fabricating and welding. He began his career working in the open air in Kansas in the early 1920's. He could manufacture in the welding shop about anything one could imagine.

Marvin Jones was the one who did the bookkeeping for the "bush planes." He kept track of the log books and scheduled the inspections in order to keep a smooth flow, instead of allowing them to come due for inspection in groups. He was also an accomplished mechanic and later, hangar foreman.

John Dull had flown copilot for Oscar Underhill in the Tri-Motor Stinsons and the Douglas DC-2. Oscar was a senior captain. John was now working as a mechanic and was quite capable. Johnnie was short and heavy-set. I kiddingly told him that if he were two inches taller, he would be square. He was very quiet and steady with a subtle approach to expressing himself.

A Woodcutter Turns Mechanic

Herman Smith was the accessories overhaul mechanic and a source of good information when a need arose. A good person to talk to prior to taking an engine mechanic's written examination. He, too, was a very small person. He had a pair of twin daughters, which gave us something in common in the future.

Eldred Quam was the engine overhaul mechanic. His advice and suggestions were sought after, not just by our crew, but by mechanics all over the field. Eldred was the dean of the round engines around the field for years.

George Clayton could explain understandably, everything about anything. That aptitude extended to flying as well as mechanical subjects. He had married his former "lady" flight instructor. His interests were such that he was familiar with about anything a person asked him and enjoyed imparting that knowledge to those of us who were less informed.

Louie Bourdon was very knowledgeable about a vast number of subjects. He was the inspector on the DC-3's and had no equal. When he took his A & E written examinations, both the same day, and scored 100% on both, I suppose the inspector could be excused for asking if he had used a "pony." (Information gleaned from the written exams by others who had taken the test before him.) His indignation had no bounds. Before his clarification was complete there was no question in the mind of the inspector whether or not he knew his subject prior to taking the examinations.

We had a fabric shop presided over by Josephine Jacobson who had also worked for the company in Anchorage. Josephine grew up on the Kuskokwim River and had the typical Eskimo patience and love for people. She was an accomplished fabric worker, both with the fabric itself, and the dope and painting process. She sewed engine covers, wing covers, upholstery, and about anything one could run through the shop or under the head of her sewing machine.

Margie Browne also worked in the dope and fabric shop with Josephine. She didn't have quite the years of experience, but was very accomplished and a nice addition to the atmosphere. Her accomplishments paralleled those of Jo. She was very pretty and Marvin and I quite often took the two of them fishing, then we all converged on their little cabin for a fish fry that was surpassed nowhere.

It would be impossible to overemphasize how fortunate I was to be working with such a crew of perfectionists. I watched, listened, and tried to incorporate as much knowledge and professionalism as I could, for I knew I would never again be working with such an assembly of superb professionals.

Since the ten thousand hour overhaul was taking place under the direction of Harold Herning, he was able to observe my working habits and capabilities. When that project was finished so was my job with Wien. He gave me an opportunity to work for Northern Consolidated Airlines on some of their rebuild work.

One day the crew found themselves looking at an awful pile of junk that Harold told us was going to fly—after we finished the tasks he had in mind for us.

In short order the various parts had found a place to hide somewhere in the hangar until some member of the crew dug them out to begin the task of making them new again. When finished, we would have a huge, single-engine, nine-place airplane that would carry eight passengers and a pilot much farther than most people were willing to ride in one trip.

I thought I had the biggest and toughest job, but then, that is life. We always seem to feel the ten pounds in the other man's pack is lighter than the ten pounds in our own. My section of the hangar was a corner, close to the welding shop. I was sanding tubing, and sanding tubing, and sanding tubing. Does anyone even have the slightest idea how many miles of tubing there really are in an airplane, especially the old Noorduyn Norseman? It all had to be sanded to a new metal brightness before being primed with zinc chromate.

About the time I felt I was the only one left in the world, working in a dark corner of a hangar in the far north, here would come Harold with a big smile and a story about when things were really tough. He would grab a strip of sanding tape and sand vigorously for a couple of minutes, then someone would need his presence elsewhere. I often wondered if he really knew how much of a boost that gave me, but then he had to know, or he could not have employed the maneuver so successfully. Finally the last foot of tubing was bright and silver colored, passed inspection, and here comes Josephine with her paint gun, face mask, a towel around her hair, and did she ever fog up the hangar! We all had to clear out and let the air clear up. Now, with the tubing all primed, we can start the real work, the real work?

At the time I held a private pilot's license, but had no knowledge or experience working on the actual machine. This was a rather rude introduction to the path leading to a commercial flying career and the procurement of both the aircraft and engine license required by the Civil Aeronautics Authority (CAA), now replaced by the Federal Aviation Administration (FAA). During this period of rebuilding the entire aircraft, the process of rebuilding sub-assemblies, then combining the whole, became quite apparent as well as educational. I found all this new experience so interesting, I procured several books and began to seriously study.

There were many steps during the rebuild that could easily be overlooked by one not familiar with good procedure. My next assignment came after some of the more experienced craftsmen had completed several phases of work.

Enter Walt Eberhardt. Walt was a rather obscure person. He was a handsome young man who always wore a smile and kept to his part of the hangar. He was the carpenter, rebuilder of the wooden parts of the aircraft, manufacturer of ribs, cap strips, even replacement spars. He also did other jobs if necessary, but his woodwork kept him occupied most of the time.

After I completed the miles of sanding and priming tubing, it was Walt's turn. He fashioned a couple of the nicest windows to be placed, one on each side of the rear seat, which was located aft of the entrance door. Those windows not only looked nice, but considerably decreased the claustrophobia suffered by many passengers required to ride in aircraft in the original form. Those windows also became standard installation in all subsequent rebuilds. Walt continued to make little additions and changes, making the work of future mechanics

21

who followed him much easier. His expertise with a saw and draw band made life much more bearable for others. He surely must have thought the other fellow's ten pounds was much lighter than his while he was installing all that fiberglass batting for insulation and soundproofing. The fuselage was now ready for some of the rest of us.

Walt went on to rebuild the wings and stabilizers, which were both of the old, spruce construction. As he finished a member and the last coat of varnish had dried it would go into the dope and fabric shop where Margie and Josephine would recover it with grade "A" cotton fabric. As this was rather a hurry-up project, the wings were returned to the hangar after the girls had completed recovering, up through the clear dope stage, and my indoctrination as a sanding machine began. There are yards and yards of fabric on those wings and the old school taught they should be sanded to a smooth finish. It was unknown to me then but later experience taught me the sooner the sanding was accomplished after the dope was dried, the easier it was to sand. Other projects took me off the sanding from time to time. The job got harder and harder as the dope aged, but we finally finished, and the wings were ready for the girls again. They sprayed them with many coats of silver dope, which is simply clear dope with aluminum powder added and thinned enough to spray. Silver is added to keep to a minimum, deterioration from the rays of the sun. They then painted them the company colors which was the most horrible combination ever conceived: briton blue and gunmetal gray. I'm quite sure those colors had redeeming features but those features were never divulged to me.

We are getting a little ahead in the story, but, in order to get the paint onto the wings in proper sequence, now comes Johnny Dull. Josephine and Margie did not paint the numbers onto the wings as we ran into a little controversy when the paperwork was submitted to the CAA for a registration certificate.

The company had bought the aircraft from the U.S. Fish and Wildlife Service, who, as all the federal agencies were allowed to do, had their own numbers for their aircraft. They wanted to keep all those numbers for themselves, which resulted in new replacement aircraft having the same number as the retired aircraft. Before we submitted our paperwork, the Fish and Wildlife personnel were flying another NC-725. They had sold us only the junk, not the number.

To straighten out the paperwork, Marvin Jones agreed to a suggestion to add an "E" to make it 725E, or phonetically, 725Easy which the CAA approved.

OK, now that we had that straightened out, Johnny Dull could go ahead and paint the NC numbers onto the wings. He had them all masked out and was about ready to paint, when I told him he had the "N" masked backward. He looked at it a minute, realized it was, and without uttering one word, ripped it off, and remasked it. Dick Johnson scolded me for telling him. He was going to let him paint it, then tell him.

The original Norseman utilized a system of aileron droop when full flaps were applied. The idea was to make a slower approach and landing speed possible but it was achieved at the expense of aileron control. Someone suggested the aileron droop be removed from the system and the pilots agreed with that suggestion. Having since flown Norseman, both with and without the droop in the system, and nearly "buying the farm" in one with the droop, my vote is definitely for removal. Jennings Johnson designed a simple system allowing for the

Norseman 725E at Alaskaland.

removal, making full aileron travel available with full flaps down. Very little take-off performance was sacrificed but slow speed aileron control was much enhanced.

Actually, Jennings rode herd on most of the assembly procedure. He studied the erection and maintenance manual and saw to it that everything was properly adjusted. He removed the seventy gallon, rear belly fuel tank and replaced it with a cavern with a very innovative door. We used that cavern to carry the fire pots, wing covers, engine cover, starvation gear, ax, sleeping bags, and a number of other things we may need should embarrassment overtake us on the trail. Also, removing that seventy gallons of fuel, which it was inconceivable we would ever need, gave almost five hundred pounds more weight available for load.

Jennings wasn't through yet. I was fortunate enough to be his helper during the upholstery part of the project. He was a craftsman. I was an apprentice.

Eldred Quam, our dean of the round engine overhaul fraternity, made us a new engine. A zero time propeller was installed, making everything start at hour 0. It was practically a new airplane. Walt made a pair of new boards for the skis so even the winter time part of the aircraft was new.

Warren "Tilly" Tilman made one of the cabin heaters for which he and Chauncey Coleman were so well known.

No one voiced their feelings, but surely all were a little disappointed when, after test hop, the "new" Norseman was sent to Bethel. Little did I know it then but in spite of the horrible color, I would, in years to come, share many experiences with that newly restored aircraft.

An Exciting Season
✈

When a person is working on an interesting project, especially when he is learning the craft, everything he encounters is exciting. I was fortunate enough to be able to work with some energetic, knowledgeable craftsmen with varied experience.

My second winter working at Northern Consolidated hangar, the crew acquired a few new members. Among them was Chauncey Coleman, an accomplished welder, who came over from Alaska Airlines. Chauncey was an old rancher from Nevada and it still showed. He loved a good laugh.

One day, walking across the hangar floor with the legs of my coveralls draging my tracks, I stepped near an air drill and tripped the trigger. The drill bit wound up in the leg of my coveralls causing the trigger not to release as I stamped my foot. The air hose was jumping up and down, rolling and flipping all over the floor, I couldn't get loose and almost went into hysterics. The scream of the air drill was similar enough to the buzz of a rattlesnake it alerted all my dormant senses that had not seen or heard a rattler for fifteen years. I was clear across the floor and out the door before I could control myself. Watching, Coleman knew exactly what was going through my mind, and his amusement was exceeded only by my near heart failure.

Art Smith came onto the scene that winter also. He was about six feet tall, blue-eyed and his hair was so blond it was almost undetectable when he started to turn gray. After his transfer from Anchorage, Smitty and I were working the night shift. One of Smitty's strongest points was his ability to get things done in a sequence and order that required the absolute minimum of moves and time. I was careful to watch and incorporate his system into my own work habits.

On several occasions we completed, in one night, the one hundred hour inspection on an aircraft, also making a complete engine change. We always encountered patching and painting a few small holes in the fabric, plus adjusting or correcting any pilot "squawks." Of course we would start right at five in the evening and work straight through until the job was completed. At times we worked almost until the beginning of the next day shift, but the pilot could take the same airplane and return to his station after just one night in town. (A feature not always appreciated by some of the single pilots.)

It seems that in every walk of life, one encounters those who think most everyone but themselves are out of step. It does no good to try to help those people by explaining to them that not only do they not quite understand the problem, but that they are the problem.

One case in particular comes to mind. Since we were working the night shift in order to have the airplanes ready to go every morning, no matter what may have gone wrong with them during the day, Smitty and I had no chance to talk to the foreman on many occasions. The answer to the problem was to stay up after completing our shift and talk to him after the day shift had started. Wanting to discuss a personal matter with Glen Dillard, who had replaced Harold Herning that second winter, I went to his office one morning about ten o'clock.

Things were quite informal in those days and Dillard never kept his office door closed. It would be hard to not overhear a conversation in progress when one approached the door. Dillard and a CAA inspector were arguing over the necessity of procuring a ferry permit in order to fly an airplane from a bush location. After temporary repairs had been made, the aircraft had been flown to Fairbanks to effect permanent repairs. The flight had already been made, so we could go on all day about the "what ifs."

A ferry permit is simply a piece of paper an inspector signs approving the ferry flight for an airplane that a mechanic has told him is safe to fly. The inspector seldom even sees the airplane.

Dillard presented the argument the airplane was three hundred miles out in the brush under winter-time conditions of wind, snow, and temperatures below zero. The salvage crew was living in a tent, doing their own cooking, with no possible knowledge of the exact day they could depart with the crippled airplane. First, they had to complete the repairs to the point they would be able to safely fly the aircraft under normal conditions, and second, they had no way of knowing what the weather would be like upon completion of the work. Also, there was just one mechanic, one pilot, and one airplane, so how were they going to procure that ferry permit, under any condition, without first flying the airplane at least to a point of communication? Ferry permits are issued for a specific time period. If your flight is not accomplished within that time period, a new permit is required. It might be well to point out here, that ferry permits were just coming into vogue at the time and most of the old-time mechanics and pilots were still offering a stiff resistance to the government meddling.

To support his argument the inspector asked Dillard, "Just what would have happened if a wing had come off during the flight?"

Dillard's reply of, "What usually happens when a wing comes off?" really didn't satisfy the inspector's curiosity. He kept badgering him until Dillard asked him if that little piece of paper would have prevented the wing from coming off. It was obvious to everyone, except the inspector, he was badly out of his element in that discussion. No one but himself was taking him seriously.

I was new to the fraternity at the time and hadn't yet put inspectors, flight and maintenance, into a slot of their own. A few days after the ferry permit discussion, I happened to be in the same company with that inspector. It would have been a little clumsy to not strike up a conversation. I asked him if he flew those airplanes, referring specifically to the DC-3.

He assured me, indignantly, that he certainly did, "What did you think we did?"

I advised him that had I known for sure, I'd not have asked. He then expanded upon his duties until I asked if he was an aircraft mechanic also. Then his dignity was really insulted; why he wouldn't dirty his hands working on an airplane --that is what licensed mechanics were for.

Not realizing I was making no points real fast with him, I mentioned I had overheard the discussion about the ferry permit. Naturally I took for granted he was also a maintenance inspector. I didn't understand they were a whole separate breed and gender, etc. He then took advantage of the opportunity to expound the virtues of a ferry permit. It was at least fifteen years before I was able to comprehend the one thing a ferry permit could do for you, besides get you into trouble. It could remove one of the many escapes an insurance company could employ to refuse payment if disaster struck during ferry of a cripple from the spot where salvaged to the hangar where permanent repairs would be accomplished.

Down the road a way, that inspector came to me and wanted to know if he could get his car into the shop to change oil and grease it. I told him, sure — bring it around to the small auto shed and I'd fix him right up. I gave him a pan for draining his oil and showed him where the rags were, then took a grease gun down, removed the head, plunged the barrel into a five gallon bucket of grease and drew back the plunger, filling the barrel with grease. He was astounded I could fill the gun in that manner.

When I had asked him if he needed any tools, he assured me he had his own and knew everything there was to know about automobiles, but he still wouldn't dirty his hands on an airplane. Strange he had never seen a grease gun filled by employing the simple principle of suction; I didn't know there was any other way, but fortunately, that time, I kept quiet.

Louie Bourdon was the designated company inspector on the DC-3's and if a person had a need to know something about one of them he need look no further. If Louie had signed off an airplane as service ready, there was only one reason for a walk around inspection—regulations *required* the pilots to make a visual inspection prior to entering the aircraft. Louie had a good sense of humor but was one of those fellows everyone waited for someone else to approach first each morning just in case his reaction was less than amiable. No one wished to intentionally endure his scathing scorn. He was a fine person but he was moody.

One shift Smitty and I had worked right up until Louie arrived to check the airplane over and sign it off as ready to go. We finished on time, but just barely. As we were cleaning up our tools and Louie was doing his paper work, in walks our little East Coast inspector all ready to route check the Douglas crew on the scheduled flight. Louie was turning the engines by pulling the propellers through, as was normal before start up.

The inspector walked up to him and asked, "What is the voltage of the electrical system on this aircraft?"

Louie looked at him and frowned, "It is twenty-four volts, why?"

Then comes the most brilliant question of the month, "What would you think if I told you that was a twenty-eight volt system?"

Louie stopped, turned around, looked him straight in the eye, and said, "I'd think you were the dumbest SOB I have encountered for a month. You may be able to get one hundred volts out of those generators, but when I hit the switch to crank those engines, twenty-four volts is all that will come out of those batteries."

Case closed. Smitty and I made ourselves scarce.

Fred Goodwin flew for Wien and basically was a captain on the Douglas DC-3's. In the early years of establishing a scheduled operation, the DC-3 captains often filled in doing other types of flying where help was needed. One day Fred flew a Bellanca Pacemaker into Weeks Field and found it necessary to slip the airplane to lose enough altitude to make the airplane fit the field. Our intrepid East Coast inspector was watching and met Fred as he was deplaning. Right in front of his passengers, he started giving him a going over for slipping the airplane with passengers aboard. Fred asked him what he would have done under the circumstances. The inspector said he would have done the obvious, use flaps. Fred exploded, saying, "I would have used flaps too if Giuseppe[1] had known what they were when he designed the airplane!"

That was the beginning of a running feud that continued for some time.

Just incidental to the foregoing narrative, that Bellanca was one of the last Pacemakers produced by the Bellanca factory, but they still did not incorporate flaps. Sig Wien had the large Pratt & Whitney R-1340, a six hundred horsepower engine, installed and was quite impressed. He loved the airplane. I remember fondly rubbing the fabric and commenting on the fact that everything on the airplane was designed to fly, even the struts. The aircraft burned at Big Delta in 1949.

One night, in Anchorage, one of our DC-3's was parked for the night at Merrill Field. Some practical jokers entered the airplane, cranked up the engines, received permission from the tower, and flew the aircraft around the pattern, landed, parked, and beat a hasty retreat. The crew in the tower got suspicious and reported it as it didn't seem normal. No one in the Company knew a thing about it.

In one of the rooms at the front of the hangar in Fairbanks, we had a Link Trainer. A special mock-up of an airplane set up for instrument training for both Northern Consolidated and Wien pilots. It was a much safer and cheaper method of teaching instrument flying. The unit contained a normal seat, rudder pedals, a control yoke, throttle and other controls, engine and flight instruments and radio head phones. That simulator was complete with a sound that closely represented the slip stream over the cabin when in flight. It was hard to sit in one of those things, fly an instrument problem, and not feel you were in an actual airplane.

The room had one door that opened to the outside and another to the hallway of the office part of the hangar building. A person could walk straight through. One day I walked into the training room, Fred entered from the opposite side of the room, and our little inspector was standing there also.

[1] Giuseppe Bellanca designed the Bellanca aircraft.

"Hello there Gregory," Fred said loudly. "Say, I hear they caught those guys who stole your Douglas in Anchorage."

Being quite surprised, as I had yet heard nothing, I said, "Oh yeah, who was it?"

"Just a couple of those drunken CAA Inspectors," Fred said, and kept walking.

Our little inspector got all excited and wanted to hear more, but Fred just walked away. For several minutes the inspector didn't even realize he was the butt of the joke.

Blinn Webster was a captain on the DC-3's and loved to fly. His stories about flying airplanes up from Great Falls, Montana, to Fairbanks for the Russian Lend Lease Program during the war, kept the younger fledglings enthralled for hours. He wasn't a braggart, just told fascinating stories, mostly on himself when he did something foolish but got away with it. Of course, knowledge or skill had nothing to do with it. He was just that lucky young squirt, flying fighters to Ladd Field for the Russians as part of the Lend Lease Program.

One day Blinn was scheduled for a flight check and of course our intrepid inspector was all enthusiasm and efficiency. He would know, beyond any shadow of a doubt, if Blinn Webster was qualified as captain on the DC-3 before this check ride was over, you could count on it.

There is some confusion about what it means to feather a propeller. If an engine fails, naturally it causes drag, just as a car engine does if a person takes his foot off the accelerator. In an airplane there is no transmission or clutch, so if the engine fails, the propeller continues to push the engine like the blades push a windmill. To minimize that drag, which is a must to allow the remaining engine to carry the load, it is possible to turn the propeller blades a full ninety degrees to the normal position. When the propeller is in the feather position the blades are edgewise to the line of flight, thus allowing the absolute minimum drag position to be achieved.

To feather the propeller there is a large, red button, almost impossible to hit inadvertently. One of the checks a pilot must make each time he runs the checklist before take-off is to press the feathering button and leave it snapped into feather

31

position long enough to be sure that it is working. That is determined by watching the tachometer needle to see the speed of the engine diminish without moving the throttle setting. The feathering button can then be manually pulled back to the original position, restoring the system to normal for take-off. Once the feathering button is intentionally pressed, the propeller will feather, even though the pilot is busy with both hands doing something else. That is by design to give the pilot time to do other necessary tasks when an actual emergency exists.

On the check ride the inspector served as co-pilot, dutifully reading off the checklist for Webster. When all was in order and the take-off run was in progress he read off the airspeeds just like a competent co-pilot should. After proper speed was acquired, Webster eased the aircraft into the air and called for gear-up. The inspector punched the feathering button on the right engine.

Blinn Webster had been around too long and had too much experience in the DC-3 to allow that to panic him in an empty airplane. He just politely cleaned up everything,[2] closed the engine down completely, continued the climb out, called the tower for permission to come on around for a landing on a single engine, for practice. He didn't declare an emergency or ask for any treatment other than ordinary.

Our little inspector nearly suffered apoplexy and decided that Webster had shown sufficient knowledge and ability in the DC-3 to be properly certified for another six months as captain.

The real amusing part, when it came to light, was that the inspector thought it necessary to hold the feathering button down for the complete cycle. To *unfeather* the prop, it *is* necessary to hold the button down, as it pops out when full feather has been achieved. He took the rest of the day off.

I usually worked construction in the summertime, and came back to airline work in the winter, and our little source of humor was gone that fall upon my return. It was rather dull around the airport that winter and in social circles he was missed by both of his friends.

With the coming of spring excitement picked up a little.

---

[2] Cleaned up means to have landing gear and flaps in the up and locked position.

Poorman

✈

The act of retrieving from the brush broken aircraft that have been asked to deliver a little more than could prudently be expected, is in itself an art. It requires a great deal of initiative, hard work, skill, imagination, and yes, luck. Generally speaking, luck is spelled WORK.

Practically it is important for all beginner mechanics to become acquainted with the art of "Resurrecting Cripples." I coined that terminology and the fellows in our crew picked it up. It has been a frequently used phrase where accidents and salvage operations are the subject of conversation.

Some of the older pilots who flew the Alaska bush had a good knowledge of the mechanics of the machines in which they placed so much trust. Blinn Webster really amazed me on one occasion. He had a problem with one engine of the DC-3 on which he flew as captain. He had just landed at the small, remote, mining village of Flat, when the trouble became apparent. He thought the problem through, considering the fact the aircraft was now empty, he decided it was not an unsafe operation to fly the aircraft back into McGrath where facilities for repairing or changing such a large engine were more readily available. His judgment proved sound. A safe operation was maintained and much expense and adverse working conditions were averted. Today, the FAA would hang him.

The problems began to surface with the influx of military trained pilots who were breaking into the bush-flying fraternity.

Many of the old bush pilots had started by scraping together what parts and promises they could, assembling a passable excuse for an airplane from the salvaged pieces, painting it, then hanging out their shingle advertising the "Fling Wing

33

Air Service." Many of the very reputable, substantial, and reliable old timers had such a questionable beginning. *This is the voice of experience.*

It really isn't very difficult to imagine the chasm that developed between the thinking of the old timers who were determined to fly the biggest piece home, and the product of the military training which taught that airplanes were expendable.

Entering the picture is also the psychological frame of mind after an accident.

The old timers well understood it was expedient to be as thorough and truthful as possible in reporting the condition of the damaged aircraft so the mechanics could take all necessary parts, tools, equipment, mosquito dope, and fishing gear, to complete the job—on the *first* trip.

The new breed felt if they would minimize the damage in the telling, it would somehow erase the blemish in the logbook as well as to their reputation. They could never seem to comprehend that once on the scene, the mechanics would, in short order, determine not only the awful truth but the fact they had lied as well. That act alone relegated them to the darkest corner of the hangar as well as the most reprobate piece of equipment in the fleet for future flights. Some pilots, with basically good potential, completely ostracized themselves by incurring the wrath of the mechanics through devious or untruthful reports.

The most humorous incident of my early indoctrination to the role of retriever of broken aircraft, occurred in about 1949, at the mining camp of Poorman.[1] The weather was beautiful: late May, breakup conditions. The airport was built on mine tailings and all the snow had been pushed off with a bulldozer. There were no soft spots.

About noon we got a radio report from Ruby. The pilot radioed Fairbanks he needed a mechanic and a spark plug. No explanation, no report of an accident, just a mechanic and a spark plug. We presumed he was at Ruby with a fouled spark plug and was afraid he may damage the engine if he flew it further.

[1] This story previously appeared in "Alaska Magazine."

Poorman

Smitty and I saw an opportunity to possibly catch a fish, so we grabbed a small handful of tools, our hip boots, fishing poles, and some new spark plugs. We jumped into my little Cessna and headed for Ruby about an hour before quitting time. We figured a fair exchange was no robbery; we planned to work the time in Ruby that we missed in Fairbanks.

Upon our arrival at Ruby, Chris Nollner, who lived in Ruby and always helped our pilots with freight and mail or fueling if necessary, advised us the airplane was in Poorman—standing on the prop in a snow bank. Sure enough, the first thing we saw when we crossed the ridge into Poorman was the giant tail of the blue Norseman, about fifteen feet in the air, silhouetted against a background of white snow. The pilot had landed too fast and used all the runway before starting to heavily use brakes. He had gone completely off the end and stopped on his nose in the berm pile made by the bulldozer that had cleared the field of snow a few days previously.

Smitty had a sense of humor that wouldn't quit, and a temper to match. It was quite obvious to us, before we even got out of the airplane, we weren't going to be cleaning any fish that trip. We also knew we were going to have to make a trip to Fairbanks and back, before morning, to get parts and tools we could have easily brought the first trip and saved three hours flying time.

We got out of the airplane and walked around to the front of the Norseman, then Smitty went into hysterics. The engine had scooted along on the frozen ground for about fifteen feet, scooping up rocks and snow. One boulder, about the size of a man's head, had broken off a spark plug—the major damage. Incidental damage was the bent propeller, the broken carburetor air scoop, the smashed lower cowling, a rocker box cover with a hole in it, and a rocker box full of gravel. He needed a mechanic and a spark plug.

We put a rope onto the tail and pulled it back down. I left my tools with Smitty, then headed back to Fairbanks to get replacement propeller, air scoop, more tools, and other necessities.

When I got back to Poorman about midnight, the pilot and some of the nearby mining crew had come out to join the fun. Smitty, with his highly developed ability to scorn and intimidate, had the pilot back in the brush among the mosquitoes, peeking out between the bushes, watching the progress.

We had the engine running by about 6 A.M. and to add insult to injured ego, Smitty absolutely refused to allow the pilot to fly the airplane back to Ruby. Smitty had an uncanny ability to be in command when necessary, whether or not anyone had delegated him that authority. He had me fly the Norseman to Ruby while he flew my airplane and brought the pilot with him. The pilot then took off from the longer airport at Ruby and flew the Norseman back to Fairbanks.

That was one of the pilots that left Alaska at the end of the season, and, to the best of my knowledge, never returned.

The following story also is about a Norseman and includes Art Smith. However, at the last minute, I was considered so valuable to the operation at Fairbanks that I, to my disappointment, was eliminated from the salvage crew.

The story begins with Terry McDonald, who worked around Pollock Flying Service until he was able to become a full fledged, licensed, and practicing commercial pilot. Pollock was one of the companies that combined with Dodson, Walatka, Miller, and Peterson to form Northern Consolidated Airlines. Frank Pollock moved to Washington state to pursue a business enterprise which involved a Cessna dealership. Terry went with him for a time but eventually came back to Alaska to fly for Northern Consolidated. It is so hard to leave Alaska.

During a flight from McGrath to Flat in a Norseman, Terry encountered some low clouds and snow. For a brief instant he lost ground visibility and when he saw the ground again his position, speed, and direction dictated the most dignified reaction was to pull back hard, close the throttle (and maybe his eyes). He hit fairly hard, but that old Norseman is a rugged airplane. The damage was enough he wasn't going to fly it out of there. Smitty and I felt it could be salvaged if we could rely on the description Terry gave us. Terry was from the old school and we felt we had a full and accurate appraisal.

Glen Dillard, the maintenance supervisor, was the part owner of the company who had replaced Harold Herning when he moved to McKinley Park for the summer. He had endured a sad experience with a Tri-motor Stinson salvage, gone bad.

36

After spending many ducats[2] on the salvage, the Stinson didn't even make it back to the shop for further restoration. After running out of fuel a few miles short of Anchorage, landing on the mud flats, and being swallowed by the tide, the Beluga Flats claimed that one.

With that memory crowding his judgment, it was hard to convince Dillard the Norseman could be salvaged. Terry was very upset.

"Darn," he said to me, "after ten years Alaska flying, now I have to leave one in the brush." Smitty and I finally offered to buy the airplane from the company. That caused Dillard to perk up his ears a little.

Finally, after sleeping on it, Dillard told Smitty he was willing to make a deal. He really didn't want to lose the airplane, but was also skittish about putting a lot of good money after bad. Here was the deal: Smitty was to take time off, take his own airplane, a J-3 Cub, go to Camelback Mountain, look at the downed Norseman, the location, the depth of the snow, and anything else that may be a contributing factor, then report back. The first thing to go wrong was, upon landing, Smitty broke through the crusted snow and broke his own wooden propeller. Inasmuch as it was necessary to get the Cub back, as well as the information, Dillard sent him a metal prop which we sandwiched between two boards and Winkleman, an operator who flew out of McGrath, dropped to him. It worked fine.

That evening, when the DC-3 returned from the mail run, we had all the information, including the patterns for some chrome-moly[3] patches Smitty wanted to strengthen some temporary repairs he was planning to make. He already had his little welding unit with him.

After receiving the patches he persuaded a native fellow from McGrath to go with him. They rounded up some hydraulic jacks and jacked and blocked the airplane into the best position for welding. Removing the skis, they turned them

[2] Ducats. A gold or silver coin of variable worth up to as much as two dollars and thirty cents.

[3] Chrome-moly. A chromium, molybdenum, steel alloy. Very strong and withstands vibration well. Used on the steel construction of airplanes.

around backward and slowly let the airplane down the hill, backward, with a block and tackle. Once on level ground they turned the skis around correctly, ran the engine, and called for a pilot. Terry McDonald came out to complete the flight he had begun a couple weeks before.

By the time they had the engine warmed up for take-off and Terry had been emphatically assured the airplane was just as strong as the day he put it in there, he was raring to go. A few minutes later, upon his arrival at McGrath, Terry made sure the inhabitants were aware he had returned with the same airplane with which he started the mail run to Flat. He finished his career without leaving one in the brush.

Searching for Gold

✈

In the spring of 1949, Glen Dillard assured me if I wanted to work construction for the summer I would still have a job that fall. Maintenance always seemed to go up in the winter time just by the nature of the operation. Skis, short days, the necessity of heating aircraft each morning, the necessity of "putting them to bed" each night, placed a higher demand on the crew. More people were required to do the job. It was as simple as that.

Dillard, a small, handsome man, with dark curly hair, was a perpetually smiling individual. He was also an accomplished mechanic with a world of experience. In case that perpetual smile should briefly depart his countenance, it was wise to give him extra room. He could hold his own when placed in a controversial position, but seemed to always come out with an amiable solution. It appeared I had a penchant for moving from one fantastic supervisor to another. I felt indeed fortunate to have him as an employer.

The dirt moving job that came first was just outside Fairbanks, straight out Gaffney Road on Ladd Field. We were building streets and lawns for new housing. One of the first people I met was Earl Thronsen. I had heard his name on the news during the winter. His family suffered a tragic cabin fire in the village of Ophir, near McGrath, which is on the Kuskokwim River, and serves as a hub for transportation. He and his wife, Laura, lost all their children. He asked me if he could ride to and from work with me each day since I had transportation and was going anyway.

Earl and Laura were staying in the Pioneer Hotel. I was still single so we often ate together at Pat and Mike's Cafe, next door to the hotel. Laura was due to give birth to a new baby in the near future.

Earlier in the year Ted Davis, with whom I had worked at the railroad roundhouse construction job in Fairbanks the previous summer, came into the hangar. Ted, his name was Tolbert E. Davis—hence the Ted, was married to an Eskimo girl from Selawik. He was all excited about the new gold strike in the Selawik River, up near Purcell Mountain, about fifty miles north of the Arctic Circle. He wanted to borrow my rifle and other related camping equipment. That was just the beginning. Later I wound up flying him, supplies, and other people into the area, eventually becoming a partner in the venture.

Of course, my being a pilot with an airplane, it was my assignment to make all purchases and deliveries of groceries and related goods. I left Ted with a good supply of grub and equipment when I had to leave to change the airplane from skis to wheels. The snow was all gone at Fairbanks. I made the change and one more trip, landing on the ice of a glaciered overflow. I felt I could do it one more time but a fog bank

Point of departure for prospecting trip. Author and Cushman St. Bridge across Chena River -- downtown Fairbanks in the '40's.

forced me to return without being able to land. The extended period of time in the air caused me to experience a few anxious moments.

Being aware the engine used more oil than normal, the drop in oil pressure told me what was happening, but the unknown was: "How long would it run?" I figured I could probably make it to Tanana. The wind was blowing unmercifully and produced slow ground speed. The turbulence was moderate to severe, making it necessary to maintain about five thousand feet altitude. That, of course, would give me more time to get worried if the pressure dropped completely and I had to hunt for a place to put the little Cessna 140.

The pressure began to become quite erratic. I knew a decision could not be forestalled much longer. The cussed radio would not work, making it impossible to call Tanana. They couldn't have done anything for me anyway but it wouldn't have been so lonesome if I could have just raised someone on the radio to give me some bad advice. One dislikes making all the mistakes by himself.

I had just crossed the last ridge of hills into the Yukon and knew I couldn't land on the river but thought I may as well save the engine if possible. I shut it off. My glide took me out over the Tozitna River where I spied a little gravel bar with high banks and tall spruce trees on the approach end. I could get a good, low approach coming in the wrong way—down wind, but beggars can't be choosers. I got all lined up, about twenty feet too low, then flipped the engine back on, and with power, drug the airplane the last few feet to the end of the bar, shut the engine off and got onto the brakes, hard. I splashed water coming in and ran the tail wheel out into the water turning around on the far end, but we made it. The beauty of the whole thing was, down on the river, the wind was not blowing very hard due to the nearby hills and tall spruce trees along the edges of the river.

I relieved myself, a chore so long overdue that keeping myself thinking clearly was a conscious effort. I then walked the entire gravel bar, even laid a small pole across the departing end to bounce me into the air on take-off, and kicked off all extra large rocks or sticks as I returned to the airplane. After adding three quarts of oil, I cranked up, went charging down the runway, popped flaps, tugged lightly on the elevator control, exhaled, and we were airborne. I thought I had really foxed Mother Nature that time, but later experience taught me I'd have done just as well making a normal take-off, without the pole at the end.

The next trip was with floats. Earl Thronsen was all excited about our search for gold and insisted we couldn't get along without his expertise and experience. He and I landed on a small lake which had a baby sister just north. They were separated by a heavy growth of lilly pads. The lake was full of nice-sized grayling. We took a two-man tent, our packs, sleeping bags, and please don't forget the mosquito nets. It was broad daylight so we walked until about midnight when fog came in over the hills and we couldn't see far enough to keep from getting lost. We did the only sensible thing; we camped. The next morning the weather was beautiful, so we continued toward camp but my stomach objected strenuously. That was the first time I ever baked a grayling on a rock, but not the last. I have always admired the Eskimo's ability to endure hunger.

After arriving and spending a night at camp we looked for a landing area for the Cessna on wheels. I had rented the float plane. It is so much nicer to fly your own and a good landing area at camp would preclude many footprints made while carrying a backpack, a big one, from the lake.

We found an area that looked like it had redeeming features. Ted gave me his order for groceries when I returned to Fairbanks. After working with them for a while I left them to clear the trees and brush off the intended landing area.

The take-off, from the nice grayling filled lake, was fun. I just couldn't quite get enough speed on the larger lake. The bend around the lilly pads was too sharp to be able to use them both. Methinks, I'm going to try something, I have plenty of room to stop if it doesn't work.

After taxiing up into the smaller lake as far as possible and turning toward the larger lake, I cut straight across those lilly pads. To my surprise, they bounced me right up onto the step instead of creating the expected drag. I was off and gone in half the larger lake. That lesson made me popular with many other float pilots with whom I shared it in future years.

After procuring the needed supplies in Fairbanks and giving the boys about the right amount of time to finish the landing area, I made the next trip in my little two-place Cessna on wheels. Circling the landing area, the strip looked beautiful, so I made the specialized short field approach and stopped amazingly short. Everyone was ecstatic, until I got out of the airplane and walked around a little.

Mixing professions is something like mixing languages. If a person thinks partly in Eskimo and partly in English, any explanation forthcoming tends to be less than lucid.

To illustrate my meaning, let us use the instructions of an Eskimo, as opposed to one in English, for the trip from here to there. The Eskimo will tell another Eskimo he must travel a long way looking into the sun at early morning then turn and follow the river, not very far, until it turns away from where the sun was this morning, then go same way, for long way, until you see different kind bushes. After awhile you will see big lake. A new trail will cross wrong side of lake. Take that trail and go away from west wind.

A person who uses English as his thinking language will tell you to travel east for about thirty miles, then follow the river for a couple or three miles when you will come to a bend in the river. You must not take the bend but leave the river and continue a straight course the same direction the straight part of the river established. After twenty five or thirty more miles you will come to some alders, and not more than two or three miles you should see a large lake. Across the side of the lake where the snow drifts badly, will be a newly-made trail which will take you on to the east and your desired destination.

Now an Eskimo would easily understand the first explanation, but the second would be quite confusing to him. An English-speaking person could easily understand the second explanation, but would be confused by the one given by the Eskimo. Neither explanation is itself basically flawed. The communication is lacking between those who speak and think in a different language. It took me a number of years to comprehend that it was up to me to adapt my thinking to that of the basic subsistence dweller, be he Native or English-speaking, in order to communicate fluently. I slowly learned many terms that were familiar to me were not to those, whites or natives, who lived mostly in the bush. How far is a mile to a person who has never seen a road? Learning their language will not do it—one must learn their thinking, then the language really helps. Forty years' association has helped also.

When a trapper asks a pilot to take him to the trapline, the most important question is not, "What kind of a load do you have?" but, "What kind of a landing area do you have?" Now is when you have to be careful.

I once had a trapper describe a landing area to me that was just as long as from here to there. It was always smooth and the wind seldom blew in that area. It was on a slough out of the main river and the ice always froze smooth as there was hardly any current. It was fairly straight, some bend to it but nothing abrupt. Boy, how can one be so lucky? Not even any snow drifts!

I almost fainted when I saw his landing place. He had described it perfectly. I seriously doubt I could have added any superlatives to enhance his description. However, I would have added there was a fifteen hundred foot bluff at each end, blocking any possible approach. To a professional trapper it was a beautiful dream, to a professional pilot it was a nightmare.

There were other times when the description probably fit a landing area described, but the last time the trapper had seen it was when he left it late in the spring when the snow was deep. It was an entirely different situation in early fall before much snow had fallen. During the course of a winter, a five hundred foot lake could easily turn into a good fifteen hundred foot landing area, due to a couple feet of snow falling and more drifting over rough places—meanwhile, back at my new landing strip.

Those guys had left the tops of the stumps, the largest of which were about five inches in diameter, level with the moss which was about four inches thick in most places, but as much as six in others. Hitting one of those stumps would have removed a landing gear for sure. I believe this error would easily fit into the realm of miscommunication, and we were all talking, thinking, and listening, in English.

I was on a flight plan and should have taken off in order to close it with someone, but after being fortunate enough to miss all those stumps on landing, I wasn't going to press my luck so far as to hope I'd miss them all on take-off. Besides, I wanted to be sure they were all removed before I used that strip again.

By the time we had the strip in a condition that I figured was usable, I was a couple days overdue on my flight plan. To my embarrassment, a search was instituted and on the second evening, Thomas Richards and Bob Jacobs, flying for Wien out of Kotzebue, flew over us. Thomas wrote me a note, put it into a glove with a shotgun shell for weight, and dropped it onto the strip. I signaled what we intended to do and a couple of days later, went into Kotzebue for more supplies and gasoline. It seemed Thomas and I could communicate better with signals than my partners and I could in conversation.

We had a lot of fun that summer, learned much about prospecting and human nature, and produced about one half ounce of real gold. Not really a profitable season, but quite representative of many.

I had flown Laura to Tanana to stay with her mother until her baby was born. Little Johnnie Thronsen was born a nice healthy baby, Earl and Laura decided they had best go back to the trapline for the winter. H.A. "Bogie" Bogenrife steered me into a job with Transocean Airlines, a new contractor furnishing air support for Arctic Contractors, who were conducting oil exploration on the North Slope, for the Navy. Before the winter was over, I was to have more interesting contact with Earl and Laura.

Just before going up north I dropped over to Weeks Field to see how Art Smith was doing with the Piper Cub and the shotgun we had rigged on top.

The Shotgun

✈

Back in the dark ages, before Ecologists and Environmentalists were even a member of the newly classified "Endangered Species," it was quite popular, even profitable on occasions, to hunt wolves, or trap them, if that be your long suit.

During and immediately after World War II, some of the local Federal Fish and Wildlife officials in the Fairbanks area arrived at some startling conclusions. They had been studying the reports of fur shipped out of Alaska early in the century and one winter became so interested they concentrated much of their time on the study.

After reading published early-day journals by prospectors, explorers, and adventurists, all available reports seemed to point to a country which provided a miserly supply of game.

Descriptions by Frank Dufresne, who was commissioned to gather information to formulate a fish and game regulation policy, on his early trips down the Yukon, in the Norton Sound, Hooper Bay areas, were part of his daily journal and helped to emphasize the lack of adequate game.

In 1883, when Lieutenant Frederick Schwatka departed upon his survey and fact-gathering journey down the Yukon, reached by way of the Chilkoot Pass, he had less money at his disposal than it cost to publish his report upon completion of the journey. It is easy to believe those people could recognize poverty and squalor upon first hand observation.

At the turn of the century, and just before, the Coast and Geodetic Survey had a number of parties out in the field who had to terminate their journey before they would have preferred because of the shortage of supplies brought on since resident fresh meat expected during the summer had not materialized. Heavier demands were placed upon the staples they had brought with them on their pack animals and future prospects were not encouraging. The surprising part of those old journals and reports was the incredibly small number of wolf and other predatory animal pelts shipped to the Outside fur buyers. If we subtract an honest estimate of that type of fur used locally for parkas and ruffs, the amount shipped still seemed unbelievably small.

Ray Wolford, the agent I knew the best, told me they then began to try to rationalize why there were such low game numbers as well as the low predator fur production. It would seem logical if the predatory animal count was high the fur catch, and thus shipment, would be high also. Sometimes the obvious really isn't so obvious when a person is trying to determine the cause and effect of a given situation. Ray and his associates finally came to a conclusion, which they considered well thought-out, concerning the low game and high predator ratio.

There are many trappers scattered throughout the wilds of Alaska, but the fur-bearing animals on which they depend for a living are not always prevalent around the ranges of the caribou or moose. The predators are.

A trapper can catch only the animals that frequent his particular trap line and it isn't practical to ignore all the marten, mink, otter, lynx, and other producing sets, to move ten or fifteen miles to set wolf traps because wolves were heard howling in that direction a couple nights in a row. If a normal trapline produces more than half a dozen wolves in a single year, it is indeed unusual. Most traplines will produce only a couple, or none. Remember, travel was, in those days, by either snowshoes or dog team. The team size was limited to one to three dogs to keep down the dog food necessary on the trapline. Wolves in packs had been observed and documented on many occasions following the larger caribou herds, and there were always some wolves if there were some caribou. The USFW[1] personnel themselves were on the leading edge of the hunting

[1] USFWS. During Territorial days, the United States Fish and Wildlife Service was the sole fish and game management force in Alaska.

of wolves from airplanes, especially after the war when several military surplus airplanes were donated for their use. A number of private individuals began to increase the horsepower in the smaller aircraft such as the Aeronca Champion, Piper Cub, Taylorcraft, Interstate Cadet, and others. Some of the Kansas, Nebraska, Dakotas, Wyoming, and Montana ranchers had developed a procedure that worked quite well to hunt and eliminate predators from the air.

Naturally, it wasn't long until wolf hunting was a popular sport all over Alaska. The most successful followers of the trade were those in the northern latitudes because of the lack of timber. Bert Beltz, who hunted out of Kotzebue, soon became a synonym for a wolf hunter. Art Fields, also of Kotzebue, was not far behind. When we heard that Glen Hudson, from Talkeetna, had taken seventy-five wolves in one season, the thought was incredible, almost unbelievable.

There are always those who excel in any sport or endeavor. Where a shooting team was concerned, Donald Stickman and Jimmy Huntington were the unquestioned leaders in the Interior of Alaska for several years.

The USFW agents were very helpful. They were interested in predator control and any procedures or tactics they had found to work well over others commonly used, were eagerly passed on to private individuals. The agency had more money, equipment, fuel, shotguns and ammunition, aircraft maintenance, and time at their disposal. They could develop and perfect procedures much faster than an individual.

For some unexplained reason, the moose population simply exploded in the late fifties. Sighting reports began to come from Unalakleet, Buckland, Kivolina, Colville River and points North and West—places no one could remember ever before having seen or heard of moose. Strange this should happen just a few years after a concerted effort was implemented to eliminate some of the predators.

Wolf hunting was getting into everyone's blood. Art Smith and I were not immune. In those days it was the popular thing to do. There were no crowds of people who had never made a snowshoe track or observed a live moose with his intestines dragging, standing on the street creating discord, telling us we were doing something that was a crime against society, the laws of nature, or self preservation, but right in tune with their personal agenda. Sam White, a very experienced, respected, and wise old game warden, praised and encouraged every one of us.

Since Art and I were working the night shift, our days were free to work on a wonderful invention. After traipsing around town for a couple of days, we finally found a Browning Auto-5 twelve gauge shotgun, with a cylinder bore barrel. We fashioned a mount that could be clamped to the tubing of the top of the Cub, making it possible to install the Browning Automatic Shotgun on top of Smitty's J-3 Cub. A cable was installed to encircle the trigger and extend down the window on the inside of the cabin to the throttle lever, making it possible to pull the trigger without even moving a hand from the controls. The shotgun could also be reloaded in flight through an inspection hole in the top of the cabin.

By bore sighting we had positioned the gun to shoot about four inches above the tip of the propeller in a vertical position. We had sights rigged up also but they didn't really help much. They were so easily bent we soon abandoned them and just used natural instinct for shooting a shotgun. We did surprisingly well. The big advantage was, with this setup, a person could come in much lower and get off a shot before the wolf could break away to the side or underneath, a trick at which they were very adept. If they were successful once, it took an extremely good team to ever get that wolf in their sights again. Their timing was so good they could jump to one side at the exact instant the gunner shot and his shot pattern would cover the spot where the wolf had so recently been, or would have been, had he kept running in a straight line.

Before we had a chance to do much hunting and just after test firing and sighting the shotgun, a fellow came along and was watching us work. He asked Smitty how we could be sure we would not hit the propeller. I told him we always throttled down to shoot and shot while the prop was crosswise.

"Now how's that again?" he asked.

I got about half way through the explanation again when Smitty couldn't hold it any longer and burst into laughter. When the fellow left, he was convinced we had some sort of a synchronizing method we didn't wish to divulge. Actually the distance from the muzzle of the barrel to the tip of the prop was so short the shot virtually had no time to spread to any perceptible degree. We never did have a problem, but that is more than several team or individual gunner-pilots could claim. Several of them had to land and wait for a friend to bring them a new prop after shooting the tip off the one they were using. It reminds one of the old days. Noel Wien tells about carrying an extra prop because of the danger of breaking one on a gravel bar or other rough landing area.

It has already been pointed out that a trapper moving from a productive trapline to an area he hoped would produce wolves really was not even a rational thought. A wolf trap is extremely expensive and quite heavy. Pursuing wolves was not a practical approach to trapping but hunting from an airplane was an entirely different story. Snow machines were not to appear for fifteen or twenty years.

An experienced pilot and gunner could wait for a fresh snow, which would tell them immediately they were on a fresh trail as soon as they spotted tracks. They could go to a likely place to spot wolves or to a locality where they were known to be prevalent. If the wolves moved to a new area, the hunters could also move without having to abandon a productive trapline as the professional trapper would be forced to do.

A professional trapper almost always has a base cabin from which he works and it would be necessary to add a tent to his equipment as he set forth on a strictly wolf-trapping expedition. If he was lucky and actually able to catch even a good number of wolves, it would probably take place in a short period of time. Then all the wolves would be gone and he would have to return to his neglected trap line. Trapping strictly for wolves, with the limited facilities of those days, was not a profitable venture.

When the hunter-pilot team made a decision concerning the locality they wished to hunt, they would head for the area where a sighting of a pack had been reported, then throttle back, pull on carburetor heat, lean the mixture, extend a couple notches of flaps and rock along at a good comfortable control speed. That would allow them to slowly scan the country beneath the aircraft as well as do a respectable job of flying. Fly-

51

ing in this configuration would extend the fuel endurance enough to squeeze considerably more hunting time out of the available daylight, sometimes as much as two hours. The most difficult logistic to overcome was fuel. When you need fuel it is a simple matter of being where there is fuel. If a team can squeeze two more hours of cruise out of the aircraft by managing the available fuel judiciously, they can considerably improve the utility of the time mother nature gives them each day. If it is necessary to return to base camp for fuel at three o'clock, there is no point in going back out. If they can stay out just a little longer, that is valuable time.

When a pack or trail was located the order of the day was haste. By nature, a wolf pack will scatter as soon as any indication of danger is present. By scattering in different directions any pursuer will be able to follow only one of them. If there are any hills in the area they will head straight up those hills, all in different directions.

With experience, a hunter will develop a system of keeping the scattered pack mostly within his realm of hunting ability and be able to instantly determine the one he has no chance to pursue and concentrate on the others. The ones that go straight up the hills are usually lost since the brush is thick enough, that while the animal is plainly visible, it is impossible in most circumstances, to stuff your shot with any success, through the brush to the animal. Also, the airplane generally will not have the performance to follow the wolf up a steep hill. A shot, if tried, would have to be made flying crosswise of the path of the wolf. It is easy to see such a shot, if successful, was pure accident coupled with luck. Now the pilot must land down below on a lake or slough and climb that hill to retrieve the wolf. That spells spending a lot of time and effort which would probably have been much more productive if that wolf had been left alone.

As in most professions, time is extremely important, especially in the arctic, as the days are so short in winter. Once an animal has been downed, retrieval in the least possible amount of time is important. Bert Beltz could skin a wolf in two minutes, and to the best of my knowledge, that is a record.

The Shotgun

As a predator control tool the airplane is the ultimate and it really was a great sport. My own feeling is it could still be utilized with discretion, but there are always people who want to see things only from their own perspective. Therein lies the problem.

Far be it from me to use this medium to advocate policy. I can see tremendous advantages as well as some shortcomings but let it here be stated, those of us who engaged in the practice while it was legal, really enjoyed it. We kept the predator numbers down to a better balance and this was done at no cost to the government, especially after the bounty was removed. Those surviving predators were the strong, healthy, and smartest animals who helped insure a superior posterity. Most of us were successful moose hunters at our favorite spot during the moose hunting season.

I built myself a .300 Weatherby on a Springfield action and brought home a moose taken with it for the next nineteen years that I hunted. I never did even get a shot at a wolf, summer or winter, with my rifle but did hear many of them howling. I saw many tracks along the river banks and occasionally had a glimpse as one disappeared into the brush. It was a thrill to know they were still out there but not in such numbers they too were going hungry.

On my commercial flights, knowing the heavy willow thickets and moose yards of winter, I enjoyed showing wolves to many passengers as we passed over. Many people will argue that moose do not appear in herds but I have counted as many as seventy-five moose in one willow patch on the Yukon. Many were amazed the wolves would be so close to the moose and the moose be so little concerned. I never showed a passenger an attack or the results of one. Most people have such an awe-inspired perception of the wolf that I felt it wasn't my prerogative to puncture their pink balloon.

As a mechanic, after moving to Barrow, I saw few wolves. Most of the caribou were in the Brooks Range and the wolves stayed close to them. I did, however, experience unbelievable winds.

Barrow

Pt. Barrow is about six degrees south of the northern most point on the North American Continent. It is also the weather factory for the majority of the continent north of the central United States. I entertained few thoughts about a soft job when I signed up to work for Transocean Airlines and I suffered no disappointment.

If it was possible to build a mechanical device that would last forever with no failures or malfunctions, the world would be on the verge of achieving perpetual motion. It is really amazing how well most aircraft and powerplants do function. There was a time, when I first started flying, if we got five hundred trouble free hours from an engine before overhaul was necessary, we felt indeed fortunate. Toward the end of my commercial flying career, I consistently reached twenty-five hundred hours before overhaul on the Lycoming engines in the Cherokee Six's. The old timers told stories about overhauls after extremely short periods of operation.

The first comers not only faced the reality of forced landings due to engine stoppage, they expected it. In the early part of my career we constantly kept ourselves aware of possible landing spots along our route of flight. I was fortunate that my forced landings were relatively few but I never was able to bring myself to forget the possibility there may still be one more.

It seems quite a high percentage of problems stemmed from magneto malfunctions. The problems were not because of the poor quality of the unit itself, but quite often from the lack of proper maintenance. My first problem to solve after my arrival at Barrow involved a magneto.

On a trip from Barrow to Umiat with Hank Dodson, a captain and check pilot on a C-46, we encountered a situation which had plagued that particular airplane for several weeks.

Hank was a first class pilot with a world of experience. He had been in the U.S. Army Air Corps during the war, had flown practically all the steel runway matting into Galena in a C-46. His instrument and C-46 experience alone was impressive enough to cause any mechanic to listen when he analized a problem. This was a new problem, even to him.

During engine run-up before departure, one engine would break down[1] when tested on one mag, then pick up and run perfectly, with no abnormal drop. One could switch back to both, then test the other mag with exactly the same result. It seems this situation had persisted for some time prior to my arrival. The mechanics could find nothing wrong in the carburetor, the "snuffel valve,"[2] or any other area that seemed likely to cause such abnormal reactions.

The problem always surfaced as the engine was switched to one mag, either mag, but it didn't seem logical both magnetos on the same engine would have the same problem at the same time. In flight, the engine performed beautifully for fifteen to twenty minutes, then it would backfire and shake, then smooth out again and run like new for another few minutes. It always gave good performance at high power for take-off and climb.

[1] When an engine is checked before take-off, a pilot will check each magneto separately. Each engine always has two magnetos, so a pilot will switch to one magneto, then back to both, then to the other, then back to both, to insure each is working properly. When a spark plug fails, or some other problem exists to cause noise from a back-fire or post-fire, it is called breaking down.

[2] Snuffel valve. Slang for a small valve at the bottom of the supercharger chamber which drops open by its own weight when the engine is not running, thus draining any excess fuel in the blower chamber. Supercharger suction will close the valve as soon as the engine is started. A valve stuck open could cause a problem very similar to the one we were experiencing.

On this particular trip the engine broke down and picked up and ran smoothly during the check, in the same manner it had done in the past. An added incentive to push the no go button surfaced when we could no longer see the far end of the runway, which was just a mile away.

Hank ran the engine up, then sat there a few minutes and asked Danny, the co-pilot, what he thought. He was willing to go if Hank was. Hank asked me and I said I didn't think the engine was any more likely to quit than it had been in the past but battling a bad engine and bad weather at the same time was really compounding the original problem.

We taxied back to the hangar. I dragged out the long ladder. My past experience had taught me when you know the trouble is in the carburetor, always look at the mags first. All my good advice was to look at the carburetor, look at the snuffle valve, but no one wanted to share my long ladder in the wind. Those were GE (General Electric) mags, with which I was totally unfamiliar. A cautious approach was in order. When I lifted the cover of the first mag I saw the trouble immediately. I took the cover off the other one despite all my advisors, as well as my own conviction, telling me there couldn't possibly be the same problem in both mags at the same time. There was.

There is a flat, metallic spring, with a centerpiece about the size of a dime, fastened to the rotor which contacts a carbon terminal to transfer the spark from the coil to the distributor block. The little dime-sized area was broken off and lying there in both mags. The spark had to jump the distance instead of making a contact transfer. At the time of switching to one mag, or occasionally in flight, the spark jumped to the wrong spark plug wire, thus firing the wrong cylinder and the result was a little unnerving. By replacing both rotors the situation was alleviated. This situation soon became a problem widely enough experienced to cause the CAA to issue an AD (Airworthy Directory) note requiring two springs be installed where formerly there had been only one. That cured the problem.

Wind, as defined by the meteorologists, is the flow of air from a cool to a warmer location. This flow is caused by unequal heating at different locations of the atmosphere at different latitudes and altitudes. Winds of concern to pilots of

small airplanes flying in fairly localized areas will be those created by temperature differential at different altitudes. However, this is a general rule only, to which those who fly in the
Arctic will attest.

It is extremely difficult to visualize wind created by a
displacement of air caused by an altitude differential at Barrow or Barter Island. Fifty feet of altitude above sea level will
clear anything for miles around, and the temperature reading
may be minus forty degrees over a sixteen hundred square mile
area. Much the same situation prevails around the mouth of
the Kuskokwim and Yukon Rivers. When the temperature is a
minus forty degrees for fifty miles up or down the coast or
anywhere inland, and presumably out over the ice, the theory
of wind caused by the rotation of the Earth comes into play.

Working at Barrow during the winter of 1950 gave us
ample opportunity to see, feel, and analyze wind most of us
thought was strictly relegated to a hurricane. The force of the
wind was almost unbelievable. During a typhoon on Guam in
1944, the mechanics and pilots sat in the bombers all through
one night, continuously pumping hydraulic pressure by hand
to activate the brakes. The wind was allowed to weathercock
the airplanes as it swung from southwest to northeast. That,
however, was not a practice to which the pilots or mechanics
at Barrow would take too kindly in a minus twenty degree
temperature with such a wind.

We had a number of airplanes tied to the ice on the lake
by employing the most efficient method possible by freezing a
loop of cable into a hole in the ice we made an extremely strong
tie down. Most of the airplanes were tied in this manner, faced
into the wind as it was blowing when the airplanes were parked
for the night. Fortunately the prevailing wind was from generally the same direction and once the tie down loops had been
frozen into the ice they could be used daily. However, we had
one Stinson tied in a manner not detrimental at the beginning
but as the wind swung from west around to the northeast the
situation became a concern. We discussed several options, even
that of tying two full drums of fuel to each wing, then turning
loose the ropes tied to the ice and allowing the aircraft to weathercock, then secure them more positively. I was in favor of this
procedure, but those with more experience than I vetoed turn-

ing loose an aircraft, once secured, in such a wind. I didn't argue. As a result the wind blew the rudder off the airplane but we still had an airplane on which to install a new rudder when we were able to procure one. Had we turned it loose we may have lost the entire airplane.

We also had a Grumman Widgeon, a twin engine amphibian, well tied down. For the first part of the big blow it was protected by being in the lee of a C-46 to which we had a Caterpillar D-8 tied to each wing with double three-quarter inch ropes. The Widgeon, being an amphibian, was necessarily used sometimes in salt water so it had a good protection of primer and paint. After the wind swung around to a fairly direct approach to the Widgeon, we noticed white spots appearing on the side of the hull. It appeared as though small pieces of snow would fly through the air, hit the side of the airplane, and stick. I finally stopped and watched for a couple minutes. To my surprise, the wind would pick up a small ball of hard-packed snow, lift it into the air and when it struck the side of the Widgeon, it would take a patch of paint about two to four inches in diameter off the surface of the hull as clean as a sand blaster would have done.

That C-46 was grossed out with a full 48,000 pound load plus the three-quarter inch ropes tied to the drawbar of the D-8 Cat. on each wing. When a gust of wind hit the wings, the aircraft would raise into the air, stretching the ropes to the extent the main landing gear struts would fully extend. The tires would not quite come off the surface but the weight they were suspending was certainly minimal.

After having undergone this experience it makes it easier for me to understand and appreciate some of the stories by Admiral Byrd or Sir Douglas Mawson describing wind in the Antarctic.

The sound of the waves pounding the shore line across the runway to the north was very much as sound affects portray them when showing hurricane movies. Ice had been blown inland in huge blocks which had formed a dike along the shore as far as one could see. In some places this dike was as much as fifty feet high. A strong gust of wind would crash the water into the ice dike and water would come completely across the runway to our side by the hangar. It has been so long ago I'd not hazard a guess about the distance but do remember being very impressed at the time. We never did find a set of floats that, before the storm, had been parked outside, behind the hangar.

After serving an apprenticeship in the weather factory at Barrow, a decision was made to return to civilization for Christmas. During the Holidays, Orville Tosch, representing Northern Consolidated Airlines, insisted I not return to Barrow but go to Bethel to again work for Northern Consolidated. I knew most of the pilots and mechanics and was familiar with the airplanes, plus the fact I didn't like the working conditions at Barrow. I allowed myself to be persuaded to accept the offer so I gave Bill Word, Northern Manager for Transocean Airlines, proper notice.

Bill was later killed in a Douglas DC-4 which exploded in flight between Wake Island and Hawaii. That was the first in-flight sabotage I can remember.

On the way to Bethel in my own airplane, I took Jim Gilbertson, a cat skinner with whom I had worked during the summer, to Ophir. Jim and Earl Thronsen had planned to trap together on a trapline Earl had been running for several years on the Innoko and Dishna Rivers.

I think no one was ever guilty of declaring there was a dull New Year's Eve party in Ophir in 1950.

Bethel

✠

e spent the night of New Year's Eve, 1950, in Ophir and of course there was a New Year's Eve party. Not being a drinking man I fared quite well, but I fear without me and a couple other cool heads, someone would have been digging graves the first of the new year. It would be appropriate to say that wild party could be better imagined than described. Just replay Jorgy Jorgensen's rendition of "I 'ust Go Nuts At Christmas."

I did take a rifle, loaded and cocked, away from one individual in a rather novel manner. He had made a threat which only Jim Gilbertson took seriously, but he convinced the rest of us we should also be concerned. We blew out all the lights when we saw him at a distance, approaching with a rifle in his hands. The night was clear and cold. The moon was full. Objects on the horizon were plainly visible. I stationed myself just inside the door through which he would enter, then used the old military system of grabbing a rifle out of the holders hands with one fast, strong, sweep of the arm. I had the rifle completely free of his grasp and the bolt open before he realized what had happened. Someone else grabbed him. I dashed upstairs, unloaded the rifle and hid the bolt. That action alone saved him from standing a trial for murder. There is no question about it. From then on the party got interesting. In successive days the party started anew every morning.

I finally got out from under my obligation to see everyone on the trapline by just cranking up my airplane and leaving. I could never get enough of the players sober at one time to make any progress. I did have a job responsibility which took precedence over waiting for them, so I continued my journey down the Kuskokwim to Bethel.

Never Too Late To Be A Hero

Upon my arrival at the Kuskokwim River village things were not really in a neglected state but there was ample work to make sure accounting for spare time was not a problem.

Things were moving along in a fairly normal fashion until the evening of Washington's Birthday. I had gone to bed about ten o'clock. It was fairly windy when I last checked, but the airplanes were all well tied and the wind always blows in Bethel. I was just going into a deep sleep when Fritz Awe, a miner from Marvel Creek who happened to be in Bethel, awoke me and announced that a hurricane force wind was blowing.

I jumped out of bed, dressed, and headed for the river ice, where all the airplanes were parked. Things weren't yet in a serious condition, but it was apparent that attention was necessary or the situation would get worse.

The Norseman was tied to the ice with three-quarter inch ropes. The right wing had broken loose, allowing the aircraft to swing around far enough for the tail to crash under the wing of the Lockheed Vega[1] which tie down ropes were still holding. The first priority was to secure the Norseman. We drove the Dodge Power Wagon, with a cable winch in front, under the wing of the Norseman and tied it to the wing with a double one-half inch rope, then secured another three-quarter inch rope to a tie down in the ice. The wind would stretch the ropes enough to lift the Dodge front end right off the ice but it held from then on. The rest of the airplanes were holding their positions well and didn't seem in any danger of being damaged.

Now we could return to the chore of tending to our own equipment. My little Cessna, fortunately, was facing directly into the wind as it was now blowing. I put a full drum of fuel across each ski to add weight and stability. The wind was blowing the propeller around, not whirling, but it would be standing crossways, then a moment later, straight up and down.

In order to negotiate the trail from the river bank to the airplanes it was necessary to crawl. An attempt to stand and walk normally ended in abject failure. We usually found ourselves sprawled on the ice grabbing for something to stop our

[1] Lockheed Vega NC 12288 was one of only two all-metal fuselages built by Lockheed. Paul Manz later bought and restored the airplane to use in movies.

62

progress in the wrong direction, so we crawled. Going back up the trail was simple—just try to stay on your feet and aim for something to grab to arrest your progress upon reaching somewhere near your destination.

A true compliment must be paid to the ground crew. They voluntarily appeared to help prevent damage or further damage to the aircraft. There were many volunteers on the scene as well.

The weather bureau anemometers at both Barrow and Bethel were not capable of reading the highest wind gusts but the steady wind at both locations was well over one hundred miles per hour during the peak of the blow. How fortunate I was to experience these two unusually strong winds, both the same winter.

There was a very interesting occurrence concerning an Alaska Airlines Bellanca, which was parked on the river bank. It was still on floats, just sitting there, not tied down, and it rode out the entire wind with no problem. They had a Stinson SR-9 tied on the ice, on skis, which was upside down by the time we first got to the river.

George Thiele, one of our pilots and my room-mate, had a J-3 Cub on skis which blew into the upside down position very early. That was probably partly my fault. Not being

Alaska Airlines Stinson SR-9 on its back after Bethel wind.

from a windy country, I didn't fully understand the aerodynamic and physical theories that help one keep his equipment in one piece. I tied the control stick of George's Cub with the safety belt, which is exactly what my primary instructor had taught me. I was like most students, the instructor's word was absolute (until sad experience taught me better). He also was not from a windy country and believed, without question, things he had read or been told, until they proved unsound, as was the case with the Cub. The airplane was stronger than the ropes, so when a strong gust hit the Cub, the ropes broke and the Cub with the stick tied back tried to perform a loop but with insufficient speed and altitude.

In the village, from end to end, there was trash everywhere for a few moments, then it would fly away!! There were full sheets of corrugated iron roofing sailing along the streets about four to six feet in the air. They would have cut a person in half, had they encountered them in a standing position. Some windows, frame and all, blew out of the wall into the room. Some roofs were removed. Empty fuel drums, garbage cans, boxes, about anything a person could imagine, went sailing by from time to time.

Norseman breaks loose in big wind at Bethel on Washington's Birthday, 1951.

The Northern Commercial Co. maintained a quonset hut on the tundra, behind their main store building, which they used for the storage of pressure appliance fuel, kerosene, and cased gasoline. When the wind settled down and everyone took a look to see what was left of their town, the quonset hut, all except the base floor and the fuel which was mostly still stacked on pallets just as it had been shipped, was completely gone, never again to be seen.

The river at Bethel, being close enough to the coast to experience daily tides, was also affected by the ice moving up and down with the tides. The ice along the shore would crack and bend as the ice in the center of the river floated up and sank back down with the tides. Wind blowing from the coast naturally held the water back from flowing out to sea, which in turn raised the level of the water at all points for over one hundred fifty miles from the mouth of the river. The on shore wind blew the level of the water much higher than the high-tide level. Small rivers formed on each side of the main ice along the shore on both sides of the river. It became necessary to use a boat to get from the river bank to the solid ice and the airplanes. We could not get the Dodge Power Wagon back to the shore so the simple solution was to bring all passengers, baggage, and freight, out to the main ice with the boat, then drive them across the river to the larger airport, which accommodated the larger passenger carrying DC-3. Another boat would transport them from the ice to the shore near the DC-3. After a few days the water level dropped and froze along the shore to a strength great enough to support the truck.

The task now was to get all the airplanes back into operation. The Lockheed Vega had only minor damage which did not require removing it from service. A few surface patches would suffice until it was due to go to town for a regular inspection. The Stinsons and the Aeronca were unscathed. The Norseman was a different story.

I removed the rudder from the aircraft and welded the top of the tubing framework in order to recover it with fabric, and it was again safe to fly. The wooden spars on the left stabilizer were both cracked longitudinally, right where the landing and flying wires attach. By removing enough fabric material to work on the spar itself and fashioning a plate of chrommoly steel for each side, bolting them into place, George and I flew the airplane to Fairbanks, without a ferry permit, for further corrective surgery. We turned it over to Walt Eberhardt who decided complete amputation and transplant, of both front and rear spars, was in order.

Wind, like fortunes of life, sometimes comes to us in doses greater than our ability to appreciate, utilize, or even tolerate—yet on other occasions it seems to be in such short supply, like when one attempts a take-off with a heavy load, on floats, from a small lake.

With the coming of spring, water ran on top of the ice about a foot deep on some occasions. Naturally, water turned to ice each night. During the take-off run in the mornings, the skis would break through the thin ice and the propellers would throw chunks of ice, like so many meat cleavers, against the bellies and tails of the airplanes. I tried to get the operation to close down for a couple of days to allow the ice to float up on top of the increasing surge of fresh water.

No one was very sympathetic to my requests. I guess mostly because they were not the ones who had to go around town scrounging bed sheets to replace the fabric torn off the airplanes during the morning take-off. After a couple of days the ice floated up and the problems were over, but our supply of nitrate dope and bed sheets was becoming rather meager.

In a couple of weeks the ice was gone and the airplanes were on floats. Now comes the real Chinese fire drill.

Flying Floats

✈

S alvation came in the form of Bob Lindsey. Bob had been working for a mining company at Nyac.[1] He was a self starter and could work well without supervision. He set up a five hundred gallon gasoline fueling facility, which really made the fueling of the aircraft on floats a simple task, something Northern Consolidated Airlines really needed. Things were just getting lined out nicely when Alden Williams appeared in a Norseman on floats. He had brought it over from Dillingham for the purpose of repairing a cantankerous starter. Alden was an old friend whose permanent station was Fairbanks. He was a rather small man with piercing blue eyes and a friendly smile. He had started flying in the twenties back in the plains states of Kansas and Nebraska. He loved to fly—had even courted a beautiful girl named Dorothea by giving her rides in his airplane. She once told me how he had demonstrated a loop—and the engine had quit, precipitating a forced landing. The loop and forced landing had no negative effects. They married, reared two children of whom they were justly proud, always following the flying trade.

Just give Alden an airplane, an assignment, and turn him loose—you would see him again in a few days—coming home with a load of passengers and a handful of money he had gleaned handling business along the way. When problems arose, such as the starter on the Norseman, he would figure out a solution.

[1] Nyac. New York Alaska Company owned and operated a gold mining dredge, on the Upper Tuluksak River.

The engineering that went into that starter was extremely fascinating. It was not only a heavy duty, functional piece of equipment, but a work of art as well. Several companies were manufacturing the starter. The most common ones we encountered were Leece-Neville, Jack & Heinz, Eclipse, and probably several others that do not immediately come to mind. All would fit the same engine, and were very reliable if properly installed and utilized. They were heavy with a flange containing many holes around the perimeter to accommodate almost any installation position the mechanic may choose. This made it very nice, as they were so compatible with other accessories installed on the rear case of the engine. They were referred to as inertia starters, since they incorporated a steel flywheel that contributed the inertia for rotating the engine once speed was built up with the hand crank or electric starter motor.

The most disturbing part of the installation or removal of said starter was the fact it simply could not be accomplished without a special wrench. Yes, of course, those wrenches were available commercially, but were rather expensive and used only for that purpose. It was a simple matter for a mechanic to dig through his tools and find an old wrench of the proper size, cut it off to a handle length of about three inches, drill a three-sixteenths inch hole in the end of the handle and install a simple clevis to which had been welded a three-sixteenths inch diameter rod with a tee welded on the end. This tool could be used for many close quarter purposes, but was essential for either removal or installation of the starter.

It was late in the evening when Alden landed in Bethel. He told me after take-off at one of the stations in Bristol Bay, he noticed an intolerable amount of radio noise. His search for the source disclosed the starter switch had not centered upon being released after the last startup. To prevent misuse of the starter, the switch is spring-loaded—designed to return to the center, or off position, when not actually held in the cranking mode. However, this time it had stuck, not automatically returning to center, thus continuing to turn the starter motor and creating radio noise.

Flying Floats

After the next stop the starter would not function for startup. True to the traditional enterprising nature of all successful bush pilots, Alden placed some planks across the floats and propped the engine. He carefully removed the planks and delivered the problem to me at Bethel. It was quite late and nothing was revealed after a quick once over in search of a burned or disconnected wire so we all went to bed for another try in the morning.

The next morning about six o'clock I went down to the river and tried the starter and it worked like a charm. The station manager came running out rubbing his hands with glee. He announced that with such beautiful weather, we should be able to catch up on some of the back logged mail to Hooper Bay.

Alden returned to Fairbanks on a regular scheduled flight and Elmer Nicholson, a pilot stationed in Bethel, was assigned the flight to Hooper Bay.

Elmer had grown up in the Bristol Bay, Kuskokwim, Yukon River area. He was a small man with bushy hair and blue eyes—always sporting a cigar which was seldom lit. We often called him "stogy." He had fished and flown in the area for many years.

I fetched a tray of tools and my hip boots preparing to go with him. The station manager announced that I couldn't go as they had more than a load of mail and could not sacrifice my weight worth of pay load. I explained I wasn't preparing to go on a pleasure trip. I had done nothing to cause the starter to function, consequently it may not work next time. I could not repair the starter, but I may be able to get the engine going so Elmer could at least get the airplane home.

The station manager was adamant that I could not go as the company simply couldn't afford for me to be taking joy rides, so I tried again. I told him the only thing that had changed was the temperature of the engine and starter. After a flight, the temperature would again be up and the starter probably would again refuse to function. I had done nothing to correct the problem. The argument continued until I finally had to tell him in plain English—if I didn't go, the airplane was not going. I would not sign it off as airworthy. Elmer then spoke up and said if I didn't go, he didn't want to fly the trip either. The station manager was more than a little disturbed, but Elmer's words saved an airplane.

Upon arriving at Hooper Bay I was simply astounded at the thickness of the ice. The tide was going out and the wind was light, but blowing toward the ice. We left the engine running until a group of Eskimos approached in kayaks. I never did see how they got their kayaks from the top of the ice down to the water. They took hold of the floats and kept the airplane away from the ice while we unloaded their mail and loaded the outgoing mail. You guessed it—upon trial the starter would not work.

The Norseman has a plate on the firewall[2] that can be removed from the cabin by turning a number of dzus[3] fasteners from the inside, allowing access to the rear of the engine. The starter is mounted right in the center of the engine. Lying on the floor of the cabin, I removed the rear of the starter, exposing a shaft that operates the cranking pawl which engages the engine when the operator wants the starter to turn the engine. The procedure for starting is to 'energize' the starter, which means wind it up to top speed, then engage for starting.

In my thinking there was a dead winding in the starter motor. By disturbing the position of the starter motor, I may be able to make it work one more time. By doing everything in the starting procedure backward, I could move the starter motor position. I manually shoved the shaft forward, engaging the cranking pawl. Then I had Elmer carefully turn the propeller backward a slight amount, and stand clear. Presto, when I reached up over the bottom of the switch panel and groped around until I found the starter switch and tried it, the starter began to energize. Magic! I told Elmer to get into the pilot seat and get everything ready for start, then let me know. Upon his signal I forced the pawl into engage position with the heel of my hand and the engine started, just like uptown.

[2] Firewall. The metal divider between an engine and the cabin. Most airplanes employ stainless steel for its fire resistant qualities.

[3] Dzus. A trade name for a patented, quarter-turn fastener used on most cowlings and quick removal panels.

70

After closing the firewall door and climbing back up into my seat, I could hardly believe my eyes. The ice was now another ten or twelve feet above the airplane. The tide was now fully out and the wind was perceptibly stronger. There was not a ghost of a chance of our saving that airplane from total destruction had we not been able to get the engine running. My real regret was that the station manager wasn't able to see what I saw when I climbed back into my seat.

A replacement starter arrived while we were at Hooper Bay. I had it changed before morning and the airplane was again safe to fly solo.

The accessories overhaul mechanic in Fairbanks later told me there was indeed a dead winding in the starter motor and disturbing the position from where it stopped was enough to make it work repeatedly, provided you wanted to go through that charade each start-up.

Larry Rost dropped in a few days later with his SRJR Stinson, on floats. It is the same airplane that now sits in the Gold Dome at Alaskaland, in Fairbanks.

Larry was a solidly built man, a little less than six feet tall, weighing around two hundred pounds. His beautiful, white, evenly spaced teeth caught the eye of everyone on their first

Stinson SRJR put away for the winter after engine repairs at Kipnuk in 1951.

meeting. His coal black hair was combed straight back under a baseball cap. He had flown in the Army Air Corps and at the end of the war had started his own flying business. He flew mostly floats out of Anchorage and Bristol Bay. He had a contract to fly his Stinson for the U.S. Coast and Geodetic Survey. When refueling at McGrath on the way from Anchorage to Kipnuk, his fuel tank cap had apparently not been replaced; at least it was gone now. He needed one desperately in order to be available to fly on the Coast Survey contract the next morning. With Larry, price was no problem, just — can you come up with a gas cap?

I was in a foul mood since the shop was in such a mess. A person from the higher echelon in Anchorage had visited our station while I was away and had told Emmett Shaw, a helper soon to leave for the mines at Platinum, that he wanted the shop all cleaned up, painted and put more in an order of display. Upon another trip through Bethel a couple weeks later, that job had not yet been accomplished. He arbitrarily took everything off the wall, out of the drawers, out of the bins, and piled them in a huge mess on the floor of the shop. It appeared to me that the fact the airplanes had never been unable to perform when scheduled, even though I was working alone and sometimes worked all night, had totally escaped the attention of the Anchorage headquarters. Being a little stubborn myself, I still felt the care of the airplanes took precedence over putting my shop on display, so I ignored the mess and worked around it. I just looked at Larry and told him if he could find a gas cap that he could use among that mess, he was welcome to it.

A short time later, maybe a couple of weeks, Larry was back at my shop. "Can you come and help me out?"

"What seems to be the main problem?" I asked.

"Oh I can't get the engine started. It's trying to jump out of the mounts, it is catching fire. It ... it ... look, if you can just help me so I can get it to Anchorage, I'll just change the engine."

"How old is the engine?" I asked.

"It has about thirty five hours since installation," he said, then added, "Look, I just want to get it to Anchorage. Ben Walker can't come out here, but he can, and will, help me make the change in Anchorage. I have several spare engines already overhauled."

"Larry," I said, "I can't even listen very well on an empty stomach, much less think. Let's go get a bite to eat, I'm hungry."

Well, Larry wasn't, but he had to be near someone who talked his language, so we went over to Marsh's Cafe. Marsh's Cafe was located just beyond the Alaska Airlines office and shop which was just down stream from our own. Most pilots and mechanics gathered there to seek their own kind and trade news. It was small and quite informal, ran by "Bergie" Marsh. The family lived in the same building and a friendly, relaxed atmosphere was always present.

I kept casually asking Larry questions until I had it fairly well established in my own mind that the problem was in the mag, or someplace in the ignition system.

When I asked him, "How is your radio?" he exploded. It was partly because, to him, it was so totally unrelated, and partly because of what his answer revealed.

"Please don't get me started on that! When I left Anchorage it was working just like a telephone and now I can't hear a thing for static."

"Did this all happen at once, or was it progressive?" I asked.

He admitted it was definitely a progressive thing.

I drew him a mental picture of the way a set of distributor blocks could break down if they had happened to be subjected to improper storage. Once the spark from the magneto began to follow an errant course, it would cause horrible noise in the radio. As this malady progressed, it would begin to cause the more obvious problems, such as he had described. If the path of the spark was so misdirected as to travel to the wrong spark plug and fire a cylinder with an open intake valve, the fire would be carried through the intake pipes to the impeller section, then out through the carburetor, causing some anxious moments for all parties involved. Due to the retarded firing feature for cranking, the situation would be amplified during the starting procedure.

Larry scheduled himself to go to Anchorage on our return flight to secure a pair of new distributor blocks and someone to come out to change them for him. I was sorry I couldn't help him, but I just couldn't spare the time, especially that far from home base.

Bethel being located about one hundred miles from the mouth of the Kuskokwim River and affected by the tides of the ocean has a problem to overcome. At high tide in the ocean the water level at the river bank in Bethel will raise considerably. Naturally when the tides are low, the water level at the river bank drops accordingly. This is not just an interesting phenomenon, it is a serious problem if one wishes to secure an airplane equipped with pontoons, along the river bank.

It is easy to see that some system must be employed, other than having a person on duty at all hours to keep moving an airplane either in or out to maintain safe parking and comply with the whims of the incoming or outgoing tides. We elected to use an anchor and buoy system. A weight sufficient to stabilize our largest aircraft was sunk to the bottom at high tide, then the attached rope was fastened to a buoy to mark the spot and allow plenty of rope to secure an airplane. This worked quite well and the airplanes would even swing around and face down stream during a stiff up-river breeze.

On the particular afternoon Larry was waiting for the 'turn around' to be completed so he could board the DC-3 for Anchorage, the station manager came out to the shop and asked me to get the Twin Cessna in to the beach as he had a charter and the pilot was on his way down. I told him I would try, but our boat was across the river where the boys were attending to the DC-3. The station manager mumbled something I did not understand and returned to the office.

I tried to procure a boat from anyone I could find who may be able to drop me at the airplane so I could untie it and taxi to the beach. I don't think I have ever seen so few boats on the river. A few minutes later the station manager returned demanding the airplane immediately. I guess he expected me to produce a boat by magic.

Flying Floats

Looking back over forty years of maturing, I can see he was under a lot of pressure and his experience in his job was considerably less than mine was in mine. He was so frustrated he just wanted to lash out at anyone, and I was handy. He felt I was a subordinate. I really didn't see it that way. I was chief of maintenance, he was chief of operations—just two separate jobs for the same company.

I really didn't feel the company was being very fair to me. I was working about seventy hours a week to keep the operation running smoothly and we had never had one of our airplanes out of service for mechanical reasons except when we experienced the devastating wind storm and once when I had to change an engine on an airplane brought in from another location. The company was paying me a monthly salary. They had recently even tried to discontinue furnishing the free room at the company owned roadhouse which had been part of the original enticement to get me to take the job. All this, on top of my still seething reaction to the mess in my shop, pushed me over the edge.

Remembering none of the actual words exchanged, it would be hard to reconstruct a conversation, but I think it fair to admit that probably neither of us employed a generous amount of diplomacy. The end result of the conversation was, I was now free to go help Larry, and he was free to start looking for another chief of maintenance. One thing I do know, I felt more relieved than I had in months. Later the company paid me a nice compliment. They hired two mechanics, both paid by the hour, to replace me.

I went out to our local municipal airport where we kept the smaller airplanes, got into my little Cessna 140 and flew over to the airport where the DC-3 was being loaded. I told Larry I'd go to Kipnuk with him. He elected not to go to Anchorage, but sent a telegram to his regular mechanic in Anchorage to send out a couple of new distributor blocks on the next airplane.

Larry rented a three place Piper Super Cruiser on floats and we went to Kipnuk as soon as the parts came. We were able to eat and sleep at the Coast Survey camp where Larry held his contract. The actual work of replacing the distributor blocks was not particularly difficult, but I did thoroughly con-

75

fuse Larry when I started tracing out the wires and attaching them. He didn't want to sacrifice the time for an explanation, if I knew what I was doing, just do it. Finally I told Larry to jump in and crank it up.

Larry was so skeptical, he stationed me with a fire extinguisher, just so—"The fire is going to be right here, be careful of the prop, don't fall into the lake..." he primed the engine, yelled "Clear!" and hit the starter. That prop went through about two cylinders and the engine was running just like a self respecting Lycoming always does. It sounded like a well-oiled Singer sewing machine. Larry shut it down, cranked it again, shut it off, cranked it again, then shut it off and fell out onto the float, grabbed me around the neck and pounded me on the back until I wished it hadn't run quite so well. I could see what was coming so I just turned loose and jumped. We both went into the water over our boots but no matter, that engine was the most beautiful sounding thing this side of Anchorage.

Still slapping me on the back as we waded to shore he said, "Look, I'm going to tell you something you had better learn if you want to live working around float planes or fishing boats. I haven't said anything before, but now I think you are really worth saving. Cut those cussed straps off your hip boots so if you fall into deep water and have to swim[4] you can at least get your boots off."

I took out my knife and cut them off and have done so on every pair of boots I've owned since. It was thirty two years later[5] but that little bit of advice, one day, saved me from drowning.

Looking back over operations like this one, it is amusing the things a person will remember. I recall a little bird nesting right along the trail. Every time we passed the nest to or from the camp, the broken wing act was performed for us.

---

[4] All hip waders are made with straps that fasten tightly above the calf of the leg. That makes it difficult to remove hip boots and swim at the same time.

[5] After retiring, the author once swamped a boat while moose hunting, wearing insulated hip waders, was able to kick them off while swimming, then made it safely to shore.

Larry told me later he went out to the airplane early one morning and there was nothing but feathers and egg shells where a mink had been during the night.

One day at lunch we had fresh duck. I think the fellow who shot the duck was the only one at the table who didn't know it was a loon.

I think the thing hardest for Larry to abide, and about which he said nothing, was my constant absent minded lapsing into whistling a tune, especially when I was almost stumped over something. It was not lost on me that Larry would pick up the tune I was imitating and whistle it or sing it in clear, on key notes. I could recognize his accurate rendition, but just didn't have the ability to duplicate it. As concerned as he was about the engine, it must have really been trying for him, but he never once mentioned it.

I had gone to Fairbanks to see Dr. Shaible and returned a few days before Larry first approached me. While there, Dr. Shaible advised me I had a condition not uncommon to people who worked in bush communities. He suggested I take some time off, go out to my cabin on the Salcha River to watch the breakup, and stop working so hard. He gave me the liver and iron to combat anemia, but told me the real problem was revolving too tight in my circles and not enough diversified circles.

I didn't have any help and the company didn't seem willing to send me a mechanic or even a mechanic's helper. I had a crew that was beyond reproach but their duties took up all of their time and there was none left over to help me. I didn't see any way I could keep all the airplanes flying and slacken my pace.

Considering the events of the past few days, and with Larry now happy again, I loaded my little airplane and headed for Fairbanks. I owned my own pickup truck and my own cabin out at the Salcha River, plus a couple of city lots close to town. Besides, I wanted to get married. I had already given the girl the ring, but no specific date had yet been established.

Coming into my Own

❊

fter arriving in Fairbanks, the company didn't want
me to quit. They wanted me to work in the Fairbanks
hangar, but I worked rather half-heartedly. I didn't
really have an assignment and nobody told me which
airplane needed attention or where they wished me to work. I
sensed the foreman felt intimidated and that made me uncomfortable because he was a good friend of mine. He knew more
than I did about airplanes and engines but I had supervised
more jobs than he so he seemed to feel less secure.

My fiancée, Lena Laraux, was half Eskimo and half
French. Her mother, Lena, after whom she was named, was
born and raised in the Bethel area. Her father, Arthur, had been
in the Dawson, Flat, Opher, and various other mining districts,
but had never made the big strike. He was a fox and mink
rancher when she was born. The original French-Quebec spelling of his name had been L'Heureux. I thought she was really a
cute little girl. Later I thought she was pretty. Still later, after
I had matured a few years, I realized that I had married the
most beautiful woman I had ever met. Her patience with me
has no bounds. Her manner of accepting responsibilities as a
wife and mother, and later as manager of a trading post, is
beyond reproach.

After I was able to coordinate marriage plans, I turned
the wedding arrangements over to Clara Johnson and her daughter, Betty Wood, mother and sister of the flying Johnson brothers, Art, Wally, and David. George, who had suffered death
with David in an aircraft accident, did not fly.

Clara and Betty took over the "woman's" part of the
arrangements and the ceremony was held in the Johnson home.
The atmosphere and arrangements suited both our personali-

ties well. Neither of us were impressed by lavish affairs. Clara was an Eskimo from Haycock, near Nome. She well understood how the Eskimos enjoy any excuse for close association with others.

Holger Jorgensen and I had roomed together, worked together, and flown together since I had been in Alaska, so it was a privilege to have him as best man. His wife, Rosalie, was matron of honor. Bill Vehmeir, a local contractor and personal friend of everyone in attendance, substituted as father, to give the bride in marriage. Reverend Thomas, of the Church of the Nazarene, performed the ceremony. I would have to say they all did their parts well as the marriage has lasted well over forty years. We haven't yet had our first argument; however, I always assure people that is all her fault.

I sent my new wife back to Akiak, about forty miles up the Kuskokwim River above Bethel, to spend the summer with her mother. I had promised her I would. She loved her youngest daughter so much, and, with her husband working at the

mines at Nyac, she had planned to have her company all summer. I could understand her feelings, but she could also understand the feelings of a young girl wanting to get married. I thought she was being very unselfish. I later learned she didn't know the meaning of the word selfish.

Morrison-Knudsen Co. Inc. had a contract to build a communications repeater station at Campion, a

Author receiving the first bite from the new cook -- June 28, 1951.

location just above Bear Creek, about ten or twelve miles up the Yukon River from Galena Air Force Base. I had worked on the beginning of the job the fall before. A special request came into the union hall asking that I be sent to Galena to again work for MK Co., so everything was falling into place beautifully. I had been married less than a month when I began work there.

I had exactly thirty dollars in my pocket when I landed at Galena with my little airplane. I sent every paycheck to my new wife and when I quit the first of September to start flying commercially, I had fifteen hundred dollars in cash I had made flying, all right around close to the job.

I met a number of new people on the job, but the ones who had the most influence upon me in the next few months were Edward Pitka and Sidney Huntington.

Edward was a fairly large, raw-boned fellow. His father was Polish and while Edward had been raised strictly on the Yukon, he inherited many of the features of his fathers ancestry. He was a hard worker and exceptional trapper. His wife, Laura, was a very pretty girl who later became good friends with my wife.

Sidney was not a large man, but he was such a bundle of energy and strength that he was always able to accomplish much more than anyone against whom he may be pitted. He didn't know there was such a thing as something that couldn't be done. I learned many things from Sidney that helped me in the future.

Sidney and I went to Koyukuk one evening and were returning to camp after dark. It was late in the fall of the year and salmon strips (smoked salmon cut into strips the length of the fish, salted, and smoke-cured to a taste that is beyond my ability to describe), had just became available for the season. In those days they were available at fifty cents a pound, the going rate. Sidney and I stocked up. Sidney also had a couple cases of beer.

On the way back to camp, in the pouring rain and darkness, we were sneaking up the bank of the Yukon River feeling quite smug. The engine was running smoothly and everything else seemed to be under control when suddenly we heard a loud explosion-like sound and a tremendous increase of exhaust, or propeller echo. We really couldn't identify the noise or its origin. All the engine instruments told us everything was normal but—from whence cometh the noise? I thought a spark plug had blown out of a cylinder but the engine power and temperature seemed normal. The sound was similar to a blown exhaust gasket on an automobile engine.

Naturally, I was trying to look as professional and competent as my bewildered assessment would allow. I looked across at Sidney and I'm sure I must have had a look of consternation on my countenance when he shrugged his shoulders, pointed into the baggage compartment, and calmly stated we had plenty of emergency gear, so why worry. About that time I noticed a patch had blown off a hole in the windshield, so I placed my hand over the hole and presto, all was quiet and serene again. The echo of the prop was coming through the hole.

That hole was a factory installation into which was placed a special air scoop to bring fresh air into the cabin in hot weather, a forerunner to air conditioning. By turning the scoop backward, the flow of air was diminished to *almost* nothing. We had removed them in the winter as it was too cold to tolerate *any* leakage. Alaskan summers were not so warm we couldn't do without them, but we didn't need any cooling drafts in the winter. We covered the hole with a fabric patch and dope. The dope had deteriorated and the patch had blown off.

As Labor Day rolled around we all had a few days off. Since I had only been married a short time, I considered no place to go other than to visit my wife, who was still staying with her mother until the close of mining season in the fall.

On the way to Akiak I flew down the Yukon to Holy Cross, then crossed the portage to the Kuskokwim and on down to Akiak. After a couple days visit it was necessary for me to get back to the job if I wanted a job to get back to. Retracing about the same route followed coming down, I flew right over a Gullwing Stinson parked on a gravel bar on the Yukon. A pilot standing out front, looking a little dejected, was waving his arms vigorously.

Naturally, I stopped and asked him if he was having a little problem. There was no damage to the airplane, no holes in the cowling, no tell tale puddles of oil, so I didn't think the engine had come apart. His explanation was humorous as it was obvious he didn't expect me to actually believe him. He stated the engine began to surge and act as though it was growing weak, but didn't appear to want to stop, then surge again. The only word that seemed to apply was sick. He had ample power to easily reach the gravel bar of his choice but the sound of the engine was not encouraging. His trust for further flight was minimal, at best.

I always carried a set of tools with me in those days so I opened his cowling. I had considerable experience working on those R-680 Lycoming engines and had worked with some of the best overhaul men and trouble shooters. A quick check told me the magneto had been secured with plain washers and flat nuts with no pal nuts or safeties of any kind. They had loosened. One was completely missing while the other was so loose the mag itself was moving back and forth on the slots of the base mount. The slots are necessary for adjustment for timing the unit to the engine. The mag was badly out of time.

Some of the old heads had taught me how to align the propeller with bolts on the nose case to establish exactly the right degrees of advance for timing the mag and how to use a piece of cellophane between the points to know exactly when to secure the mag on the studs. I had his mag timed in about fifteen minutes and asked him to crank it up. He gave me a strange look, but I'm sure he didn't want to insult me so he gave it a try. He was the most surprised person on the Yukon when it ran smoothly with normal power.

I neglected to tell him I had copped a couple of nuts off my landing gear which were really just precautionary fasteners to me. I didn't even get his name and don't think he got mine, but I'll bet he didn't forget me for a few days.

The rest of the summer work was just a normal dirt-moving job. I told Carl Going, the foreman over the airport job, I would be leaving the first of September. He tried to pretend he understood me to say the first of October, but I knew it was just a ploy. I went over to Akiak and helped little "Granny" and my wife "Cutie" harvest their garden. What a harvest! I never saw such turnips — anywhere.

Granny was named Lena, and my wife was named Lena. At first I called her Little Lena and everyone thought that was cute at first, but some people thought I meant Granny since she was only four feet tall herself. Everyone who knew my wife called her "Cutie" and since she was about the cutest thing I had seen so far, I fell in line with the rest.

Nat Browne, an old bush pilot who in his younger days had delivered Tri-motors to South America for Ford, and once had an operation in Bethel, contacted me to help him get a crippled airplane off a hillside. He was now conducting a fairly large operation with thirteen Super Cubs on floats and special Whittaker landing gear, supporting the Coast and Geodetic Survey party. That sounded like only a few days, so I agreed to help him but things backfired a little.

We landed at Unalakleet on the way to Kotzebue, and one of the pilots at Unalakleet told Nat he had to leave in order to get enrolled for fall term at college. Nat left me to fly his airplane and he took the other pilot back to Bethel. We never did get to the wrecked aircraft, but I helped them finish the season at Unalakleet.

We tied all the cubs down at McGrath for the winter, all thirteen of them, and I headed back to the Yukon to start my winter flying operation at Koyukuk. Dominic and Ella Vernetti were still vacationing in Italy. Jack and Mary, their children, ran the trading post until they returned. Dick Pitka, an old handy man who had lived in the area all his life, helped me build a special warm-up device to preheat the airplanes. Ella had a Standard Oil concession so stockpiling fuel was not necessary.

Business was pretty slow until late October, then it only picked up slowly. Finally, after trapping season became serious business, there were not enough hours in a day. There was a nice school house and quarters building in Koyukuk but there was no school that year. I made some inquiries, and largely due to the recommendation of Art Johnson, was able to rent the school building for living quarters for the winter. Art had established a flying business in Unalakleet and happened to be flying the man who made the decision about renting me the school building. When he received my request, he had asked Art if he knew me and he gave his recommendation.

My wife joined me after her father returned home from the mine at Nyac. She was accepted and loved by the community, as she has been every place we have ever lived. She had gained a little weight during the summer.

My regular routine was: up at four A.M., cook breakfast, preheat the airplane, fly all day, try to be home famished by ten P.M., eat, then unintentionally go to sleep on top of the bed. Sometimes Cutie could get me properly into bed by midnight. I'd start all over again at four the next morning. I was fast learning that a man who loved his work could have a whale of a time in this bush-flying institution.

Being alone all day and me being such poor company at night would have driven a less patient person to desperate measures, but my little wife was the most patient person imaginable. After getting better acquainted with both her mother and father, I learned that she had come by it honestly.

One night in early November, Sidney Huntington approached me to fly him and Angela, his wife, to Huslia. We did a lot of night flying. I have always had exceptional night vision, plus, if you were going to get any flying done when it is dark nineteen hours a day, night flying is a must. That was our first meeting with Angela but we have been fast friends since. Angela was Edward Pitka's sister.

Dominic and Ella Vernetti ran the trading post in Koyukuk. They had been on vacation to Italy and upon their return to Fairbanks, Dick Jones brought them back to the Village of Koyukuk.

Dick was a heavy-duty welder who had learned to fly about the same time I was working toward securing my commercial license. His experience was more limited than my own, especially in dealing with the people. I had worked and hunted with them more than he and had a better understanding of how they think. He wanted to stay in Koyukuk and fly with me. I really didn't encourage it, but I had no authority to tell him he couldn't stay.

He finally proposed we try working together for a month and see how it came out. Before the month was over, things got complicated.

Troubles

✈

I had trappers all over the country with promises to pick them up on certain dates, all as close to Christmas as possible. I had taken Jimmy Huntington, Sidney's brother, near the mouth of Hog River and was to pick him up the 21st of December. His experience with bush pilots in the past had left a little to be desired, so he pulled his traps a little early and snowshoed into Huslia. He was there when I arrived the night of December 20th. The plan was to spend the night and get an early start. It was fortunate I had planned it that way, as a fog settled over the country and we couldn't see the tree tops until the morning of December 24th, which dawned clear and cold.

I had two more trappers near Hog River, so I headed for their camp. I passed right in front of Jimmy's cabin and happened to look back as I went by. There was Cue Bifelt, along with Steven Attla, waving like crazy. They hadn't heard me until I had almost reached the cabin. They were standing right in the door. I would have missed seeing them had I not looked back just after passing the cabin.

I finished up all the commitments around Huslia, and headed for the Yukon, brought in one set of trappers and went for the boys from Nulato just before dark. As I flew over them, I could see Donald Stickman had been sent out by their families to insure they would be home for Christmas. He was on the ground, stuck with his Stinson. I knew I could get moving empty. I landed to help them get moving, then planned to go on over to Long Creek for the last trip of the day. Everyone would be home for Christmas.

The temperature was thirty degrees below zero and those little Continental engines, once throttled down, refused to run at a temperature lower than minus fifteen, without a lot of coaxing. My position was less than desirable when the little engine went into its act. There wasn't time and altitude enough to do the necessary coaxing to establish that nice, smooth roar again. My only option was to deliberately land too fast and let the airplane run off into the deep, soft snow. I knew it would stop me with no problems. There would be the chore of turning the airplane around and heading it toward the runway— but I would have help.

I walked over to the boys and told them if they would help me get turned around, I'd help them get started, then I'd go on to Long Creek.

A couple of them grabbed the rope on the tail and one was pushing on a wing strut. I couldn't kick the skis fast enough to reduce the twisting action caused by the skis not being able to turn in the deep snow. A mighty tug on the rope and one of the axles broke—now there are four of us to go out in an airplane that couldn't get moving with three.

I told everyone to get in and I would push to get us started. Donald cranked up and gave the engine full power. I heaved on the strut and the skis started to slip. Now was not the time to tarry. The wind from the propeller was diligently holding the door closed, I was riding on the ski trying to keep my King Island water boots from slipping, as well as get inside. Of course Donald could only take one attitude, "He has to take care of himself, I'm busy." The idea was to get that thing off the ground just as soon as possible. Those spruce trees were sixty feet tall and didn't really look very far away.

I finally forced my head inside the door just as the skis were getting light on the ground. The airplane was about to fly and I was still standing on the ski with only my head in the door. I knew that when the heels of the skis left the ground the front would be pulled up by the shock cords. My feet would then slide to the rear of the ski because the heels were now off the ground. It was now or never and with all the strength I could muster in my arms, I was able to get onto the edge of my seat. I then got a knee against the door and slid into the cabin.

The door was still trailing open and my belt was not yet fastened when we cleared the tall trees, but we made it. We knew we would.

Donald dropped me off at Koyukuk. I filled his airplane with gasoline and wished all a Merry Christmas. The only thing that made me feel worse than the broken axle was leaving the boys at Long Creek.

Later, after a few years more experience, I would have known after several days' bad weather in a row during and after the pick-up date, the boys would figure out I just couldn't catch up. That is what they did and they walked into Ruby. Everyone was home for Christmas.

Dick's wife, Dean, who was visiting over the holidays, became quite ill. Ella Vernetti, who was the local medical aid by default, asked me to go to Nulato where the nurse had some medicine she could prescribe for such an illness. When I returned from Nulato, the entire country was covered with a thick layer of fog. It stopped right at the mouth of the slough which ran in front of the village of Koyukuk, where it entered the Yukon River. I could only see about one hundred feet up the slough, but I knew every foot of it so I got right down over the ice and flew up the bottom, watching for a boat I knew was beached at the lower end of the area we used for landing and take-off. When I saw the boat, I chopped the throttle and was on the ice with my skis. I couldn't even see to taxi into the parking area, but I had the medicine. The down side of this story is, the nurse had given me sulfa drugs and Dean was violently allergic to sulfa. Dick insisted I take her to Tanana. I was flying his airplane because he was so emotionally upset he didn't trust himself. That was New Year's Eve. I attended the dance at Tanana and had an enjoyable time. Leaving Dean at the hospital, I returned to Koyukuk New Year's Day.

With the holidays over, everyone wanted to go home first. Haymen Henry was pretty insistent that he was going first. Edward Pitka told Dick there was danger of running into overflow water on the ice at Haymen's camp, which should dictate that trip be made last.

Overflow is caused when the weight of the snow on top of the ice forces the ice down until water runs up on top of the ice under the snow. The water cannot be detected from the top but when you walk over it or land your airplane on the snow you sink to the bottom. Extreme difficulty is encountered trying to get out of the situation. It usually involves pushing, placing poles and spruce boughs or willows under the skis, an appropriate amount of swearing, and adequate horsepower to extricate yourself. Naturally, when the engine is turning at high power it causes the propeller to throw saturated snow all over the airplane. When it is cold, as it was on that occasion, slush sticks and freezes to the airplane. What a mess.

Haymen was so unreasonably insistent, Dick disregarded the warning and took him first. When he was a couple hours overdue on his return, our suspicions were confirmed. When he did return he was so exhausted he insisted I take the airplane and make the next trip to Huslia. On the return from Huslia, a storm slipped over the hills from the coast and covered everything at once. Light fog, heavy snow, and darkness combined to precipitate the accident.

There are actually very few accidents that could not have been prevented by the proper use of common sense, good procedure, or sound judgment. Occasionally unforeseen or unrecognized developments will cause a pilot to suffer from a dry mouth, sweaty palms, and the bane of the industry, ulcers. Many times, what we term an accident, is a result of a lack of experience, but after all, how does one gain experience except through doing things?

It is my considered opinion, many people who are in a class by themselves where accomplished pilots are concerned, were at one time on the receiving end of an abrupt education definitely not planned. Serendipity often plays a larger role than we recognize. If, at an early stage of his career, a person has just one serious accident but is fortunate enough to come through it with all his faculties as well as limbs, he is very apt to seriously reflect upon the incident and learn many of the fundamentals that escaped him the first time around. There is another factor that should be seriously considered by any pilot in the early stages of his career.

Overcaution can be an insidious or distracting element in the realm of judgment. While perfecting my procedures, I found once I had thought something through carefully and, if possible, tried a procedure in good weather a couple of times, then it was imperative to do everything exactly as I practiced in good weather and the results would be exactly the same in bad. The hard part for most people is to disregard what others think or say, and fly their own limitations.

Don Jonz once wrote an article entitled "Ice Without Fear" that was criticized by some of his detractors. I deemed it an excellent article. In it, he detailed the method of going out into a situation of known icing conditions where there is a good five thousand foot ceiling below the clouds and stick your nose into the icing conditions cautiously. The beginner knows he has five thousand feet of safety net beneath him, thus giving him enough confidence to 'play with the devil' and learn something about the actual formation and results of ice on an airplane, without the usual pressure and doubt that accompanies the actual condition. This same method of learning, applied to other aspects of flying, can be a very productive learning tool.

In my own case, I was coming home with an empty airplane and encountered some low visibility combined with heavy snow fall and darkness. I used my instruments to keep the airplane on an even keel, and took a heading from where visibility became so impaired to a point that should intersect the Koyukuk River at fifteen miles above the village of Koyukuk. Intersecting the river at the exact location expected, inflated my ego considerably. From there on following the river should be easy.

About five or six miles above the village, I reeled in the drop antenna, changed to the fullest fuel tank, adjusted my seat, and checked the trim, all in preparation for the upcoming landing at home. I then made the crucial mistake. I turned the lights to the bright setting so I could read the fuel gauge, knowing the tank was full of fuel. There was no need to check the fuel level since I knew it was full, and there was nothing I could do if it wasn't. The lights turned up to bright had an adverse affect upon my vision. I could not see the ground, with any degree of clarity, for just long enough to allow the aircraft to descend slightly. Most of all, I did not see the edge of a sand bar that had a high, cut bank, caused by fall time high water. I hooked a ski on the top of the bank which had the affect of abruptly calling to my attention that it was there, as well as spinning the aircraft completely around, causing it to slide backward for the last few feet of the homeward flight.

Looking back, I have to smile when I think of the last fifty feet of that ride. Upon striking the frozen sand bar, I had been concentrating so hard on avoiding it that I thought I had flown into the bluff. While sliding backward I thought I was falling down the sheer face of the bluff.

I was thinking, "When will I ever hit bottom? This suspense is killing me."

Before figuring out where I actually was and what had happened, I thought I had been killed. It was so quiet, a normal result of an abrupt engine stoppage. I could see nothing but gray fog. The sensation was like being on top of a large dome covered with snow or some other grey medium. Every direction was down— something like looking south from the north pole. It was so quiet and I was alone— so alone.

"I knew death would be something like this," I thought, "but I thought I would be in company of others who had gone before. Where is everybody? Eternity is going to be such a long, long time with no one else here."

Upon hearing snow melting on the hot engine and exhaust, I realized I was stationary and slowly figured out what had actually happened.

The reader will be spared the details of a crumpled wing, broken landing gear, cut lip, broken clavicle, and other major and minor injuries, as the real intent of these paragraphs is to emphasize the insidiousness of overcaution.

I could see the bluffs and shore line on the right side of the airplane but, succumbing to overcaution, I had crossed the river to the side most difficult to see. The act was justified by the thought it would be more prudent to avoid the bluff, which I could see. Turning the lights to the bright setting had impaired my vision. Had I left the antenna down for just three more minutes I'd have felt the antennae weight hit the ice when losing a little too much altitude.

Silently reflecting back over the accident and being honest with myself, I realized the major cause was a combination of complacency and overcaution. During the time leading up to the occurrence, I was telling myself I was using good judgment, procedure, and caution. The abrupt stop on the gravel bar caused me to rethink the entire picture.

I was able to extract myself from the aircraft on the right side. The left side is the one that took the brunt of the damage. I took my snowshoes off the wing and saw they were badly broken so I abandoned them and started to cross the river, wading through soft snow about knee deep. Suddenly I fell right off the edge of that sand bar, down into snow so deep and soft the only way I could maneuver my way out of it was to swim. By keeping my weight spread as far as possible I could remain a little higher in the snow and make a little headway. I really don't remember too much about how it took place, but I finally worked my way back to the airplane and retrieved my snowshoes. On second appraisal I determined they were broken just ahead of the footstall. They were quite limp on the forward part. By careful high-stepping I could keep them straight and they were better than nothing.

I worked my way across the river on my broken snowshoes and located the dog trail running through the willows. I braced the framework of the snowshoes by lashing willows to them, and started home. I was knowledgeable enough about injuries to know shock could be a serious factor and I should not rush home—just keep moving. I had a badly cut lip but was spitting out all the blood, yet my throat kept getting congested with blood clots and I'd have to clear it and spit out clots of blood. I thought I may have a punctured lung so was careful to not over-exert.

Walking home on a pair of broken snowshoes, spitting out blood, wishing I had some way of erasing the last couple of hours, I kept thinking of the trauma it would be if my little wife were to have to tell my little girl her daddy had been killed in an airplane a month before she was born. (I never even considered the child may be a boy!)

Upon arriving home, I sat down on the bottom step to remove my snowshoes. Then it happened. I was quite familiar with the element of shock so I was able to hold it off by plain strong mental resistance. Once I relaxed physically it almost got away from me. I gritted my teeth and refused to succumb; stood up and walked into the house and down the hallway, opened the door, then stepped back into the darkness.

It had been virtually impossible for me to sneak in on my wife before, so when she saw me she knew I had come home, minus one airplane. She quickly came to me asking what had happened. I kept assuring her I was OK. I just looked like the Dickens. I asked her if she had anything ready for me to eat. Since she was due to give birth to our firstborn in about a month, I was trying to not excite her. I thought keeping her mind on other things was in my favor.

It was rather difficult to keep the excitement down. Ella Vernetti, who over the years had seen about every kind of injury and was unusually handy at attending to them, came right up to give me the once over. After eating my fill of a good moose stew, I went to bed to spend the most miserable night of my entire life, and that is counting both ways.

The next day about noon, Bill Carlo came into Koyukuk and stopped for gas. He had two of his little ones with him but agreed to leave them with Dominic and Ella while he flew me to Tanana Hospital. He was really concerned about them all the time he was gone.

Bill came in to see me before heading back to Koyukuk the next morning. I asked him to hand me my wallet but he said he wouldn't take any pay for what he had done. I finally got him to at least accept enough to buy gasoline to refill his tanks. Years later, Bill would come into Tanana for the night and plug his electric heater into my outlet and timer. I was happy to be able to help him be nice and toasty when he was ready to leave. He never asked permission to use my electricity and I never mentioned it. It was just an unspoken understanding I felt proud to share.

Dr. Wehler, Alaska Native Service doctor at Tanana, kept me on my back, not allowing me to move, for three days. When he was satisfied all swelling in my throat was diminishing, he allowed me to leave. I caught a ride into Fairbanks with Alden Williams. I asked Alden to tell my wife to be ready to go to Tanana when he stopped at Koyukuk on his way back to Fairbanks. I emphasized he was not to ask her if she wanted to go but to tell her she was going. I would feel much more comfortable with her waiting in Tanana than Koyukuk, especially when I didn't yet have an airplane replacement and the little Cessna was still out in the brush.

In Fairbanks I contacted Al Wright, who was the administrator for the Hanz Rutzebeck estate. I bought his Gullwing Stinson to be able to stay in business.

The holiday week, and continued snow and bad weather for the next couple of weeks, prevented any attempt to retrieve the little Cessna. I had procured, a new axle in readiness for the big rescue. The press of taking all the trappers back to their camps, bad weather, and locating someone to take me out to the airplane, continued to delay the rescue mission. Finally, arrangements were made for Bill Carlo to take Dick Jones out to change the axle and fly the Cessna home. Edward Pitka went with them.

The evening before going after the Cessna, I had checked Dick out in the Stinson. Just after the take-off he reached over and pulled the prop control all the way back.

"That's too much," I yelled, but it was already too late. The propeller had progressed to full high pitch before I could feed the control back in. The result was something like winding a car engine up as much as possible in low gear, shifting into high gear with the engine still wide open, then letting your toe slip off the clutch. Dick had been flying two position propellers. That is the way he had been taught to use them, so I couldn't really fault him too much for making the mistake. After all, I had not coached him on the procedure either. I thought he understood those props, but then, when checking someone out in an airplane, the check pilot should assume nothing. It seems none of us has an instant education.

After landing the airplane, we opened the cowling and could see nothing amiss. There is no way to detect an overstretched stud or bolt without torquing each one so we just hoped no damage had been rendered. We were wrong.

Early the next morning, Bill Carlo came in from Ruby and picked up Dick, Edward Pitka, the new axle and tools. After they departed to resurrect the little Cessna, I loaded the Stinson with kerosene, dog fish, lamp gasoline, Butch Yaska and Laura Pitka, Ed's wife, and departed for Huslia.

A pilot, any pilot, if asked to sit down and quickly list the ten things he would most like to see before he died, would have a tail wind high on the list. That day we had the wind—but it was a headwind.

On this trip to Huslia, we were cruising at about one thousand feet above the ground to somewhat minimize the loss of forward progress due to the wind. The turbulence was of little consequence as the country immediately below us was so flat the flow of air was just strong, not rolling turbulence.

The engine suddenly assumed a slight vibration, different than previous performance. Nothing to seriously disturb a person, but definitely discernible. All the normal pilot checks of the instruments revealed nothing. Carburetor heat did nothing, a change in propeller setting did nothing. After a few minutes of tolerating the increased vibration with no indication of cause or that it was inclined to become worse, it began to sound normal. After gaining another one thousand feet of 'wife and kids' altitude, I sat back and actually said to Laura, "I guess I'm getting the single engine jitters." Of course she had no idea at all what I meant so she agreed and I relaxed—briefly.

Suddenly a little gremlin was up front with a big hammer wreaking havoc in my beautiful Lycoming engine. I closed the throttle and said to Laura, "I guess this is as good a place as any to put it." She agreed again, but I'm sure she didn't have the slightest idea we were in trouble. Right in front of us was Coffee Can Lake, not more than three thousand feet ahead of us—but we weren't going to make it—too much wind.

I had closed the throttle, but the engine was still running and all I could think of was the time I had seen a B-24 come back into Guam with one cylinder completely gone, and the engine still running. Long ago I had decided that if I had to clobber an airplane, I would do it with dignity, so I added throttle, cautiously. Up to about eighteen inches manifold pressure it didn't sound too bad. It surely was helping to stretch a glide. We just cleared the scrub spruce trees on the edge of the lake when number one cylinder came right up through the top of the cowling, but we had made it to the lake.

Again my lack of experience surfaced. I didn't want to slide too far out onto the lake. I knew we were going to probably have to change an engine right there. I intentionally stalled the airplane a little high to try to bury it down into the soft snow but we only bounced and slid along on top of the hardest drifts I had seen since leaving the coast. I should have known, having spent a winter at Bethel, such a wind would leave hard drifts. Fortunately the thirty knot wind prevented us from sliding very far. We chopped some ice bridges right there and tied the airplane to the ice.

Butch Yaska was one of the best snowshoe travelers in the country, as well as being woods wise. I gave him an ax, a sleeping bag, a supply of fish, and let him head for Huslia to alert someone to come to our assistance.

Fortunately for us the rescue of the little Cessna went quite well and they returned early.

"They will be having a dance in Huslia tonight, let's go up," Edward said.

So he and Dick loaded in some more gas and kerosene and flew right over us. They saw us and landed. I quickly jumped into the Cessna, left Dick at the Stinson, and Edward and I headed out to track down Butch. I was amazed at how far he had traveled in such a short time. He was about three hundred yards into the trees beyond the last possible place I could have landed for miles. I landed and he returned to the airplane so we all quickly dashed into Huslia where we off loaded the fuel and the two men and I returned for Dick and Laura. All was quite successful and we did have a dance in Huslia that night.

Now was the time to consider a procedure for changing an engine out in the brush, specifically at Coffee Can Lake. I contacted Al Wright to bring me out the spare engine, certain hoses, a prop wrench, etc. Late one evening he arrived in his Howard, a large, single-engine, high wing, monoplane capable of hauling good loads at a speed of about one hundred forty-five miles per hour. That was real performance in those days.

He brought the engine and other gear and spent the night. We took a tent, chain hoist, sleeping bags and grub to Coffee Can Lake the next morning, then Al went straight back to Fairbanks.

Edward Pitka came to help and we pitched our tent right in front of the airplane, out on the ice. It was embarrassing for Edward to pitch a tent in such an unwoodsman-like manner, but knowing we had to do all the buildup before we could hang the new engine, I wanted the engine right in the tent with us. Jesse Bachner had put the correct prop wrench in with the hoses and such, but someone else thought it was the wrong one and changed sizes. As a result, we had to make our own out of the closest thing we could find to a wrench that would fit. Dick made the wrench, but he had to do it in Galena so we had to stumble over the prop in the tent with the engine until he had the new wrench completed.

Normally one will not encounter strong winds and bitter cold temperatures at the same time in the interior of Alaska, but this time we had both. The warmest temperature we observed, by watching the thermometer on the wing strut of the airplane, was minus thirty eight degrees and the wind was never less than twenty knots, estimated.

Gullwing Stinson purchased from Al Wright.
Author and George Thiele in 1952 at Koyukuk.

The Stinson Voyager 150 that the author wore out on the way home.
Jan. 1952

To decrease the misery and improve working conditions, we froze a couple of spruce poles, about fifteen feet long, into the ice just a few feet in front and on each side of the engine on the airplane. We then stretched a tarpaulin between the poles for a wind break. It worked quite well. We put two plumbers pots under the engine, removed the cowling and placed it inside the airplane so it would not blow away. Taking a hacksaw we separated all the rubber hoses where they connected fittings and tubing. Those hoses were so stiff and hard we would have been required to get the engine warm enough to start to remove them intact. It is prudent to replace the hoses at engine change and we had ordered new hoses. There had to be enough to do the job. The important thing was to get the engine into the tent so we could start transferring accessories from the old to the new.

By the time we had the new engine installed and about ready to run, Dick returned with the prop wrench that he had fashioned from a lug wrench originally designed to remove the wheels from large trucks. He removed the prop from the old engine and installed it onto the new one.

There are many steps, mostly miserable out there, involved in changing an engine, but to spare the reader we will only hit the important points. The main things are to check and recheck all fuel and oil fittings as well as the electrical connections. Make sure all bolts attaching throttle, prop, and mixture controls are properly safetied. The foolproof procedure involved in everything one does is to stop and think through everything one has done to that point. Almost always when one takes the time to follow this procedure, any step overlooked will come to mind. That gives a person an opportunity to correct an error before an embarrassing event makes headlines in the newspapers.

Those old engines with straight pistons, cylinders, and rings, all required a run in procedure, beginning at low speeds, and increasing speed and power at intervals. In all, a person will spend at least two hours running an engine for break in, after the installation is completed. That can serve two practical purposes. One can break in the new ring to cylinder fit and look for oil leaks that may show up with increased pressures and temperatures. In some cases, when problems are uncovered, those two hours can grow alarmingly.

While we were running the engine for the break in series, Edward and I were intently removing the good chrome cylinders from the old engine. As the number one cylinder had lifted off the base after breaking the cylinder hold down studs, the cylinder came completely up out of the main case. The piston came out of the cylinder, breaking the link rod off about the middle. The link rod went around and around the crankshaft with centrifugal force throwing it to the limit of the length of the broken piece. It struck both number nine and number two cylinder skirts. They were damaged to the degree we could not even remove them from the case so we left them for the ravens to pick over.

By the time the engine was ready we had the tent down and loaded, complete with all the salvage from the old engine. We installed the cowling and chopped the poles on which we had stretched the tarp, shoveled the drifted snow from around the skis and said, "Well, here goes."

I told Edward a couple of times it wasn't prudent to jump into an airplane with a newly installed engine and takeoff in the dark with nothing but timber under us until we reached the Koyukuk River. He almost thought I was afraid to fly in the dark. However, any prudence I harbored was overshadowed by a desire to get off that ice mattress as soon as possible.

Actually the sky was clear with a pale moon and stars. In the interior visibility is good at night, even in January. The trees are so dark and the lakes and rivers covered with the white snow reflect the light well from the stars and moon.

After take-off and climbing to four thousand feet, we circled over Coffee Can Lake for a good fifteen minutes. Everything was running like an Elgin watch, so we said, "Koyukuk, here we come." One learns so much in the wilds of Alaska.

Even though I was a licensed mechanic, I still liked to do my one hundred hour inspections in a hangar if possible. When working out in the open with no compressed air, few spare parts or material, and no heated workplace, a person is prone to leave some things in a less than desirable condition. One should never create temptation. An engine change done out in the brush, without many tools or conveniences, is usually a less than admirable job. I elected to take the aircraft into Fairbanks, and a hangar, to clean up the installation.

We usually scheduled all the family, friends, and business shopping along with those inspections in Fairbanks. On that trip I learned the inside information on a recent fatal accident near Fairbanks.

Bob Warren was a flight instructor in Fairbanks for some time, but it is so nice to have a steady meal ticket. The winters are long in the interior, and it is sometimes rather difficult to gain the necessary cushion to carry one through the long, cold winter when flight instruction is at a stand still, or slow at best.

When Transocean Airlines won the contract to supply the Arctic Contractors on the North Slope in the late 1940's, the need for co-pilots appealed to Bob. He qualified by having most of the necessary ratings and certificates and felt this was the one break for which he had been waiting. His experience was totally in small airplanes, but after a year and a half as co-pilot on the Curtiss C-46 with some of the most competent captains in the business, he was considered for check out as a captain. The company was in need of experienced captains and Bob had been on the same run since first hired, so his familiarity with the route could not have been questioned. I talked with Hank Dodson, who gave him the check ride, and he said he had turned in a good performance.

Shortly after beginning flying as captain, he and Erwin, his co-pilot, were scheduled to fly the 'line haul', the freight and passenger flight from Fairbanks to Barrow, and return. The line haul was a daily run providing the weather was cooperative. On the return trip that night, there were only two passengers, a Wien pilot by the name of Wheeler, and a mechanic named Cross, who were 'dead heading' or flying free, a common courtesy between companies. I briefly knew Wheeler, but had never met Erwin, or Cross.

Weather reports and winds aloft were not quite as reliable then as they are now and that lack of reliability came out and bit him on this trip. Unbeknown to them, they were blessed by a sixty knot tail wind. That is something for which all pilots pray but so seldom see, then when he got one he did not recognize it.

In those days most navigation was on the Low Frequency Range, backed up with an Automatic Direction Finder. Since both Umiat and Bettles were Non Directional Radio Beacons, an unusual wind could cause them to pass the station on course, but finding it necessary to hold a considerably different heading than normal. When they passed by Umiat, they reported their ADF was a little erratic and when they passed Bettles they reported the ADF was seemingly getting worse.

The author's "Fleet" -- Cessna 140 and Gullwing Stinson in 1952.

When they passed Fairbanks and the ADF turned around to signal a tail null, as it should have under the conditions, they again reported on the ADF. It had completely ceased to function with any degree of reliability. In actuality, they had arrived at Fairbanks about thirty minutes ahead of schedule and hadn't yet recognized the fact, but had they trusted the ADF—it was telling them exactly what was happening.

Radar was something that had not yet come to the civilian aids to navigation, but there was one at Ladd Field. After a report of a missing aircraft was received, information was made available to the CAA. The radar operator on duty at Ladd had seen the aircraft approach and pass Fairbanks, then turn left to disappear off the screen. Bob was apparently confused and didn't know it. The approach plate showed only right hand turns allowed east of the Fairbanks Range. He had not called for an approach clearance so he wasn't attempting an approach pattern. He must have been trying to do some sort of an orientation as both captain and co-pilot should have known of the location of Chena Dome and the fact all maneuvering east of Fairbanks would be only right-hand turns. They were found about fifty feet below the crest of Chena Dome, headed west. Unquestionably they thought they were still west of Fairbanks, but hadn't yet figured out what their navigational aids were telling them all along. He could have made a check on KFAR radio broadcast station with their ADF. It is not a legal navigational aid, but really makes a dandy double check on what the CAA station was telling him.

It is not my intent to criticize the actions of those poor, unfortunate individuals, but I do feel if a lesson can be learned from such an unfortunate occurrence, it should be passed on to the upcoming captains of the future.

My troubles would soon turn into double joy.

The Twins

☙ ☙

Actually January, February, and the first week of March are usually slow times in a village made up of mostly trappers. The marten season is over, beaver season hasn't yet started, and the ebb and flow of life, for a while, is rather sedate. After returning to Koyukuk with the Stinson there was a lull in business. Dick had taken the little Cessna back to Fairbanks, so I told him to have an inspection done and I would pick it up later. There was no need of us both batching in Koyukuk and making no money. He may as well stay in town.

I went in to Fairbanks and spent the night with George and Mary Lou Thiele. While in Bethel George and I were roommates. He played the part of cupid in causing my wife and me to be constantly aware the other was there. Mary Lou was the daughter of the proprietors of the Marsh Cafe in Bethel and a close friend of my wife. They also had been roommates.

Those were the days when the government was still drafting young men for a two year military orientation. George had been drafted about the time I left Bethel. He was feeling low about having to leave his job as pilot for Northern Consolidated Airlines and possibly losing his seniority but definitely losing the experience the two years would have provided. I told him to not let it bother him too much. There was nothing to do about it so just go in and do it, one day at a time. He would soon have it half done, then the other half would be all downhill. He was sent to cooks and bakers school and loved it. He turned out to be an excellent cook. After his schooling he was stationed at Ladd Field, right in Fairbanks, and was able to live off-base with his wife. Things weren't so bad.

Never Too Late To Be A Hero

I left Fairbanks about nine o'clock in the morning of January 29th, 1952. My destination was Koyukuk, with a stop at Tanana, estimating Tanana in one and one half hours from departure. Over Manley Hot Springs I called Tanana on the radio, giving them a position report and estimated arrival time. The communicator at Tanana answered me, "Roger Cessna 72567, have you over Manley Hot Springs at zero five, estimating Tanana at three five. For your information you are the father of twins, I say again, you are the father of twin girls."

I dropped the nose of the airplane, advanced the throttle a little, and called back, "Make that estimate twenty minutes instead of thirty."

After landing the communicator assured me things were fine with all concerned. I walked to the hospital and the nurses started to usher me in to see the twins. My first thought, which I kept to myself, was that I wasn't interested in the babies—I wanted to see my little wife. As I looked down into those two tiny faces it was like looking into two pools of water reflecting the image of my own face. I think the feeling that came over me as a new father cannot be conveyed to a person who has not himself had the experience. Once I saw those sweet little faces, the nurses had difficulty getting me in to talk to their mother.

My wife was in her hospital gown, repeatedly blowing up a balloon (doctor's orders), looking like a child herself. She is five feet two inches, if she stretches a little. She had lost considerable blood, so she was given a transfusion. The only person they could find with type "O" blood, was the local U.S. Deputy Marshall, Frank Wirth. She kidded me about going back and becoming marshall of Koyukuk. Frank liked to drink, and didn't try to hide it, so I kidded her about her blood now testing ninety proof.

We named the girls Lois and Dolores. We called Lois, Robin and Dolores, Dolly. When they were two weeks old, I picked them up at Tanana, along with Frank Wirth, and took them back to Koyukuk. It was forty degrees below zero. I had not yet installed my special heater and the airplane was really cold. We just wrapped them well, my wife held one, and Frank held the other. They didn't even awaken until we arrived at Koyukuk.

The Twins

Frank Wirth had been working as a Deputy U.S. Federal Marshall since the early 1940's. He was a large man who played the guitar and sang. He loved a party and enjoyed being with the people of the Yukon River and tributaries. His headquarters was at Tanana, but he covered a vast amount of territory. I never saw him carry a gun or any form of weapon. He asserted the authority of his office by sheer confidence and personality. His size helped.

I took Frank on a charter up the Koyukuk to investigate a suicide. I made a few other trips around the country, but it was evident the flying season was over until next winter. We decided to move back into Fairbanks. As soon as we could, we started making arrangements for a place to live until we could move our own cabin from the Salcha River to a lot we owned near the new International Airport.

I worked for Jesse Bachner in his new hangar on the newly built Phillips Field. Later "Swede" Blanchard, chief pilot for Northern Consolidated Airlines, contacted me and wouldn't take no for an answer; I just had to go to work for Northern Consolidated as a pilot. (I think he thought I was going to go back to flying in Koyukuk and wanted to eliminate the competition.)

I flew out of Fairbanks for a while, but all good things seem to come to an end, especially when someone else is calling the signals. I was destined to fly relief for permanently stationed pilots who were on vacation. I was first sent to Bethel. There again, I met my old friend, Norseman 725Easy.

The next story isn't quite qualified to fall into the category of being humorous, or a tension builder, but is so interesting and totally true, that including it seems quite in order. I was scheduled to make the coastal mail run to Eek, Quigillingok, Kipnuk, and back to Bethel. The airplane for that trip was the old Norseman 725E. Upon landing at Quigillingok, I discovered the National Guard members had been alerted and advised to report into Bethel preparatory to going to Anchorage for annual training. No one at the office was aware of the situation and it was fortunate I was flying the Norseman, as it would just handle the load. The leader of the group was very persistent and wanted me to assure him I'd stop for them on my return from Kipnuk. He assured me they could all pay their own way if the National Guard did not.

There were five of them. The weather really didn't look as it was going to hold much longer, so I told them to jump in now and I'd take them to Kipnuk, then go straight to Bethel.

"Who is the best navigator?" I asked.

They all pointed to the same person and said, "He is, he is." Guess who got the front seat so he could sit close and assist me making navigational errors.

We flew over and landed at Kipnuk. The new postmaster brought us the mail but didn't know that, in order for us to get paid for hauling the mail, we had to have a mail bill from each post office, each trip. It was necessary for us to wait for him to make the trip to the village and back to the lake where we had landed. The round trip was two miles and there were no snow machines in those days. There wasn't a dog team in sight. We waited, the weather deteriorated, and four more National Guardsmen boarded the flight, bringing the total to nine.

By the time we again got into the air, visibility had dropped to almost nothing. It didn't appear so bad before we took off because we could see the grass along the edge of the lake. Once in the air all we could see was the little streaks of grass that grew along the edges of the lakes but one couldn't tell which side was lake and which was tundra.

I was working at keeping the airplane level with the ground and high enough to clear everything in the area. Fortunately there were no obstructions higher than twenty feet above sea level. I was wishing we hadn't taken off at all. Now the wise thing to do was get inland as fast as possible—perhaps we could get ahead of the storm again.

That Eskimo in the front seat began motioning to me which way to turn to go to Bethel but I wasn't yet prepared to put my complete trust in the signals of a total stranger although I knew he was motioning a more direct route than I was preparing to pursue. I took a bisector heading that would intercept the SW leg of the Bethel low frequency radio range.

Those old low frequency ranges worked on the principal of combining an "A" and an "N" signal. The "A" is a dot dash, the "N" is a dash dot. The "A" is sent out in two opposite sectors and the "N" is sent out in the other two sectors. Divided equally, each sector would be one quarter of a circle. When a receiver, meaning the airplane, is placed right where the "A" and "N" signals merge, the pilot will hear not the dash dot nor the dot dash, but a merged signal which is a constant tone. When the aircraft moves off the range leg, or beam, as the merged signal is called, the listener will begin to hear the signal that is predominant in the sector toward which the airplane is drifting. It was rather a tedious task to stay right on the range leg if wind was a problem, but one could do a surprisingly accurate job if he was consistently articulate. When I look back, it appears quite crude but at the time it was heralded as a wonderful aid to navigation.

My newly acquired navigator kept motioning me a little further to the left and I would shake my head, point at the ear phones, and continue. When we bisected the range leg and turned to the inbound heading to Bethel, he displayed a big smile and motioned straight ahead. Just to test him, I would slowly feed in a little left rudder and as we headed slightly off course, even before any tone change was discernible, he would motion me back to the proper heading. As we reached the proper heading again he would motion straight ahead, and smile, as only an Eskimo can.

After landing at Bethel I asked him to stick around for a few minutes. After getting the mail and my paperwork in order, I took him off to one side to question him. I asked him how he knew just where the proper course was. I was well aware of how to establish course by visible means. The common direction of small creeks, the direction the brush all leans due to the prevailing winds, the angel of the snow drifts, all are indicators very useful—when you can see them—but we could see nothing but occasional tufts of grass. I was quite sure, even if he could determine our location and direction by listening to the low frequency radio range, he could not hear it. I was confident he could see nothing I could not, but the only answer he gave me was, "We know."

"Yes," I said "I know you know, but can you tell me *how* you know, so under the same circumstances, I can know?"

All he would say was, "We know." HE KNEW!!

It seems in all walks of life, the desire to pull a joke on the new member of the crew is an irresistible urge. One day I was scheduled to deliver a cook stove to Chukfaktoolik, a small village between Bethel and Hooper Bay. One of the pilots assured me I couldn't find the place. I asked why they were sending me out if they were so sure I couldn't find it. The pilot serving as temporary station manager told me it would be good practice for me. I asked where the stove was. I was told it was already in the airplane and when I brought it back I shouldn't feel too badly, it had already been out that direction three times, without being delivered. I took the clipboard and departed the office with a firm determination I was not going to bring that stove back.

I should point out, in the Yukon-Kuskokwim-Hooper Bay area, anything over twenty feet high is classified as a mountain. There are no trees and the brush is quite short and sparse. The country is well-covered with tall, stiff grass, and a few willows. After snow has drifted for a month, nothing looks like the map which depicts the appearance of summer.

As I was taxiing out to take-off, I noticed a young fellow that didn't look local. I called him over to the airplane and asked him his name. He said he was Billy Moon, from Chukfaktoolik. He was a round-faced, blue eyed Eskimo that had the look of confidence and knowledge. I told him if he wanted a free ride to jump in. We delivered the stove. I never told anyone how I found Chukfaktoolik, but will here admit I probably never would have without Billy Moon.

Reinhold Thiele, George's older brother, was flying out of Aniak, on the Kuskokwim River. Reinhold was a determined, constantly smiling, blue-eyed man about my own size-an exceptional pilot. He, like George, loved a good joke. I was asked to relieve him for a month while he took his family on a well deserved vacation. I rode with Reinhold to McGrath and back, making all stops, on an orientation ride. The next day we repeated the performance to Bethel and back, for the same purpose. Before departing, Reinhold was careful to call to my attention the Post Office was empty. The insinuation was, he expected it to be that way upon his return.

The Twins

We were using a Gullwing Stinson number 5709N which had the best useful load of the fleet. It was still only 960 pounds, which sounds good until you face up to the reality the weight of the pilot, his fuel, oil, emergency gear, etc. all are subtracted first; then you start loading mail. On occasion, it was difficult to keep the post office empty and stay within your legal load envelope. At times the mathematics involved creating a legal load manifest would have made the best of IRS accountants proud of us.

All pilots really disliked the arrival of the Sears Roebuck catalogues each spring. They weigh so much, they completely exhaust the weight available of any airplane long before the room is utilized. It would have really been nice if the catalogues had come to each village, one at a time, but we have to face life as it is, instead of the way we would like it to be. The catalogues all came into McGrath at once, so logic dictates to the bureaucratic mind that they must all go to the villages the same day. Perish the thought.

On a trip to McGrath when I stopped at Stony River, a nurse from Bethel asked if she could board the flight to Bethel. I assured her she could but I was going the wrong way, however, I would be coming back in a couple of hours and she could board then. She was adamant she wanted to get into the airplane with me right then, even if it meant going to McGrath and back. I told her I didn't mind at all but she could leave her bags until the return flight. One look at the expression on her face told me of the indignities she had suffered at the hands of one of the local residents.

"The ladies think they are plagued by harassment today!"

Upon arrival at McGrath, I went into the Roadhouse and ate lunch. The station manager prepared my paper work. Claude Demientieff, an efficient, hardworking, dependable helper, serviced the airplane and loaded the mail. After lunch I went into the office to check the manifest which seemed to be in order. I did have an unmanifested passenger but that is the way I wanted it. This should be a nice, uneventful trip. If only I had known this was the day of the Sears Roebuck catalogues.

Actually the load didn't appear to be too bulky, just a number of mail bags with a few outside packages on top, it all looked normal.

We taxied out to the longest runway for the take-off run. About the CAA Station, I lowered the tail to take-off position but nothing happened. I released pressure on the control wheel, let the airplane continue gaining a little more speed and tried again. Still nothing happened, so a little more speed should surely do it. By now we had gone so far, and were going so fast, we could not even entertain the thought of stopping on skis. The only dignified thing to do was: if at first you don't succeed, try, try again. I knew the airplane was built to fly, so at the last possible moment I popped flaps and gave a slight tug on the control wheel. We went straight off the end of the runway, out over the ice of the Kuskokwim River. We didn't lose any altitude but we darned sure didn't gain any.

We were just hanging in the air on the prop and the flaps. After using up all the straight section the meandering Kuskokwim had allotted us we didn't dare try to pull up over the spruce trees. We used up all the speed we had acquired just negotiating the bend in the river. Oh boy! Another couple miles of straight river ahead.

I maintain that being a mechanic really helps one as a pilot. I understood the flap arrangement, which was a vacuum system. You either had full flaps or none, and a terrible sinking feeling when you released the flaps to reduce drag after take-off. I had noticed that by moving the flap control just enough to hear a slight whistle in the system, the flaps would come up slow enough to allow the thrust of the engine to provide an airspeed increase sufficient to compensate for the loss of lift as the flaps were retracted, thus eliminating that awful sinking feeling.

I now employed that technique and we made it around that bend in the Kuskokwim to another straight stretch a couple miles long. We had acquired almost enough speed to pull up over the trees when another bend came rushing down upon us. Figuring it better to remain over the ice on the river than to almost clear the tops of the spruce trees, we again sacrificed our precious airspeed to another bend of the Kuskokwim.

Well, to make a long story less long, bends and straight sections of river alternated for some time but then success always comes to those who persevere. After burning off enough fuel, sweating away a few pounds, or whatever it took to decrease our weight sufficiently, we were able to acquire enough altitude to begin flying straight to Stony River instead of making every bend in the river.

Landing at Stony, we sincerely hoped the majority of the load would be off-loaded there, but that was wishful thinking. When I found an unmanifested bag of mail I began to get suspicious. Looking through the paper work I discovered that cussed station manager had given me two legal loads, complete with two legal manifests. I was exactly 100% overloaded, plus the unmanifested passenger.

The next time I was in McGrath, I tried to tell the station manager I didn't mind overloading a little but would appreciate it if he would tell me about it when he next decided this was the day for me to kill myself. He just laughed, he had accomplished his aim, it was up to *me* to look out for *myself.*

A few days later upon returning to Aniak from the McGrath mail run, Wayne House, Aniak station manager, advised me there were seven air force officers and men upstairs waiting to meet with me. The Col. told me he had made arrangements with the office in Anchorage for me to be at their disposal to fly them on charters to locations of their choice. The operation was a military secret. I was a little dismayed. It would be difficult for me to keep up the mail runs as well as fly charter for them, so I had a little discussion with Wayne. He got a clarification from Anchorage the next day. I was to be at their disposal as much as possible—after the mail runs had been completed each day.

The weather was very good, the days were getting long, and by starting early, there was quite a bit of daylight left for their needs. Most of their flights were within thirty minutes of Aniak. I landed them at several sights in just a few days, they completed their work and moved to another. They were looking for a possible location for a radar sight (but don't tell anyone). They were engineers, surveyors, electronic technicians, and most of them were also pilots. One was a paramedic, and was he ever one tough soldier. He seemed to thrive on hardship. His name was Marden, but his is the only name I still remember.

They had searched all the possible sights north and east but there was one lone, flat-topped mountain, west of Aniak, that really looked the most promising of all. We went there last and it happened to be Sunday. We had the entire day to devote to that project alone, no mail run. The plan was to take in four men the first trip, then return to Aniak for three more. The Col. went on the first trip.

The top of that mountain was as flat and smooth as a football field, with little snow. The wind really whistled across it most of the time. On the first trip we flew over at about eight hundred feet looking over the surface and to determine wind direction and velocity, which proved to be straight down the intended runway at about thirty knots. We circled and set up an approach that should land us about one hundred feet from the end, thus making it unnecessary to taxi for departure.

That mountain was formed much as many in the states of Utah, Colorado, Arizona, and New Mexico. Very flat and smooth on top, then drops almost straight down on both ends, as well as the sides. As we approached and were still about one hundred fifty feet above the level of the surface, we could feel a down draft. I immediately applied full throttle, full flaps, and some back pressure on the control yoke. We landed with the skis just making contact with the crest at the end of the runway, a short bounce and we stopped about fifty feet from the beginning of the airport. I would probably have made a good poker player because I pretended that was just the way we always did it. I received and thanked them for congratulations on such a nice landing with a composure and nonchalance that would have done justice to Sitting Bull.

After unloading, I returned to Aniak and brought out the rest of the crew, three in all, but made sure we touched on a little further down the runway. The Col. jumped into the airplane as soon as we had it unloaded and pushed back to the beginning of the take-off area. He said, "Let's get this part of the crew back to Aniak as soon as you can. It will only take these fellows about twenty minutes to do what they have to do and it isn't too comfortable out there in that wind with no shelter."

"If they can be done in twenty minutes we may as well just wait for them," I said.

He was astonished to think I would actually consider taking all seven of them in a five-place airplane, in one load.

"Can you really do that, will this airplane haul that much, where will we all sit?"

I explained gross weight was only a factor to consider under adverse conditions, and to be used by inspectors intent upon filing a violation on someone. After all, the airplane was trying to fly right then, and we didn't yet have the engine cover off. Wait until we open the throttle and get to the end of the runway to start worrying. If it isn't flying by then, all we have to do is point the nose down, we have four thousand feet to gain flying speed. (Of course, he didn't know the story about the Sears Roebuck catalogues.) Considering how light we were on fuel, we had about the same load but we also had a thirty knot wind to assist the take-off. Needless to say, we had about two hundred fifty feet altitude when we went over the far end of the runway. I had difficulty fitting all seven names onto the first trip on paper so I just did the easy thing and made it look like two trips.

As an afterthought, the Col. wanted to check out one more place. We landed and the crew took off to check out whatever it was they wanted to see. One private was the slowest in getting into his back pack and snow shoes, so I asked him to help me get turned around by giving the tail a little push. I suggested he really didn't need his snowshoes in only eight inches of snow, but he insisted. I showed him how to push on the end of the elevator just long enough to get me started into a circle and the airplane would continue thus until I straightened it out. Well, of course he fell down, grabbed onto the stabilizer and created a totally negative effect, so I had to chop the throttle. I could see we were going to hit a small spruce tree, which we did. It broke off but dropped straight down and remained between the propeller and the cowling, slightly bending the cowling. It probably took me twenty minutes to get that thing out from between the cowling and the propeller. Neither was really damaged beyond a blemish but I wished it hadn't happened.

As I pulled the airplane into the parking area at Aniak, Buster Vanderpool, who helped me fuel and load the airplane, asked me how I had bent the cowling. Again "Sitting Bull" declared we had hit a ptarmigan on take-off.

Not showing one bit of expression nor saying a word, Buster pulled an eighteen-inch spruce limb out of the cowling, looked at me and said, "Ptarmigan huh? He must have been roosting in a tree."

Before leaving, since Reinhold had been so careful to call to my attention the post office was empty, I was also careful to be sure it was empty when I left. I even had to make an extra round trip-Kaltag to Aniak-to do so. The next time I saw him, Reinhold really gave me a bad time about leaving a mountain of mail for him. I never did know for sure if he was pulling my leg or if a load had come in just as I left, but the last time I saw the post office, I took the last bag of mail from the building. You win some, you lose some.

Upon leaving Aniak, I went back to Fairbanks. April was rushing down upon us and spring was in the air. Little Granny came up from Akiak to stay with Cutie and the twins when the new baby came. The new little bundle of joy was another girl. We named her Vicky.

I made myself available at the office but was never scheduled out on any flights. I read that as an omen so I called at the union hall and had been working on a construction job for several weeks when "Swede" notified me the company no longer needed me as a pilot.

Don Hulshizer, Chief Bush Pilot for Wien, came to see me one day, offering a job flying out of Barrow. A good friend of ours, Walt Baer, had been killed in an accident right in Barrow and his death left quite a hole to be filled. I really didn't want to go to Barrow and was working on a good construction job. I asked him if he could wait about a week. He assured me he could, but would like to get something lined out as soon as he could.

I recommended he go talk to George Thiele, who was in the process of finishing up his last week with the Army. It didn't appear Consolidated had planned to honor his return after completing his military obligation. As it turned out, he hired George and everyone was happy.

About three months later, Don again came to see me. He said he didn't want to talk me into anything, just check to see if I had changed my mind. He needed another pilot, in Barrow. Well, now things had changed a little. I had most of a construction season behind me and the weather was getting a little nasty for skinning cat. Also the construction season was almost gone and George was in Barrow, why not? That was the beginning of a very interesting year.

Flying for Wein

✈

After arriving at Barrow, George checked me out on floats in the Cessna 170. This airplane happened to be the "B" model, which indicated a fairly new air plane at the time, but most important, it incorporated the new Fowler flaps. The older models used a drag flap which were not nearly as advantageous on take-off. George was occupied full time in the Cessna 195 on wheels.

I found Barrow a fairly easy place from which to fly. Most of the flights were along the coast to the villages on regular mail runs. The flights which took us inland were mostly charters and the time could be adjusted to take advantage of weather. We flew a lot at night due to more stable temperatures and less fog.

If I were a cartoonist, I could here create a story of considerable humor, but since I am not so endowed, the word picture will, out of necessity, have to suffice. One day we loaded the 170 with mail for Wainwright and Point Lay and a lady passenger and her baggage for Wainwright. We taxied out and took off from the small lake between Barrow village and Browerville. The lake was not large, but quite adequate for our purposes. The weather was good, the fuel tanks were full, the floats were empty, the engine was running smoothly. All indications were this would be just a routine flight.

We usually kept the seats positioned all the way forward to allow stowing mail and cargo forward, in consideration of weight and balance. The seats fit onto a track attached to the floor on which rollers built into the legs of the seats would smoothly roll the entire seat fore and aft. Making the

119

adjustment from short to tall pilots was a simple matter of pulling a small lever and pulling or pushing with the feet. Therein hides the gremlin.

One must be especially careful to secure the adjustment lever after seat position has been established to insure the seat will not slide back into the baggage compartment on the take-off run. The normal procedure is to press downward on the lever and shake the seat with the legs to see if it will move back, and when it does not, you feel as though you are home free. Imagine my consternation and surprise when a situation developed far worse than having the seat slide back.

On this day it was fortunate I was flying a "B" Model Cessna because of that much longer and more sturdy flap handle. That handle made it possible for a pilot, who had not been pumping iron regularly, to lower the flaps on approach with only one good arm.

There were power lines near one end of the lake but nothing about which one should be concerned under normal conditions. However, once a pilot has had a bad experience with power lines, just the sight of them tends to make him uneasy. We were about thirty feet off the water when my seat turned completely over backward. The two front legs had moved forward and become disconnected from the rails while the two rear legs still held fast. Lying flat on my back, unable to return to the upright position, not being able to see out of the airplane nor reach the rudder pedals with my feet, I was convinced it was decision time.

The lake was not large enough to land again straight ahead, even if I could see. Thankfully the engine was running smoothly, but the airplane was going much too fast. Being able to reach and adjust the elevator trim made it possible for me to get the airplane to climbing at both a higher rate and angle. The instruments gave me the information needed to nudge the control wheel to remain level. The passenger was so calm I wondered if she was accustomed to having her pilot lean back and take a siesta immediately after take-off.

After reaching five hundred feet, I deemed it safe, possible, and appropriate to rearrange things so I could at least see. By grasping that sturdy flap handle with both hands I was eventually able to get the seat back into an upright position but could not get it to slide aft enough to re-attach the front legs to the rails. Facing reality, I flew the airplane around to approach position with the rudders, my left hand making all the aileron as well as engine control adjustments. I was not about to let go of that flap handle again, I had almost lost it twice more after achieving an upright position.

Once back on the water, it was a simple matter to taxi into the beach, replace the front legs to their proper position and install the keeper that had apparently been lost. Now to continue the trip. I still think it would make a humorous cartoon.

A couple weeks later there was another experience which needs to be passed on as it may save someone else some embarrassment. I am not sure the same problem did not cause the death of a friend of mine in the same area a few years later.

I was flying the regular mail trip from Barrow to Wainwright. The weather was reported as good at Wainwright, but I was encountering some sloppy fog and low clouds in the Peard Bay area. I was so close to Wainwright I thought I would just climb out on top of these few clouds as the weather at Wainwright was reported so good. I could see the sun plainly up through a hole and started climbing. My engine began to overspeed so I steepened the climb a little but still the engine was racing. I could see the sun above me but couldn't understand why my airspeed was also increasing. Suddenly a bunch of ducks exploded right in front of me and I could then see the water. I got the airplane straightened out and figured out what had happened. The air was so calm and the water so protected within the bay, that I was flying right into a reflection of the sky on the surface of the placid water. I have always liked ducks.

During the ensuing weeks, I experienced a number of interesting situations. Some were worth recording for posterity. Some may increase longevity for aspiring pilots. The C-170 on floats had a number of idiosyncrasies which a pilot seems to have to learn for himself. Like so many situations, it is totally impossible to check out a pilot and name all the pitfalls he may encounter. The check pilot has to appraise him to determine if he has the basic instincts and abilities to handle unusual circumstances on extremely short notice and hope he doesn't encounter too many of them all at the same time.

My first encounter with a strange behavior was when I was asked to take the doctor from the Barrow hospital and Roland Heatherington, of the U.S. Coast & Geodetic Survey, out to Teshekpuk Lake. Both were huge men. Without weighing them, I would estimate I was in the vicinity of two hundred pounds overloaded. We had a terrific wind, so I thought I could make it. The airplane would not rise up onto the step on floats, so, after abusing the engine about the right amount of time, I closed the throttle and the airplane simply jumped up onto the step. I was so surprised I almost waited too long to add power and continue the take-off.

After I got into the air, I thought to myself, "Now what happens when we get out there and I can't get this thing up onto the step?"

We landed at Teshekpuk Lake and taxied up the beach until we spotted the object of our inquiry. Two Coast Survey men had disappeared a couple years before when their boat overturned on the lake. They were never found. We were to check out a report of a body on the beach. It was a body and we did bring it back to Barrow for identification.

We prepared for take-off and room was not a problem since Teshekpuk Lake is about twenty-five miles long. We faced the same strong wind we had at Barrow. I had to use the same technique to get the airplane onto the step.

Later I learned that was an idiosyncrasy of most airplanes using both power and floats that were barely adequate. A few days later I almost turned that same airplane over backward while parked at the loading dock. The passenger didn't understand what I meant when I shouted for him to get up front when I felt the heels of the floats sinking. He wasted so much time trying to get into the front seat of the airplane I could not get past him to run up to the front of the float to get weight enough forward to establish a balance. Fortunately that time, the water was so shallow that the heels of the floats hit the bottom and when I finally got to the front of the float, the heels resurfaced. Otherwise, the entire airplane would have gone completely over backward, floating with only the floats visible after a few minutes.

About a month later, I took a couple of mechanics to Liberator Lake, about one hundred fifty miles south of Barrow. They were to make a repair on a weasel which had been left there two years before. I learned two things on that trip. The battery had been completely disconnected during the time the weasel had been sitting out in the weather. After completing their work, they reconnected the battery and started that machine just like it had been parked the evening before. When they left, they disconnected the battery again.

As we prepared to depart, the mechanics wanted to bring the tools with them that had been left out there for so long. I told them I didn't think we could get off with them but we could give it a try. I cautioned them to not step on the bilge covers on top of the floats as doing so would possibly cause them to leak. The way the airplane was parked, I had to be the first one to enter, but I heard the last passenger step on one of those covers. It was such a hassle to get out and check, I thought it would probably be OK. Carelessness (or laziness), yes.

The south side of the lake was located at the base of an almost vertical mountain with low tundra shore on the north. The weasel was on the south side, at the bottom of the bluff. A strong wind had been blowing from the south. The surface of the lake was extremely rough, but it was the residual action of a large body of water set in motion. The wind had let up to a fresh breeze, still from the south. We had to taxi about a mile north in order to have safe room to take-off and make a turn before encountering a down draft caused by the proximity of the bluff.

I extended one notch of flaps and applied full power. Normally a float pilot will attempt to help the aircraft rise up onto the step by slightly pumping the control yoke. In doing this I noticed the nose of the airplane would come a little higher and fall a little less with each cycle of the yoke. Conclusion, we are sinking.

I appraised the passengers of what was transpiring, raised the flaps, pushed forward on the control yoke and held it there to keep the heels of the floats up and applied all the power my mechanics conscience would allow. I told the passengers to open both doors, let them trail in the prop blast, but for now, to stay in the airplane. I advised them to consider swimming as an absolute last option. The attitude of the airplane seemed to be stable, so I calmly advised them to get out onto the shore side float when we were about one hundred yards from shore. I cautioned the fellow in front to be sure to jump to shore at least three feet before we hit the beach, for if he waited too long there was danger of being thrown into the prop when a float hit shore. Above all, stay behind that wing strut until the right float hit the beach.

Because of my familiarity and experience with the airplane, I had a better idea than they, when the float would hit the shore. I pulled the mixture control to kill the engine and was on the shore ahead of them both, before the floats hit the beach. I grabbed the wing, then had one of them hold it while I ran to the stabilizer and lifted for all I was worth. I caught it just before the float completely submerged and got the heel onto the shore, then the front of the floats would support the weight.

We unloaded the tools and started pumping the floats. It took us forty-five minutes of steady pumping to again render the floats dry. Second lesson—I got in last, making sure no one stepped on a float cover.

After the end of float season, I wrote a very detailed letter to Bud Seltenreich, a highly qualified CAA inspector in Fairbanks, telling him of my experience and opinion of the cover. I flatly stated that I thought they should be declared unairworthy, now that we had time to formulate an alternative before the next float season. The next year a new means of fastening the cover came out for the Edo floats.

As the season progressed, the hunting seasons were all about over. It was getting cold and ice was closing the lake at Barrow. The weather was bad through Anuktuvik Pass, so the decision was to take the float plane to Fairbanks through Kotzebue. We had to beat about six inches of ice off the floats before leaving the beach. The lake was frozen out about twenty feet from shore. The rest of the lake was free of ice. A breeze had been blowing toward shore, causing ice buildup on the floats and forming only on one side of the lake. We were somewhat worried about the airplane getting frozen in. Of course, after we got the airplane safely out of Barrow, the weather warmed up for another three weeks but it really didn't cause a problem. When I talked to Sig Wien about it all he said was, "I thought it was a little early for the lakes to be freezing over at Barrow." Fifteen years experience in an area will usually give a person that kind of insight.

I flew as directly to Kotzebue as possible. The weather north of the mountains was very good, we just couldn't get through the passes between Barrow and Bettles. I saw so many caribou in one herd, I thought it would be novel to count them. My indicated speed was one hundred five miles per hour, with very little wind, so I timed an area, counted the caribou within that spot, then multiplied it out. Later Ray Tremblay, of the U.S. Fish and Wildlife Service, indicated they did it the same way. I figured there were one hundred twenty thousand caribou in that herd. Ray said he felt I was probably close on my count.

When I arrived at Kotzebue, the crew at that station was in need of a Cessna 170 on floats. Fortunately, their requirement for the Norseman they were using was now fulfilled. They then called the company office at Fairbanks and got permission to keep the Cessna so I followed John Cross to Kobuk, traded there, and flew the Norseman on into Fairbanks. After arriving at Fairbanks, I was sent to Nome to replace Johnny James for three weeks.

Flying Out of Nome
✈

Johnny James was stationed in Nome. He was a young man who had grown up at Hughes on the Koyukuk River. I had known him from encounters in Fairbanks and at Hughes. We had fished together in the Koyukuk and I was astounded that the mosquitoes never bothered him. He owned his own Stinson Station Wagon that he used to supply the trading post his parents ran and do some local charter work. Life became rather blasé as there really wasn't much charter work in the area. He had been flying for Wien for a couple of years by the time I arrived to relieve him at Nome.

One of his regular mail runs was to Kotzebue. He met a young nurse who worked at the Public Health Service Hospital and the inevitable happened. The date was set and my arrival in Fairbanks was an answer to the prayers of the chief bush pilot, Don Hulshizer.

The aircraft we used at Nome was still the Cessna 170, but of wheels configuration instead of floats. One of the sights we regularly served was Tin City, so named because that was the location of the most productive tin mine in the country.

Representing the U.S. Geological Survey in Nome was a geologist named Mulligan. It was my good fortune to service him on many occasions. I was constantly amazed at his walking ability. He was a tall, tough, lean man with long legs. After dropping him off on a hilltop fifty or sixty miles from Nome, he would appear a couple of days later at the office in Nome to arrange a prospecting trip to another locality. All he ever carried was what he could fit into his backpack and on his belt. A sleeping bag, a little grub, and a prospectors pick was all I ever saw. I never saw a gun of any kind. I can only presume he had a good, binding peace agreement with the grizzly bears.

Never Too Late To Be A Hero

One day Marley Lincoln, an Eskimo fellow from Kotzebue, and Mr. Mulligan were scheduled to go to Tin City on the regular mail run. There was a terrible wind blowing off shore from Tin City, right down the mountain, over a bluff, and down onto the beach. Before I learned how to get behind the wind and come in close to the hill, I figured the best way was up the creek that ran past Tin City to the ocean.

Before reaching the mouth of the creek, a down draft caught us and we were going down at fifteen hundred feet a minute with the stall warner screaming. The turbulence was terrific. I was applying full attention, full flaps, full throttle, and full faith in Orville and Wilbur's wonderful invention as the down draft slammed us toward the beach with such fury I was actually surprised when our wheels didn't hit the sand. Just as I was ready to close the throttle and take what mother nature had in store for us, we hit bottom with a jolt—not the ground—the bottom of the downdraft. Without having experienced it, it is probably difficult for a non-flyer to comprehend the suddenness or solid feeling the bottom of a downdraft can give you. We went along the beach for about half a mile with the wheels about ten or fifteen feet above the sand. The stall warner was screaming, then the airspeed showed one hundred, then the stall warner was screaming again. I eased in a little left rudder and headed the airplane out over open water where the wind could spread out and cease to roll so much.

Things smoothed out enough for us to gain back about five hundred feet of our altitude so I turned my head slightly and asked, "Does anybody want to go to Tin City today?" Neither of them spoke so I looked at them more directly. Mr. Mulligan didn't look too bad, but Marley was the whitest Eskimo I have ever seen. His eyes looked like two ripe olives on swizzle sticks. We returned to Nome just as John Cross came in from Kotzebue. I told him the story and he told me the trick of getting behind the wind close to the mountain and let it pass over us, similar to standing behind a waterfall. Later I used that system several times with good results. Neither of those two passengers ever again asked me to take them to Tin City.

I was fortunate to have John Cross handy to coach me. He was a quiet man of rather small stature, but an abundance of energy and knowledge. His flying career began with the first

128

World War and he had extended it through the second as well. He was an A & E mechanic, but had always flown either in the military or in civilian life. He was a family man who enjoyed his family and worked well with associates.

During that same period of time, one day I was making the mail run from Nome to Kotzebue and return, making all stops in between. I was flying the old, reliable Norseman which was really quite noisy and to carry on a conversation it was necessary to talk directly into the ear of your companion. It was also prudent to shout.

Of course in flying circles, the same as traveling by ship or any other means of transporting the public, some rituals become established to have fun with the passengers when crossing such theoretical lines as the Arctic Circle, Equator, or the International Date Line[1].

Most pilots of larger aircraft are somewhat discreet, giving the aircraft only a gentle roll or pitch—just enough so the passengers are aware that something other than normal has been experienced. Some pilots of smaller craft get a little more enthusiastic, and most passengers enjoy letting the pilot think he has really put one over on them.

On this trip from Kotzebue, there was a passenger for Nome who represented the Department of Education, Bureau of Indian Affairs. His home office was Juneau. He was new to the area and this was his first trip to the North. Since he had boarded at Kotzebue this was not his first crossing of the Arctic Circle, which lies about twenty-five miles south of Kotzebue. However, as we flew across the peninsula near the location of the Circle, I pointed and told the gentleman we were crossing the Arctic Circle. He just nodded and mumbled, "Yeah."

His blasé manner triggered my instinct to jar him out of his lethargy. I have always tried to see the humorous side of things and have found this a contributing factor to retaining my sanity on numerous occasions.

A tundra fire had raged from the mainland toward Kotzebue earlier in the summer. The fire fighters had cut a fire break, just a ditch really, about eighteen inches wide in the tundra and there stopped the fire. Of course all the dead grass

[1] This story appeared in Alaska Magazine.

had been burned and new, green grass had replaced it on the south side, while the old, dead grass remaining on the north side, was still brown and drab.

I slightly banked the plane, so my passenger could see clearly from his side and indicated the line, insisting it was the Arctic Circle.

"Yeah, yeah," he said, "I'm onto all the tricks you guys try to pull on cheechakos but I'm not going to bite on one like that!"

I showed him the Arctic Circle on the map and suggested he locate it on the ground for himself. Just by coincidence the line was only about two miles north of the actual Circle and I doubted he was adept enough at map reading to distinguish the difference. I was careful to not circle or tarry, thus giving him little time for a thorough scrutiny.

He folded and sat holding the map for some time. I had decided my little joke had gone off completely flat when he turned to me, wearing a very serious expression, and said, "You know, I really thought you were pulling my leg. Never in the world could you have convinced me, if I hadn't seen it for myself. Who would have believed the vegetation actually made such an abrupt color change at the Arctic Circle? I wish I could have taken a picture."

He was so convinced, I just didn't have the heart to tell him he had really been "had," but down through the years I have wondered how many hours he has spent trying to convince others of what he actually saw with his own two eyes.

During the time I was at Nome, my wife and three girls came over for a few days. I was able to get my wife in to apply for a driver's license. She did quite well on the written test. The issuing officer wouldn't even give her a driver's test. He said anyone who could fly one of those airplanes could surely teach his wife to drive. I could have walked right under the door without even bending over. I had taught her nothing, I didn't even know she was driving until I spotted the tricycle before she took it to the dump. She had figured it all out on her own, using the Don Jonz approach. Just go a little at a time and when you become comfortable, go a little further. She would park the car at the edge of town and walk to the store pushing a baby carriage full of daughters until she felt capable of handling more. That was in 1953. She has never received a traffic ticket of any kind. Not even a parking ticket. Remembering what that kind old-timer said; I have always tried to emulate his perception of a bush pilot.

When Johnnie came back from vacation, I was sent to Kotzebue so Thomas Richards could also go on vacation. Thomas was a WW II veteran, an Eskimo who became one of the first Alaska Natives to break into the flying fraternity. He was truly a remarkable person. He was quite tall and slender. Actually his carriage and demeanor made him appear taller than he really was. He had a wry sense of humor which left some people laughing at his joke long after he had gone home. He graduated to flying the larger scheduled aircraft and himself established many firsts.

Even after Thomas returned from vacation, I stayed in Kotzebue all winter and had the family come over to be with me.

Kotzebue

✈

During the time I was flying out of Kotzebue, the general trend of thinking among most of the pilots was that flying instruments in a single-engine airplane was pure anathema. Being yet rather green but having relied on them on several occasions with positive results, I felt instruments, properly utilized, could be a valuable tool. I confided my convictions to John Cross who began flying in 1917 and had vast instrument experience. He assured me if I was careful to gain confidence and ability before getting into heavy situations, nothing could be a kinder friend. He cautioned me to be careful to learn about ice on the wings before I did too much actual instrument work. I listened carefully but was not totally devoid of experience with ice, first hand.

One day on a trip to Point Hope in a Cessna 195, such strong wind and turbulence was encountered it would make your eye teeth rattle. I stayed quite high to minimize the turbulence. One thing I always loved about the C-195 was the speed available. In case of bad turbulence one could throttle back to 120 knots and still be going someplace and make a smooth ride out of one that may otherwise be almost intolerable.

As I continued on course this day, cloud cover became more and more solid underneath. The decision was made that the next hole in the clouds I encountered, I'd go down to the beach and follow it the rest of the way into Point Hope. By that time I was almost beyond the hills that caused the air to roll so badly thus causing such turbulence. A strong, smooth wind is quite tolerable.

The awful truth faced me at the bottom of that hole. There was absolutely no ceiling under the fog. Of course there was no way I could climb back up and stay within the hole through which I had descended. A rather tight spiral was required going down. The immediate future was dictated by the circumstances: fly instruments, whether or not you are capable, just do it. I knew what each of those gauges told me, but this was my first offense trying to make the airplane hold still while the gauges told me everything was proceeding in a sublime manner. I was the recipient of a very quick familiarization course flying instruments with no possibility of taking a little peek at the visual references—there were none. I became so engrossed in the act of orchestrating the parts each instrument played in the symphony of telling the pilot, 'all is well,' I forgot to increase the power when tight spiraling descent was traded for climb for the stars. The strange sound of things alerted me to the fact I was only going sixty knots. Full power was definitely in order.

Suffice it to say, with the wonderful performance and sweet, forgiving nature of the C-195, the top of the clouds was reached and a return to Kotzebue was accomplished.

That night I sat myself down and ordered the Pan American manual for properly learning instrument flying. Since John Cross began learning in 1917 and was finishing out a terrific career with Wien, his encouragement influenced me tremendously. I loved it! I placed maps over the windshield and practiced daily. I was amazed at how close I could hit all my destinations flying strictly by reference to the instruments combined with the time, speed, and distance factor. The practice that winter paid huge dividends later while I was flying on the North Slope during the construction of the Distant Early Warning "DEW" line.

Later that winter a phenomena presented itself for a study by the bush pilots of the area who encountered it. The situation was very insidious, inasmuch as it would present itself on cat feet, totally unnoticed, until the results became apparent. Then they were so misleading in character a dire situation had evolved before even the most studious mechanic was equal to analyzing and rectifying the situation.

There is a formation in very cold weather some long-time pilots have never seen, or they were in the situation for such a short period of time the results were not far enough advanced to give them moments for pause or anxiety. When flying in clear weather at temperatures of around forty below zero or colder, occasionally ice or frost crystals will be suspended in the air, but one cannot see them unless he happens to be looking toward the sun through a shadow. Occasionally a pilot can look back under a wing toward the sun and see the crystals plainly. Looking forward he will detect nothing. Often in Arctic flying there is no sun, just daylight, so detecting those suspended crystals is not easy. When flying within them, one may only notice a little less visibility. I had seen the situation on the Yukon a couple of times, but had always been unaffected due to the formation being so local and of short duration.

In rare situations those crystals will cling to the structure of the aircraft to the extent considerable airspeed will be sacrificed—sometimes as much as twenty knots. One day, on a trip from Barrow to Wainwright in a Norseman, I passed Frank Gregory who was flying an Aeronca Sedan. The airplane was painted the horrible blue that Aeronca painted some of them, but that day it looked almost a light robin-egg blue, so strange looking, almost translucent. He landed at Wainwright just behind me and taxied over by my Norseman. We were surprised at the thickness of his accumulation of frost. He said he kept it in the air long enough to get to Wainwright, but thought it would have gone little further. We used a wing cover to rub all the frost off the aircraft. He flew the rest of the day with no problems and I had none on the Norseman—insidious I say. I didn't see a similar situation until the winter flying out of Kotzebue.

I was about to depart Kivolina in a Cessna 195 when I looked up and saw John Cross in a Cessna 170, coming from Point Hope. Smoke was trailing behind him for about one hundred feet. He landed complaining about his engine, but he didn't think it was carburetor ice as carburetor heat had made the situation worse. I got my tools and we removed the cowling, but could find nothing. We replaced the cowling and ran the engine which seemed to be just fine. John and I were both A&E mechanics with considerable experience, but we couldn't even entertain a plausible theory. The engine ran well from there into Kotzebue.

We had a new mechanic fresh from the states, an old crop duster, who immediately knew the answer to our dilemma: John had neglected to properly use carburetor heat! Not really too likely for a man with thirty years and twenty thousand hours experience, a considerable amount of which was Alaska experience. Besides, John had already told me carburetor heat accentuated the problem.

A couple of days later I was flying the same airplane and the same problem appeared to haunt me—same reaction, carburetor heat made the situation worse. I was forced to land at Noatak and didn't make the most graceful landing of my career. We ran off the end into alders of a diameter from two inches down. Being so cold, they broke off easily, rendering little damage. I did however, make it to the airport. Again, the mechanics diagnosis was carburetor heat improperly used.

Being a person of such inquisitive mind, I refused to go to sleep that night until I had formulated at least a reasonable theory of the cause of such a performance by an otherwise perfectly reliable engine. My diagnosis was that ice crystals had formed on or within the air filter, thus being undetectable, causing a choking effect. Applying carburetor heat compounded the problem. Well, I only had about three days to wait to test my theory and this time, I had better be right.

Behind Candle and Deering, on the route to Nome, there is a large area known as the lava beds—an ancient volcanic formation so rough a conscientious pilot will not even entertain the thought of a forced landing into such an environment. Not only can you not walk out, even if you do cease sliding and tumbling unscathed, no one can get in to get you, even with a dog team. Nothing grows, the only tracks you will see are occasional tracks of a curious fox along the edge, or a raven, teasing as usual. In those days helicopters were something the military flew and over which we only drooled.

Flying the mail from Kotzebue to Candle, Deering, Nome and back again, making all stops took me over the lava beds at about one thousand feet. A good covering of snow and a smooth running engine were conducive to a false feeling of security, which was just beginning to pervade my consciousness when the engine began to lose speed. It not only would not respond to any of my commands, it actually became worse, right on schedule, as carb heat was applied. My mother said something about proof of the pudding, so I felt now was the time to prove my theory. I really couldn't do it much earlier and from the looks of things I'd best not wait much longer. Test that theory—now.

My theory told me the engine was dying from a rich mixture caused by the ice crystals imbedded in the air filter. Essentially the engine was choking to death simply because it could not get enough air. When the carburetor heat was applied it made the situation worse because that, too, increased the richness of the mixture. So, leave the carb heat off and lean the mixture a little. It had to work, there wasn't time to try another option, even if I had one figured out. I pulled, and pulled, and pulled.

That cussed engine was gaining speed in complete idle cut off. I even started climbing the airplane to a higher altitude. The engine smoothed out and we kept climbing, but finally it was necessary to feed a little mixture back in as the engine began to starve. I listened and did what sounded appropriate.

Suddenly, we popped out on top of a layer of ice crystals at four thousand feet. It was so thick, when observed from the top, it was amazing one could not see it while flying within the mass. I cruised at four thousand feet and the engine straightened itself out and performed normally for the remainder of the flight.

I wrote a brief letter to company maintenance department explaining what we had experienced and recommended the air filters be removed for winter operation. Word came back: LEAVE THOSE FILTERS ON THE ENGINES. Well, always being accused of being too practical for my own good, I figured I'd much rather the company fire me than bury me, so I would remove the air filter at the first stop of each trip and replace it at the last stop before returning to home base. If things didn't look just right sometimes the actual change was made at the home base. I experienced no more problems for the rest of the winter.

I mentioned to John Cross what I was doing and in his soft spoken manner he confided, "Yes, that is what I've been doing also, since you told me of your experience and corrective action over the lava beds."

We had two scheduled runs with mail to the north and east. One was to Selawik, and up the Kobuk River to the village of Kobuk, the other up the Noatak River and over to the coast, then on up to Pt. Hope. After having made the flights several times, and having previously known some of the people who lived in some of the villages, I was able to establish a source for procuring certain delicacies for the table. Shee fish, trout, and an occasional caribou steak were available. On one trip up the Noatak River and to Pt. Hope, I put in an order for some fresh trout to be picked up on the next mail day.

We didn't have any priority for which pilot would fly which routes. We just took them as they came, but it was my good fortune to be scheduled for the Pt. Hope mail run the next time. I picked up my fresh fish on the way up the river instead of waiting for the homeward leg, mostly because my friend had the fish at the airport and I had the room.

The fact that my friend delivered the trout to me on the upriver leg of the flight was really a blessing in disguise, because I never did get to Pt. Hope. I stopped at Kivolina as intended, but then the blowing snow and poor visibility kept me right along the beach. I thought I was doing well, but suddenly flew into an area well sheltered from the strong wind and open water stood near by. Fog mixed with blowing snow pasted ice over the windshield so fast I suddenly found myself with visibility out the side windows only. I turned around, returned to a long, narrow lake, and landed. The temperature really wasn't bad, so I wasn't too worried about getting the engine started later. I put the engine cover over the cowling, and set about cleaning the ice off the windshield. It was fairly early in the day but time stands still for no man, regardless of his anxiety or desires. It soon became late afternoon, which seems to be the habit in the Arctic, long before the clock said nighttime was near. Also, my stomach began to rather insistently remind me it had been a long time since breakfast. I didn't want to break into the emergency food package we always carried in the airplanes. I kept telling myself this weather would let up after a while, but it didn't. I became more and more hungry.

I had spent some time prospecting in the upper Selawik River and had been privy to much talk about native habits and foods available out on the frozen tundra or along the coast or rivers. Much of this talk had involved the stories about eating foods raw, which we normally cook. I had seen many of the natives of the Pacific Islands eat raw fish right out of the nets, so I figured I could eat some of my frozen trout, but not really! How do the Eskimos do it? I had eaten raw roe taken from lake whitefish, or herring, but I couldn't swallow that trout— so how do we cook it? Forget the plumbers pot in this wind.

After looking along the coast near the airplane some drift wood was located and we always carried a good ax in the airplanes so a fire was soon crackling but more wood was needed. To cook, I felt coals would be desirable to high flames. After piling all the available wood onto the flames I went in search of more wood.

It is amazing how far a person can go so quickly without noticing he is lost. Suddenly I realized I could no longer see the airplane, the fire, or worse yet, my own mukluk tracks in the snow. The wind had completely wiped out all visible tracks. I was down behind some hills and alongside the ocean where a mass of house-sized chunks of ice were standing at all angles. The wind was so squirrely it was no use at all as an indicator of direction. Boy, was I in trouble. No airplane, no fire, no sleeping bag, no sense of direction whatsoever. I had no stars to go by, but I did still have my ax and my appetite— ——and my head——think, darn it, think! At least it was warm.

OK, now I felt the airplane was in that direction, but if it wasn't and I went that way, I could become more lost than at the present time. If I listened hard, maybe the fire would make enough noise crackling as it burns, to be heard. Silly boy, but I was thinking. Finally, I climbed as high as I could get onto a huge chunk of ice and saw the reflection of the fire off the bottom of snow swirling high in the air. At least I thought that was what I saw. Going toward the reflection I stumbled over a large chunk of driftwood that would make a nice fire for a while. Taking it up, I kept watching for the reflections off the bottom of the swirling snow and soon came to the airplane. Really I wasn't far from it in the first place, but it could just as well have been ten miles. I had no inkling which way to go or how far. OK, now it was time to cook a fish.

The fire burned down to some fine coals and since it was as close to the lee side of a large chunk of ice as possible to place it, the wind was not an overwhelming deterrent. Of course, I had no frying pan or boiling pot. It was necessary to revert to the age old problem-solving medium and ... think. Finally, the thought came to me that one of those heavy aluminum log book clipboards should make an ideal reflector oven.

These were a unique kind of clipboard with a hinge as well as a means of clamping the very heel of the log book semi-permanently. The hinged cover could be lifted to open the log book and write in it without even removing the heel from the clamping device, which was spring loaded. I removed the log book and placed it in the seat of the airplane. I then split the fish from head to tail fin and clamped the tail fin in the heel clamp. By placing the entire assembly about two feet from the fire, on just the right angle to reflect heat from both surfaces onto the fish, I had an oven. By bracing it well with driftwood, all I had to do was watch and drool.

Trout truly is a wonderful fish and when the thickest portions appeared to be cooked completely I had a picnic right there on the ice, in the wind, with snow blowing all around me. I was hungry, but I still contend I'd cook another trout in that manner in an instant. There was no mess to the log book cover either.

About two o'clock in the morning, the wind died down to a point a pilot could appreciate and, considering the time, I felt it would probably be best to head back to Kotzebue, rather than take a chance on someone being up and around in Pt. Hope. (Now, I would go on to Pt. Hope.) About half way between Kivolina and Kotzebue I ran into fog again and had to turn back and land on a nice lake about half a mile from the beach. The stars were bright now and the moon was out in full glory. A beautiful setting to just say, "To heck with it" and go to sleep.

About eight o'clock the next morning, I got out to try again. The weather had deteriorated considerably, but it was a different kind of weather — a slight breeze, high clouds, and light snow. I couldn't see far, but there was little danger of running into fog again.

After checking the airplane over and kicking the skis to loosen them from being stuck to the hard packed snow, I started the engine and warmed it up. I then shut it off and replaced the engine cover for a few minutes to thaw any frost that may have formed in any of the breather tubes. Just the heat from the hot cylinders trapped under the engine cover does wonders if frost is in the tubes or if snow has sifted into the carburetor while sitting in the wind and no preheat is used before startup.

After about fifteen minutes, I took the engine cover off and cranked up. I was ready to go home. I couldn't get that cussed airplane to move. I was flying a Cessna 170 and not only are they horribly under-powered, that lively landing gear makes bouncing the tail in the normal fashion to jar the main gear into motion, just a joke. It will not move unless everything, including the temperament of that particular airplane, is just right. I unloaded all the mail and personal gear thinking to taxi around a while to smooth the bottom of the skis on the surface of the snow. I couldn't even get the empty airplane to move. OK, knowing the tricks of the trade, I know the answer, I need some blocks.

Shutting the engine off and replacing the engine cover, I grabbed my ax and headed for the beach. I walked about half a mile each way up and down the beach and could find only one chunk of driftwood. It was a log about six inches through, about fifteen feet long, waterlogged, frozen, and weighing about two hundred pounds, more or less. I didn't want to ruin a good ax trying to cut off some chunks.

Staggering back to the airplane, I placed that log in front of the skis and worked it under until the front of the skis were just tipping down, ready to slide off the log forward. I started the engine, taxied off, and kept full throttle on the engine until I could feel the 'pull' on the bottom of the skis start to diminish. I then turned a few circles and came back and parked on top the log again. I threw the mail into the airplane and roared off for Kotzebue.

After arriving at Kotzebue and enduring about the right amount of kidding from the boys, the Eskimos told me they didn't eat raw trout too well either. They just take a frozen chunk, chomp a few times to insure they don't choke, and swallow it. The idea is to stay alive, enjoy it cooked later.

It seems that I'm either a fast learner or else I just plain had lots to learn. At any rate, new learning experiences kept coming my way that winter. One was to again involve Pt. Hope.

After delivering the mail and heading back for Kotzebue with the return mail, I was going up the Kukpuk River and doing quite well I thought. It was a few minutes before four o'clock and beginning to get dark as is normal at that latitude in February. The wind was blowing very hard, but the turbulence was tolerable when it seemed all of a sudden, the blowing snow was so bad there was nothing visible but the black ice of the river straight down. The wind had polished all the snow off the river for about a mile, then it became drifted again and so white it was impossible to distinguish anything but white. I landed and called Fort Yukon on the HF radio to report my location and well being.

Naturally it was necessary for me to really hustle if I was going to establish any sort of a respectable sleeping quarters for the night. You don't even consider sleeping in the airplane unless you are a true glutton for punishment. My experience and practice at building igloos was very neglected and I didn't have a tent, but did have some good luck. I had two wing covers and with a wind like we had at the time, I was not going to entertain any foolish thoughts of installing them on the wings. I took the tops of several alder bushes and pulled them together and tied them. I then wrapped the engine cover and wing covers over the top, clear down to the ground, and covered the skirts with snow. There were about five sleeping bags in the airplane and only one of me so that was no problem. I burrowed a small hole to make an entrance, lighted a Coleman lantern. Reilly had nothing on me.

During the night, I started the engine several times to warm the oil and insure it would start with no problems, come daylight. I dislike diluting oil unless it is absolutely the last alternative and I had more time than I did engines, so I just sacrificed a little sleep.

It seems the wind usually diminishes about daylight so I was up and ready to go at the crack of day. Upon arriving at Noatak, on the way back to Kotzebue, Art Fields asked me where I had spent the night. Everybody in the country listened to the radio traffic, so there was no question in his mind where I had spent the night. He just wanted to see what I'd say, and make an opening for a little kidding. I told him that I had slept up on the Kukpuk River.

"Is there a hotel up there?" he asked.

I grinned and assured him, "There is now."

One of the changes Jennings Johnson engineered on the Norseman was to remove a seventy gallon rear fuel tank. Another was to remove the aileron droop when in full flap configuration. Wien had incorporated neither change and I had to change my procedures a little.

My sister-in-law, Bessie Laraux, worked for Alaska Airlines in Bethel. She came to Kotzebue for a short visit, so one nice day I invited her to accompany me on the mail run to Kobuk. As we approached for a landing on the Kobuk River ice in front of Shungnak the wind was quite strong and squirrely. Suddenly we had a wing down without sufficient aileron control to raise it, nor the speed necessary to bail us out of our problem. The only alternative immediately available was power. Using all the aileron control available to me, I combined it with more power and suddenly we were headed straight for a small patch of cottonwood trees that looked to be three hundred feet tall. Bear in mind, it is a much greater thrill going up a tree than down. That exhilarating, bird-free feeling after clearing the top fills one with far more rapture than the sudden stop at the bottom, so I applied **full** throttle. Full throttle is utilized with that engine only to compensate for altitude, or in a dire emergency. By now I calculated we were fast approaching the emergency category, if we hadn't already arrived.

We cleared those trees with a full six inches to spare and at least two miles airspeed above a stall. We immediately reduced power, rolled up about half flaps for a second try, which was a success. Next stop was Kobuk.

After landing, going up to the post office and then into the living quarters of the Burnharts, I introduced them to Bessie. I explained who she was and noticed Tony really acted strange and May began to laugh.

Bessie had a beautiful radio voice and the Alaska Airlines Station, KWF-5, was a strong, clear signal which Tony could hear every day. Many times when she was broadcasting, he would tease his wife, he was in love with her even without seeing her, but someday ... Today was the day and we all had a good laugh. Bessie, always one to enjoy a good laugh herself, was really a good sport, especially since the joke was on her, kinda.

In the early months of 1954 I was still flying for Wien and we really liked it. The company had just given me notice, I was now established as a permanent employee after one year of successfully keeping the schedules acceptably up to date and the airplanes right side up. I had been filling the slot of relief pilot for those on vacation and help for the ones who had a high work load due to extra traffic for short periods, like hunting seasons. It appeared that I would be stationed in Kotzebue and we were planning to build a house.

The company president, Sig Wien, made a business trip to Washington D.C. and upon his return he brought bad news. The Civil Aeronautics Board had told him to cut down one pilot. Naturally, with me being low man on the seniority list, that meant I had a vacation coming. I was to have thirty days notice, then furlough.

From the standpoint of a realistic person, the entire idea was ridiculous. By the end of my thirty days notice period, spring acceleration of normal business would be at hand. Sig knew that, and I knew it, but the CAB had spoken. Since I had to feed my little ones, and the company offered me nothing concrete, it was necessary to look for something else.

I was making an addition to my house while extending feelers for a job when Sig stopped at the house one evening on the way home. He brought me some good news.

The Coast Survey

✈

arry Rost had just been awarded a Coast and Geodetic Survey contract for four Piper PA-18 Super Cubs
with both floats and tandem 'Whittaker' gear and one
Norseman with floats. Larry bid the contract, all or
nothing, and when told he was successful bidder, he contacted
Sig Wien to arrange for a Norseman to fulfill that part of the
contract. While talking to Sig, he asked him if he knew of any
available, reliable pilots. Of course Sig told him they had been
forced to furlough me just a few weeks ago and I may still be
available. Larry asked him to have me call him, so Sig stopped
at our house on the way home and told me about the possibility. I called Larry and he told me to come on down to Anchorage the next day.

I asked him if I could make it day after next, since I
didn't yet have my wife home from the hospital after the birth
of Lolita, our number four daughter. Larry agreed, which gave
me time to get a number of things lined out so my wife could
manage without my help. When I arrived at Anchorage, everything was ready to get into the airplanes and go to Galena. The
other two airplanes were going over to the Kuskokwim area.
He had sold one and given the buyer the contract. Eddie Olson
was flying the other Cub for Larry. Eddie was a small, wiry
man whom I had not previously known and we flew on separate parties.

On the way to Galena, it was necessary to fly through
Rainy Pass, with a stop at McGrath. We were about half way
through Rainy Pass, where it opens up into the Kuskokwim
Valley above McGrath, when Larry started down, down, down.
I couldn't imagine his problem. We didn't have radios, so I
figured it would probably be discreet for me to circle until he

hit bottom. I could at least tell someone where to go to pick up the pieces. There certainly was nowhere either of us could land. At about two hundred feet above the ground, Larry started flying a little better. Then he started to climb, so I figured he had the problem under control.

After we landed on the Kuskokwim River at McGrath, I let Larry taxi in first as I was unsure of his original problem. It looked like he was killing snakes in the airplane at the time. I may still have to throw him a rope. When he finally opened his door, still some distance from shore, I thought for sure it was the door to Fibber McGee's closet. I maneuvered into position behind him, jumped out onto my float and picked up jackets, maps, rope, gloves, and about everything imaginable that would float and looked as it could have come from his airplane. We laughed later, saying it was a good thing the tool box was not on top.

We refueled, and while eating lunch Larry told me what had happened in the pass. Those airplanes were brand new. Of course there were a number of things we didn't want left in them for our operation. The date of delivery, float installation, and flying them to Galena, didn't leave time enough to take care of all the little things. The decision was to take the airplanes to Galena and make the little changes in our spare time.

PA-18 Super Cub on floats in Galena--parked on Yukon River in 1954.

One of the first things necessary was to remove the rear throttle control. That was the culprit where Larry was concerned with the loss of altitude. The turbulence was unbelievable in the pass, a rope encircled the rear throttle lever, a shift of other gear and the throttle was pulled closed. He was unable to clear the problem quickly.

We flew out of Galena for about a month then moved to Iditarod, on the Iditarod River, just a few miles north of Flat. Harold Nash, one of my co-workers my first year with the Road Commission, who once mined in the Flat area, told me that in the native tongue Iditarod meant crooked waters. A river well named.

The summer of 1954 was really a paradox. The first part of the summer was so sunny and dry the whole country appeared to be on fire. Later in the year there were not three days straight which would be considered good flying weather. Rain and low clouds prevailed. Fortunately, with the Cubs, we could fly low ceilings and visibility as they would fly so slow one could react before being completely out of time, room, and ideas. Heavy smoke was as bad as low clouds—sometimes worse.

There were times when the flying assignment would keep a person away from camp for so long breakfast and supper were the only meals we could take for granted. For this reason I usually carried a can of peanuts in the airplane. The Cub is so small there is no place to secure things, so they usually wind up on the floor. That is where I carried the peanuts. When I'd miss the noon meal the can of peanuts on the floor came in quite handy and we did it so much no thought of any problems ever occurred to us. That changed after the encounter with the smoke, the peanuts, and later, the jade.

One day I was coming back into camp late in the afternoon, empty, and all done for the day as far as I knew. I ran into smoke about fifteen miles from Iditarod but thought I could make it if I slowed down and played it cool. The smoke finally got so dense I put down full flaps and flew that thing just as slow as I could. The flight developed into a practice of left wing way down then immediately roll the right wing way down and be ready to reverse again. The river is so crooked there aren't even any straight stretches between the curves in most places. As I began to sweat a little, I started to make a correction from full left to full right, and the control stick would not even center, much less move to the right side to roll into a right turn. As hard as I pulled, it wouldn't budge. I grabbed with both hands and heard a crunching sound, but the control stick moved to the right. I then thought of the peanuts. The can looked rather sad. Once I removed the top, it was never going to fit again but we made it back to camp and I logged that experience as one to remember.

After finishing the arc to the Kuskokwim, we moved to Kotzebue. We flew many trips into McGrath and once everything was moved the rest of the party went to Kotzebue on big airplanes and we flew the Cubs over. Of course, I got lost on the way and wound up in Fairbanks. I was forced to spend the night at home with my wife and new baby daughter, Vicky and the twins.

The next morning I took off at 4:00 A.M., planning to refuel at Hughes, as I had several five gallon cans of fuel with me. As I approached the Koyukuk River, the weather began to deteriorate. I could hardly believe it. Fairbanks was CAVU[1] and Kotzebue was very good at four o'clock. I was afraid to land at Hughes. I knew if I ever stopped where other people could influence my decision about the weather, I'd never take-off again. I went on across the Koyukuk River and landed on Lake Tokhakklanten, northwest of Hughes, and refueled.

Soon after take-off, the cloud cover became so low the map was useless—I couldn't see far enough to orient anything. I'd picked up a small stream with spawned out salmon all along the shoreline. I knew I was still on the Koyukuk drainage. I was going upstream, which was generally northerly and that fit, so I just kept going. Soon I was over a stream that didn't seem to be much over three feet wide but looked fairly deep with heavy grass trailing into the water from both banks. I then thought I could see a stream running in the opposite direction, just over a small ridge ahead. I entered sort of a pass formed by higher hills and knew I was on the Kobuk drainage. Terry

[1] CAVU—abbreviation for Ceiling And Visibility Unlimited.

McDonald had described that pass to me a few years before. Also, there were no more spawned out salmon. I followed the Pah River down until it ran into the Kobuk and soon came to better visibility. I could see the village of Kobuk ahead.

The Kobuk River makes a loop south then swings back to the north. The village is located on the northern part of the loop. The location of the village and the direction from which I was coming made it appear, to people on the ground, that I was coming from out in the tundra. To those observing my approach, this and the early hour, translated to a pilot having spent the night out on a lake in his airplane. In those days, before the time zones were changed, Kobuk time was one hour earlier than Fairbanks. It had taken me three hours to arrive at Kobuk, so that made it six o'clock at Kobuk. The people were just coming out to meet the new day. Sam Gamblin, an old miner and prospector who had spent a lifetime following the dream, mostly in the mountains of the Fortymile, was the first person I saw. He was rather unfamiliar with the lay of the river. By his question, it was obvious he thought I had spent the night on a lake in the airplane, due to fog.

"A little lost, are you son?" he asked.

I looked up and said, "Heck no, I'm not lost, this is Fort Yukon isn't it?" He almost fell into the river, though he did catch on after I started talking to Tony Burnhart and Harry Brown. They lived in Kobuk and I had known them for some time. That was an opportunity I couldn't let pass.

Enough interesting situations developed during the summer to write a book, but then we would be leaving the reader wondering what happened to the jade mentioned earlier in the story.

Gene Joiner was a pilot from the '20's era, a newspaper publisher, jade miner and cutter. He was a general entrepreneur and self-proclaimed only citizen in Kotzebue not dependent on the Federal Government. He owned the only Ryan B-1 I ever saw. It was almost an exact replica of the one Charles Lindbergh flew across the ocean in 1927, wicker seats, plate glass windows, and all.

151

Gene flew the airplane to Fairbanks for the annual re-license, but Bud Seltenreich would not approve it due to poor structural condition. The Wright engine was well along in the past tense also. As a result Gene left it at Weeks Field. I noticed kids were breaking out all the glass and tearing it up in general. I had met Gene briefly in Kotzebue, so I pulled the airplane down to my yard to salvage what was left of it, then wrote a letter telling him what I had done. I felt it could at least serve as a temporary museum piece.

Paul Manz, professional provider of many antique aircraft for movies, eventually bought, restored, and used that airplane in one of the Lindbergh movies.

One day on a street in Kotzebue, I was talking to Gene and eventually wound up at his house talking about various subjects when he handed me a jade necklace.

"Here, give this to your wife, best girlfriend, or whomever you think really deserves it," he said.

Being dumbfounded, I asked him, "Why?"

"Let's say, a payment for a debt of gratitude."

"For what?" I asked, mystified.

Gene gave a typical, humor spiced reply. "For saving my Ryan B-1 from being ravished by fun and games."

As a result of that gift, I was able to sell several jade necklaces for him. He also had curiosity pieces of jade cut into squares. They were about the same size as a can of peanuts, but that similarity was to surface later. I kept several necklaces and jade squares in the airplane. I sold several to people on some of the other survey parties during the summer. The squares were intriguing as they had small deposits of platinum which stood out quite silvery within the green jade.

One day while caching gas for the helicopters on a sand-bar along the Kobuk River, I experienced a few moments of anxiety. After landing, I turned the airplane around backward and pulled the heels of the floats up onto the sloping sand. I didn't bother to tie the airplane as the weight alone would keep it in place for the short time necessary to unload. Upon completing the unloading, I stepped into the airplane and attempted to start the engine. The intent was to pull off the beach with power, continuing on for take-off and return to camp on the

Noatak River. The cussed engine simply would not fire. I finally took a spark plug wire in my hand, put the heel of my hand against the engine and turned the engine over with the starter. There was absolutely no spark whatsoever.

On smaller engines, an impulse coupling is employed in the magneto to give it a sharp spin during the cranking mode. This sends a hotter spark in a retarded position, thus enhancing starting of the engine. This coupling is installed on the left mag and the right will contribute to the system as soon as the speed of the engine increases just a little above that achieved during cranking. It is almost impossible and, at best, difficult to start one of those engines without an impulse coupling on one mag.

Since the impulse coupling mag was the one that would not fire, it was evident that I was going to have to remove both mags and perform some alterations. The easiest approach was to remove both coils and trade them. I was quite sure that was the problem. It was my hope that the bad coil would contribute after the engine gained more speed and it was necessary to replace the mag anyway to keep oil from leaking from the engine. I assembled and timed both mags just as if they were both new.

Of course the right mag did not function but the other one started the engine and it ran fine all the way back to Kotzebue. I borrowed a coil from a friend of mine and repaired the other mag and was able to continue working the airplane. After returning to Fairbanks that fall, I bought him a new coil and sent it to him, along with a little present for the use of his.

Before leaving the bar on the Kobuk, I wrote a note in the sand with a stick so the helicopter pilots would see it and stop any attempt to formulate an all-out search when I didn't return to camp on the Noatak. I dislike publicity.

This was not my last flirtation with anxiety over an impulse coupling mag that did not rise to the occasion when asked to start an engine.

After many hours of boredom, a good deal of excitement, some well-deserved rest, and a few stories to tell the grandkids, the summer came to an end. Of course Kotzebue, being the large airport in that part of the country, was the gathering place for all the camp equipment and personnel for the Coast Survey. Everything was taken there to be returned to Anchorage or eventually back to the lower states.

Wolf hunting from small airplanes was still considered an acceptable predatory animal control measure as well as a way to make a few dollars in the winter time. It was also one heck of a lot of fun and I was able to cache quite a bit of gasoline in five-gallon cans that would be more expensive to fly back to Kotzebue than to just leave there. Of course, I lost my maps on which the caches were marked, but I'm sure some of my friends around Kotzebue probably found them, as well as the gas caches.

While moving personnel and equipment to the Kotzebue airport, I had been flying all day across the same strip of the peninsula between our camp on the Noatak River and the large lake along the edge of the runway at Kotzebue. There was an Eskimo out on the peninsula, ptarmigan hunting. Every time I flew over, he was almost close enough to a flock of ptarmigan to be successful when they would fly, just out of shooting range. Finally on the last trip, feeling anyone so tenacious deserved at least one good shot, I flew down low over the birds and thus kept them low and they flew right over him. As I started to roll out of the turn, the darned control stick was immovable beyond center. The peanuts! No, I couldn't crush it—the jade! I grabbed the control stick with my left hand, reached down and moved the jade quickly with my right, and just skimmed out over the tundra with about ten feet to spare. Some people learn slow and others remember slower—oh, but for a can of peanuts!

Good judgment is a result of experience. Experience is a result of poor judgment.

154

The Dew Line

✈

After finishing the summer flying for the Coast Survey, the season was too far advanced to entertain any thoughts of going moose hunting. Instead, we contacted our old friend, Carl Main, a dragline operator with whom I had worked on several occasions. He cut meat on the side and in the winter. We had him supply and cut half a beef for our winter supply of meat. I busied myself doing odd carpentry and aircraft recover jobs until late December. I then went out to talk to Jim Hutchison.

James T. Hutchison, "Hutch," was an authorized maintenance inspector, experienced in all facets of aircraft work, who could give practical examinations for aircraft and engine licenses. The CAA inspectors could give the examination, but much preferred Hutch give the practical for the engine license because it involved so many components such as a carburetor, wooden propeller, magneto, and cylinders. Hutch had them all, and a place to work, at his disposal. The inspectors did not. I felt better working with Hutch because I always felt more comfortable working with someone who really had the knowledge himself.

I had been working without the "E" license for so long I was almost afraid to complete it for fear the CAA would ask who had signed off all the work I had performed without really having the license in my pocket. However, a larger problem was looming. My written examination was about to expire if I didn't complete the practical soon. We never could seem to establish a date, so one morning I just showed up at 8:00 A.M. and started overhauling an engine for Hutch. I completed a major overhaul of an engine, magneto, carburetor, and refinished and balanced a wooden propeller. When that was all done to his satisfaction, the oral questions were all answered, and I thought I was through.

"Now let's see if you can work a weight and balance problem," Hutch then said.

I hadn't done one of them for two years — hadn't even reviewed the process — but I did know how. I objected, saying, "I proved my ability to do that when I took the airframe part of the test."

Hutch grinned and said, "Now we are going to find out how good your memory is."

He dug into his paperwork and gave me a problem taken right off an actual airplane that was flying at the time. After working the problem about six times, and taking twice as long as a person should, Hutch asked me if I had forgotten how to do it. I told him I knew I was working it right but the answer said it couldn't legally be done. Hutch worked it and to his surprise the installation was illegal. All he was really trying to determine was my ability to work the problem, so he passed me. I never did ask what was done about the airplane.

That airplane belonged to Dorothy Magoffin, wife of Jim Magoffin. They owned Interior Airways and were beginning to do an increasing amount of work on the North Slope for the contractors building the Distant Early Warning (DEW) Line. Jim offered me a flying job. I hoped he really needed a pilot rather than trying to keep me quiet about that weight and balance.

My first assignment was to go to Anchorage and pick up a Norseman he had recently purchased from Northern Consolidated Airlines. It was ready for delivery, in Anchorage. After inspecting the airplane, old 725E again, I went into the Consolidated stock room and asked them for a pair of wing covers, an engine cover, and two firepots.

Of course I got considerable resistance, but emphatically stated my position thus: "You would not ask your pilots to depart into the wilds of Alaska with less equipment and I don't plan to do so either. I have no idea what the agreement was between Interior Airways and Northern Consolidated Airlines, and could care less; they can work that out between them, but to accept this airplane in good faith, I need that equipment. If there is a discrepancy between my request and their agreement, work that out with Jim Magoffin, but allow me the dignity of departing with confidence."

They agreed. I used all that equipment before reaching Fairbanks. I had to spend the night in Gulkana due to high wind in the Alaska Range.

After returning to Fairbanks, I was sent to Umiat for my first assignment. Umiat lies on the banks of the Colville River, about twenty miles upstream from the mouth of the Chandler River, north of the Brooks Range. Daylight was extremely short and the mercury was deep in the bowl of the thermometer. Shortly afterward, I was transferred to a camp east of the mouth of the Colville River, near Milne Pt. A few days later, we were moved to Barrow where I remained for the rest of my tenure with Interior Airways.

The DEW line was quite an important piece of construction. It involved a string of radar and communication stations all around the coast of North America, with repeater stations clear to Colorado Springs, where the headquarters was located for gathering information concerning any possible Russian aggression. The job had a number one priority with the War Department. A good portion of the work extended into Canada.

Leonard Sarja was the handyman around the operation. He was quite intelligent, but also willing to put on the foul weather gear, pull heaters and prepare the airplanes for flight in minus forty degree weather. He loved to fly and would climb aboard an airplane with the slightest provoction. One day he jumped in with me on a trip to a camp near Corwin, a little east of Cape Lisbourn, along the coast of the Chukchi Sea. Before leaving, he grabbed his rifle and a box of ammunition—we may see a *parlor bear*! In those days it was not only legal to shoot polar bears, but also legal to shoot the same day you were airborne.

After delivering the passengers and freight to the designated camps, we were returning to Barrow, empty. Sarja wanted to fly. I scooted over and let him take the controls.

Sarj was studiously watching for *parlor bears*, when I noticed tracks in the fresh snow on my side of the airplane that did not come out on his side. Conclusion, there has to be a bear right under us!

After showing him the trail on my side he rolled one wing up a little and spotted the end of the trail with a polar bear standing in the last set of tracks. I thought he had taken leave of his senses. He pulled the nose of the airplane up to an alarming angle, jumped out of the seat and said, "Come fly this thing."

I reclaimed my seat and descended to a couple hundred feet above the ice, looking for a likely place to land which would still leave us in the same country as the bear. There was a long, open lead in the broken ice that had frozen over again. The far side was bordered by open water. While flying low over the open water to check the thickness of the newly frozen ice,[1] Sarj kept shouting, "Land this thing, land this thing." After determining the ice was about thirty inches thick, we landed right in front of the animal. Sarj jumped out and shot the bear in the neck but he didn't go down. Of course the bear started to run straight back through that horribly broken ice which was difficult for a man to negotiate. It was the salvation of a long wheel-based, soft-footed bear, with three-inch claws for traction. Naturally Sarja was losing ground trying to maintain a short shooting range and get off a shot every time the bear appeared on a chunk of ice high enough to present a reasonable target.

I was counting the shots and as they were getting further and further from me, I cranked up the airplane and took off trying to help keep the bear in sight in hopes a wounded bear would not escape to die later. The sun was coming back to the north country and this was a nice clear day. I noticed the shadow of the airplane made the bear hesitate, so I used that device to help delay him enough for Sarja to close the distance somewhat. On one turn, trying to keep the shadow in front of the bear, I stalled that cussed Norseman. That was the only time in my life I inadvertently stalled an airplane of any kind. I

---

[1] Salt water ice will float about two thirds submerged. Ice visible above the water will indicate one third the total thickness of the ice.

pushed the nose down, opened the throttle, pulled back on the control yoke and was extremely surprised when the skis didn't bounce off the ice. (We never did tell the boss that part of the story.)

After counting nineteen shots, feeling that in all of my maneuvering I could have easily missed one, I landed and climbed up onto a block of ice about fifteen feet above and in front of the bear. He was so tired by then he seemed to appreciate an excuse to take a rest, so he stood nice and still for me while I shot him in the eye with my Smith & Wesson K-22 pistol. Sarja actually did have one shot left.

I always carried a 'little lifter' set of rope blocks in my flight bag so we opened the big doors of the airplane, took the one-half inch plywood floor protection to use as a ramp, secured the 'little lifter' to one of the rings welded into the structure of the airplane and started 'lifting.' Fortunately for us, this particular airplane had been used for ambulance duty during its military career, so adequate rings were welded in various places to attach ropes and snaps.

Leonard Sarja and his 8 foot Parlor Bear, killed near Icy Cape, Alaska.

Man, what a job! That little lifter was rated for one thousand pounds and we were moving about that much weight, I think. The cord used in the lifter was one-quarter inch parachute shroud. It was very strong, but it cut into a persons hands so badly we had to use three mittens to tolerate the pain.

We finally got the bear into the airplane, took off, and landed at Barrow about six o'clock. We casually parked the airplane, told the ground crew there was a load in the airplane for warehouse nine, and went to eat.

The excitement around the airplane when we returned from supper was all we had anticipated. The real joke, however, was on us. Rigor mortis had set in and we couldn't get that cussed bear around the corner to remove him from the airplane. I had about decided we were going to have to dissect him in the airplane when Rodney Lincoln, one of our mechanics who lived in Kotzebue and had dressed many polar bears in the past, came to the rescue. All is well that ends well. A number of the local Eskimos who worked around the airport jumped in to help, so we gave them everything but the rug for the parlor. That made everyone happy.

One day while flying that same Norseman near Cape Simpson on top of a thin layer of fog, I called for a weather report. They were giving a five hundred foot ceiling and three miles visibility. We knew we were getting close to the camp, but since navigation aids were something yet to come to most of those locations we had no accepted way to determine an exact location by any means other than visual. We couldn't see the ground, so I asked the radio operator for a long count. By asking for a long count and turning my volume to the lowest discernible reading, it should be possible to discover whether we were approaching or departing the area of the radio transmitter. The length of time we had been flying should have put us approximately over the camp. If approaching the radio station the volume should increase, we called it a build. If departing, there should be a fade or decrease of volume. A person will usually turn the volume back down, or up, whichever the case may be, to twice get the same indication, to avoid errors.

On this particular occasion we got a fast build, which told us we were quite close to the station, inbound. I had asked for a long count. Now a long count is normally a slow count from one to ten and back down to one. The radio operator was unfamiliar with the terminology, so he gave me a count to one hundred. That was adequate time for me to definitely establish we were approaching and were quite near. When he stopped counting, I asked him to stick his head out the door and see if he could hear the engine. He reported we were about five miles south. That made it simple. He had given us a good altimeter setting so we just let down to four hundred feet, looked over the side, and there was the airport. The airports were usually made on ice of a lake or the beach along the sea shore. In this case, the sea shore was the airport and the black sand mixed with snow was quite visible. I never did explain to the radio operator exactly what a long count was, but it was never necessary to again revert to that means of assistance.

Flying, just like most other things in life, presents situations where there is a trade-off. For example: The pilots enjoy variety in their scheduling as in that way they are able to see different people and scenery, rather than allowing the same routine to become a bore. On the other hand, if a pilot flies the same route every day, especially in the dead of winter when daylight is so short, it is easier to stay current with the changes caused by weather. For example, the wind may drift snow around some fuel barrels on the trail and form a certain 'picture' a pilot can use to positively establish his position along a route in poor visibility.

A few days after the 'long count' approach at Cape Simpson, I was again flying Norseman 725E to Wainwright, Point Lay, and a camp on toward Cape Lisburne. The weather report for both Wainwright and Point Lay was dismal, but unless it was a foregone conclusion, the weather was unflyable, I disliked canceling a flight for weather. One reason being the longer you waited for a better report, the less daylight you would have to make the trip once a decision was made to go and we usually eventually went anyway. The worst part of Arctic weather was the scare. If a person didn't allow the weather to scare him, he could usually figure out a way to deal with the rest of it. For a pilot, ice is his most bitter enemy. It is a rather scarce problem in the Arctic. A person can figure out a way to deal with blowing snow, if there is no partner called fog. The weather that day was severe turbulance and blowing snow.

There was considerable pressure to make the trip, despite the inclement weather and short days. The best approach to the situation was to use a little psychology. Take-off and go until it was plain foolishness to continue, then return and say nothing. Let the passengers tell everyone how glad they were the pilot finally had sense enough to turn around instead of continuing to fight impossible weather.

Oh, the best laid plans of mice and men—both passengers went to sleep and we were almost to Wainwright before either awoke. By then I knew we could make it to Wainwright, at least. We made the Wainwright stop, took care of the business there, and figured we may as well give Pt. Lay a try since we were so close. The wind was extremely strong, but not turbulent at three hundred feet. Visibility was unlimited on top of the blowing snow, but we knew it was extremely limited on the ground. From the beautiful world in which we were flying, we could see straight down quite well. The blowing snow was only about thirty feet thick. The problems arose once a person dropped down into that strata and tried to see forward. Visibility was less than fifty feet horizontally.

Approaching Pt. Lay we could see the runway marked out on the ice of a large lake. On the western end, fuel drums were placed every one hundred feet, in a straight line, clear out to the beach. On previous flights, I had noticed there were thirteen of them from the first to the end of the runway. Empty fuel drums also marked the edge of the runway on the ice. Looking straight down this was all plainly visible.

I have, on several occasions, been accused of taking chances while flying in inclement weather. The truth is, I never took a chance in my life. I have always thought out what could be done to successfully effect a landing at all the locations I was likely to utilize. If there was much likelihood I'd be visiting a facility with any degree of regularity, while the weather was good, I would go out and fly the approach I had in mind. If it worked to my satisfaction, then it is only logical if it were flown in exactly the same manner in poor visibility, it would still be reliable. After all, the first instrument approaches were established in like manner.

Every day I flew, I would watch for things that could give me a clue as to where I was in relation to where I wanted to be. In the case of the runway at Pt. Lay, in previous flights, I had worked out an infallible approach. Fly straight down the runway on out over the marker drums at the end, go one more minute, pull the airplane up into a wing over maneuver, close the throttle at the apex, come on around and as the wings became level, smoothly feed in enough throttle to be able to control the decent. The maneuver would place you in exactly the same line of flight, going the opposite direction. Hold about one hundred feet of altitude and start counting drums, as they appeared through the blowing snow. After counting thirteen drums count three more seconds and smoothly close the throttle enough to just ease the skis onto the surface of the lake.

After touching down that day, the visibility was so low we could not see from one drum to the next, but it was easy to hold the airplane on course by articulate use of the gyro compass. The wind was straight down the runway. By watching over the side, the scratches on the surface of the ice made by the skags on the bottom of the skis during previous landing and take-off procedures, were easy to follow, and an excellent guide. The wind was so strong, forward speed was soon lost and power was necessary to continue to taxi.

I was almost at the end of my commercial flying career, before I realized many other pilots didn't do the same things to help them safely defy death and the laws of nature. I wanted everything I had in that airplane working for me, then I tried to add all that was available on the outside as well.

On this particular day, we simply looked straight down through the blowing snow, got ourselves lined up and executed the aforementioned approach, landed and taxied for what seemed miles. When we thought we must be almost at the camp end of the runway, I called the camp on the radio. Bill Wagner, the camp foreman, answered the call so I asked him for his weather.

"Well I'll tell you, you won't make it today," he said.

I asked again what they were giving for weather. Bill came back with, "We have a ceiling of zero and a visibility of about fifty feet."

"Can you come down and get us?" I asked.

A long pause, then Bill asked, "Come down **where** and get you?"

"We are sitting down here on the airport," I told him.

A longer pause, then Bill said, "Well I'll be a SOB! OK, I'll be right down."

"Thank you."

We sat there running our engine at fifteen inches manifold pressure to keep from blowing backward. It was also necessary to keep the radio turned on in case someone called us. Those old radios took a lot of power and to run a radio with the engine off, or the generator not charging, was to invite trouble, like not having enough battery to crank the engine the next morning.

After about twenty minutes, we called the camp again and were advised Bill had left in the weasel immediately after we had talked to him the first time. After waiting twenty-five minutes, we called again. They advised us Bill had left right away and still had not returned, so we presumed he was still looking for us. We exercised a little more patience. Finally, we could stand it no longer and called camp another time. While we were talking, we saw the weasel Bill was driving emerge like a phantom from the dense flurry of blowing snow.

Bill told us he had made it to the airport with no trouble as the trail was flagged. Not being able to see us, he went out onto the ice to try to find us and got lost himself. After about forty-five minutes of wandering around trying to find the airport, us, or the trail, he finally figured out we must be sitting there running the engine. He shut the engine off on the weasel and stepped out and away from it to see if he could hear our engine. He didn't hear our engine, but did look up and saw the windsock, so he engaged in the 'follow the drums' procedure and crept down the edge of the runway until he saw us. We followed him back to the end of the runway, parked facing into the wind, and chopped an ice bridge under each wing in order to secure the aircraft to the ice. When I throttled the engine off to shut it down, the entire aircraft moved backward until the ropes were so tight I could hardly untie them the next morning.

We spent the night and the wind blew unmercifully all night, but right at eight o'clock, just as the crew had predicted, there was a lull. We took off, only to be very surprised when in about fifty miles down the coast, the wind let up and the weather was clear with unlimited visibility. It was just a beautiful spring day at the camp where we landed about thirty miles up the coast from Cape Lisborne.

Upon departure, an experiment with the weather was in order. Instead of flying along the coast in all the blowing snow and turbulence, a decision was made to move further inland, closer to the mountains. The hope was that the wind had not picked up so much speed further inland. About fifteen miles out onto the flats, while crossing a lake about five miles long, a huge grizzly bear appeared about a quarter of a mile from shore. When he heard the engine, he turned into the wind and headed for shore with all the speed and power he could muster. Slowing the airplane and lowering flaps made it possible to almost hover over that magnificent animal. He was slipping and sliding on the glare ice. Even with the extension of his three-inch claws, his traction was poor.

The sight of that beautiful fur flowing over his neck, back, and front quarters, while he executed those fluid moves propelling himself forward, is a sight I shall always remember. The strong wind and our reduced speed made it possible to overtake him slowly, giving an ample opportunity to observe him for a fair amount of time. As we passed beyond him, we raised the flaps and increased the speed to normal and kept going. We did not wish to intrude upon his solitude. My passenger got a very gratifying picture.

To pay proper respects to old Norseman 725E, this story must be a part of the tales here related. The setting was near the area where the *parlor bear* was taken, west of Barrow. The story will help the reader to understand the various types of loads the airplane could handle.

I was scheduled to take a cook, a helper, considerable fresh and staple groceries to a camp near Skull Cliff, west of Barrow, close to the location where Wiley Post and Will Rogers met their death in 1935. I no longer remember what we called the camp. We also had one of the old style Herman Nelson heaters on board. They were a huge, gasoline operated heater, which had a small, engine driven fan to move vast amounts of air to the location where heat was desired. That airplane had a huge rear door which could be easily removed to accommodate large, clumsy loads. The Herman Nelson heater was too tall to even go through that opening so the mechanics had drained and removed the fuel tank and loaded it in beside the body, separately. Bob Rice, flying the DC-3, had left the mechanic and camp manager off a couple hours earlier, and they were supposed to meet us with a D8 Caterpillar tractor and a sled to take the cook, helper, and the rest of the freight into camp. They were not there and did not make any appearance or noise by the time we were unloaded. The camp was far enough away that I knew even if they had the cat running, it would be twenty minutes or more before they could arrive at the airport and they would still have to go back to camp. We couldn't hear a cat running, so that meant at least an hour before the 'boss' could possibly get them into camp and warm quarters. It was extremely doubtful there were any warm quarters yet, as the starting of the cat and moving freight and people off the ice was the number one priority. The cook was dressed just as you would expect to see him in the hot kitchen, with one exception; he was wearing his parka. That called for a decision which was really beyond my realm of jurisdiction, but I made it anyway.

I told the cook to get back into the airplane and keep the doors closed. I always had a small roll of tools with me just for self-preservation. I put the tank back onto the Herman Nelson, then pulled it under a fuel drain and rigged up a system whereby we drained about ten gallons of gasoline out of the airplane into the heater and I lit it for them. I adjusted the heat to what I thought would keep them from freezing and still not cook their fresh produce. Using an extra pair of wing covers, we wrapped the entire mound of groceries and I told them I'd pick up the covers on a future flight. Thank goodness that airplane carried a good supply of fuel.

Since I had considerable experience starting cold equipment which hadn't been running for some time in cold weather, I knew if I didn't leave the crew with some means of keeping warm, I'd be making an emergency flight to that camp as soon as they had functioning light plant and radio. I never learned what time it was when the crew arrived at camp, but I left them on the ice at ten A.M. I do know when I stopped at that camp in the future, anywhere around dinner time, there was no refusing a meal and nothing was too much trouble to prepare.

On the fifteenth of April, I notified Jim I'd be leaving on the first of June. I felt I shouldn't be away from the family so much. Jim tried to talk me into moving them to Barrow, but I owned my own home in Fairbanks and thought my best future was in staying closer to home.

I realized flying around people with more knowledge and experience than I was a good way to increase my qualifications, but I had reached the point where the learning process had considerably slowed because of knowledge already acquired. Watching and listening to Bob Rice was an education in itself. Bob loved to groom co-pilots and a good story was unfolding all the time. There was no question in the mind of anyone who flew around Jim Magoffin whether or not he could fly—any airplane—anyplace. My respect for his ability went up a notch one day when he hand propped my Norseman for me. Not many of us were able to do that, but he could.

I really enjoyed flying out of Barrow. Showing whales, polar bear, seals, and white foxes to the passengers was always a thrill. I was privileged to see the submarine, Nautilus, one day when flying along the coast, east of Barrow. I didn't, of course, know it was the Nautilus then, but by putting later emerging facts and memory together I was able to determine what I had seen.

Back in Fairbanks, I became a heavy duty operator again.

Marquita

☠

After returning to Fairbanks, before I was even able to make a visit to the union hall to see about a job in construction, Bud and Lenor Conkle, from Tanada Lake Lodge, came to visit me. They were in the process of recovering the J-3 Piper Cub they used in their guiding business and desperately needed help. Could I help them for a few days? Dope and fabric work was my long suit, so I agreed. Later appraisal of their work told me they could have done quite well without me, but I know the feeling of confidence instilled by having a professional around dispensing encouragement.

Bud and Lenor had a little boy named Colin. His nickname was "Bugsie," and he was a corker. He was about four years old, had spent most of his young life in the shadow of the Wrangell Mountains. He could swear just as well as his father who had spent WW II in the Marine corps. He had acquired the usual bad grammar practiced by men who have been living in close association with other men. Such grammar was less than appropriate in polite society. A few years later, I noticed Bud had exerted a conscious effort to add a better flavor to his conversation and Colin had also done so as a natural result.

Colin grew up to become an accomplished pilot and he and his family are still living and flying in the Fairbanks area.

Lenore had previously owned an interior decorating establishment in Fairbanks and her ability to work with fabrics shone through when she attacked that Cub. They really didn't need me.

Bud had worked with heavy equipment, but they wanted their own guiding business, for hunters, fishermen, and just plain sightseers. They had written back and forth about doing that while Bud was bouncing around out in the Pacific during the war. They had started with this second hand Cub and now it needed recovering.

About the time we got the Cub flying, it was looking as if I had best get busy job hunting.

Joe Clark, foreman for Boen-Eggie-Cummin & Koon (BECK) Construction Company, came down to our house one evening and asked me if I wanted to go to work for him. We were old friends, had hunted moose together, helped each other construct our houses, and worked on other jobs together. The idea appealed to me. The job was right in Fairbanks, so that was an added incentive. There were really two job sights.

During the saber rattling days, when National Defense was the number one favorite political justification for almost everything, much construction of secret installations was carried on in the Fairbanks area. In some cases, the men working on the job didn't even know what they were building. One of the jobs was building what was called igloos. They were domed, concrete and steel storage areas for the atomic weapons that could be delivered by aircraft from local air bases. They were built into the hillside and covered with several feet of dirt.

The company also had the job constructing the Austin E. Lathrop High School building. The dirt work consisted of streets, lawns, sidewalks and dressing the perimeter. I was moved from one job to the other, as was necessary, to keep each job on schedule.

On the morning of September 30, 1955, I took my wife to the hospital before I went to work. I was working right in front of the high school building where the company maintained an office. At noon I went into the building and called the hospital.

At that time, the Cushman Street bridge across the Chena River was of the steel truss construction and quite narrow. If a driver of an eighteen-wheeler was very brave and articulate, he could cross on one lane while other traffic used the other. Most bus drivers, however, blasted their air horn a

170

couple of times and straddled the three-inch pipe placed down the middle as a divider. In so doing, he was briefly occupying both lanes of traffic. Most people waited patiently for the one half minute it took the bus to cross the bridge, then everyone went on their way.

The receptionist at the hospital who answered the phone said, "You better talk to the Sister in charge, she just came from the delivery room."

"Oh yes, Mr. Gregory, we have been having quite a time here with your wife," the Sister said. "It seems one of the city politicians drove onto the bridge after a bus had started across using both lanes. The politician refused to back up for the bus. Traffic pulled up behind the bus, and the driver couldn't back up, the doctor drove up onto the bridge behind the politician not knowing of the impasse. More cars pulled up behind him, the stork was flying around over here, but you, you, Mr. Gregory, are the father of a beautiful little baby girl. Now everything is in order and under control."

Little Granny was home watching the four older children. I went straight home from work and after supper, Granny and I went over to meet our new daughter and granddaughter. We named her Marquita Loy. Who would have dreamed she would grow up to be an FBI agent?

The next day, the job came to an end. We had done quite well that summer and fall. We had started out in the spring with a good winter behind us, had a good construction season. Joe and I had been able to work the weekends to our advantage and each brought home a moose for the freezer. George Thiele, Gean Starkweather, Joe, and I were all successful, hunting in the same area.

When a person lives in country where they have nine months of winter and three months of bum trail, it is a good feeling to have a good supply of groceries. Good fortune shone on us again on the twelfth of October when I went to work for Wien again, only this time as a mechanic. I was again working with people I had known for some time, both mechanics and pilots. I was also well acquainted with the management. It was a good winter with one exception, and that turned out very well. It depends on how a person looks at life.

About the tenth of December, Bill DeWitt, a city policeman, came to our door, showed his badge identifying himself and stated he was off duty but his car was stuck in the snow near our house. He wanted to use our telephone to call a wrecker. I offered to take my car and pull him out, but he didn't want to even try. His lady friend was waiting for him in the car which he had left running. He would not entertain the idea of letting her come to our house in the interim, let us just call a wrecker.

The problem was, we did not have a telephone. At the time we were a few miles out of town, but I did take him to a nearby grocery store to make his call. He wanted to pay me but I was not in the business of making money off other peoples problems and I may want the assistance of a good city policeman some day. He wanted to buy the kids some candy so I told him we didn't like them to eat too much candy, but if it would make him feel better we would accept a can of peanuts.

Later Bill learned to fly, was working at Clear and commuting from Fairbanks. He was killed in an airplane crash near Phillips Field traffic pattern. From all appearances, the windshield blew out, and he lost control.

After my return to the house, the little ones were eating nuts like a hungry squirrel when Vicky coughed and I saw her inhale some nuts. A couple days later, she started to become lethargic and run a temperature. I took her up to see Dr. Fate. He could find nothing wrong. He tried to convince me she may have aspirated a husk that would cause irritation for a while. He felt it would clear up. It didn't. I was looking straight at her when she inhaled after coughing — I knew she had inhaled a nut. He took X-rays, but could really see nothing. Finally one day, he took an X-ray before she coughed up the phlegm that had formed. He could see the outline of the peanut as plain as day.

The good news was: we had the problem definitely isolated, the bad news was: there were two child bronchoscopes in Alaska. One was at Elmendorf Air Force Base in Anchorage. It would take an act of Congress to get permission to use it. The other was in the Seward Sanitarium. The doctor was not even in Alaska. All flights to Seattle were booked solid until after the first of the year.

Marquita

Both my wife and I have always been able to keep our panic threshold at a reasonable level, but things didn't look too encouraging until the morning of December the sixteenth. Dr. Fate called to say the doctor had returned to the sanitarium in Seward.

It pays to have friends. Alaska Airlines took us to Anchorage for one half fare, Cordova Airlines took us to Seward for nothing. One thing I loved about the flying game was the opportunity and privilege of doing favors for others just because it made you feel good to do it. Jack Wade was the pilot of the Cessna 180 in which we rode to Seward. He was later killed in an Aero Commander when the engine air intakes iced up and both engines quit while he was on instruments over mountainous terrain.

The doctor at Seward wouldn't allow me to watch the procedure when he crushed and removed the peanut, but showed me later how it was accomplished. Very interesting. The tools he used very much resembled tools we often use in the engine overhaul shop.

It was forty six degrees below zero when we returned to Fairbanks, but we had our little girl back in one piece and she showed no ill affects, physically or emotionally. She was still the boss. Her love for doctors had not increased.

I worked the rest of the winter for Wien and was crew chief when spring arrived. We had been planning to take our first trip Outside[1] as a family so I gave Wien notice I'd be leaving and took another construction job to try to amass the fortune necessary to travel for a few months.

In the late spring, John Cross and I had traded some property for a Gullwing Stinson once used by Byers Airways. Jim Hill, a friend of mine who loved working on airplanes, helped me change the engine and do some fabric work to return it to an airworthy condition. We had worked on it in the evenings and weekends, most of the summer. In September, we used it to accomplish a very rewarding moose hunt. John, my wife and I, and the twins went to a good location we knew in the Alaska Range, gathered berries and a moose into the

[1] To Alaskans, Outside is anywhere outside the borders of Alaska. Originally, the lower states -- vacation land, or visits home.

larder for the winter and proceeded to get snowed in for a couple of days. When the weather began to break, we crawled out on the wings, removing ice and snow until they were clean enough to fly, then quickly returned home. We left the tent set up. Joe Clark and I later returned for the meat and the camp.

A couple days later, we departed on our trip Outside. John and Clarence Procite, another old miner, prospector, heavy equipment operator, drove one car and we drove one. We had an uneventful trip and those five little girls, all under five years of age, had the time of their lives. We told stories, played games and had fun all the way. Marquita, the youngest, could say "cow," and a few other words. I would say, "Look," she would point and say, "cow," regardless of the object at which I may have pointed.

After visiting our fill we headed back for Alaska in December. As we proceeded north the weather got colder. It finally got so cold, we were afraid to stop. We drove the last thirty eight hours without stopping. As night was coming on, we topped off the fuel tank at every station we passed, no matter what the price or what the gauge read. We wanted to have enough gasoline to keep going until stations started opening the next morning. It was not possible to get into a warm storage unless we were willing to stop about 3:30 or 4 o'clock in the afternoon.

We pulled into the Forty Mile Roadhouse a little behind Bill Egan, Ralph Rivers, and Bob Bartlett. They were driving to Washington D.C., hoping to influence Congress to favorably entertain the Alaska Statehood proposal. They were having power steering problems and had their car in the shop for correction of the problem. Bob Bartlett was the delegate to Congress while Alaska was still a territory, later elected senator from the state of Alaska, Ralph Rivers was successful at being elected to the House of Representatives as soon as statehood was attained. Bill Egan was elected first Alaska State Governor.

We were having oil pressure problems, but our priority was so low, I was forced to effect corrections with bare hands, outdoors, in the minus 60 degree weather.

174

After getting thawed out in Fairbanks, the rest of the winter was fairly uneventful. I made one charter to Bethel to pick up a dog team for Phil Pentacost, a school teacher at Minto. I had known him at Tuluksak, on the Kuskokwim. In fact, Reinhold Thiele and I were guests at his dinner table on the trip when Reinhold was route checking me from Aniak to Bethel.

Those were the most beautiful, white, evenly marked dogs I have ever seen. They were well mannered, gentle dogs. We stopped at Akiak to say "hi" to little Granny and "Papa" Laraux.

A sad, sad note — Phil Pentacost and Al Tovey, a professor at the University of Alaska, were killed in an aircraft accident a couple years later. The aircraft stalled, spun, crashed and burned. They were not found for several weeks, but on the positive side, they did not endure any long period of suffering.

My wife took a sabbatical that year, there were no children born until the next year.

Years of Uncertainty

?

The summer of 1957 was a year of several different jobs. A couple igloo building jobs at Eielson Air Force Base, a street job at Ladd Field, a parking lot, and the correction of a road alignment that caused much anxiety and hardship for Chuck Strandberg, a contractor friend. Then came the end of the season. To finish out the few weeks left, I contacted the Bureau of Public Roads, the organization replacing the old Alaska Road Commission.

Gordon Anderson, a friend who had assisted me on several building projects, Joe Clark, and I, managed a moose hunting trip with the big red and green Gullwing Stinson. We brought home two huge moose, which was plenty for the three families. Then, back to work.

I bailed gravel with a dragline, operated a road patrol, and ended the season by marking the ends of culverts so the snow removal equipment operators could locate them in winter. Sandy Roberts, a lifelong resident of the Circle area, and I, spent days cutting alder poles and anchoring them into the earth on each end of the culverts. We then tied engineers tape to the tops as well as peeled the bark off in rings so the poles would be easily seen against either a snow or no snow background.

Both Sandy and I were fighting off a cold and fever in order to get those last few days of work before the season ended. By the end of each shift, we would both feel that today was the last day we could work, but by morning we could make one more day. Finally one day, Sandy couldn't make it, so I finished the week by myself. That was the week Stephen was born.

I left my unassuming little wife at the hospital as I went to work. By the time I dropped in to see her on the way home, she had presented me with a manchild. Everything was normal. He weighed in one ounce over eight pounds, continued to be strong and husky, and almost impervious to cold.

The summer of 1958 was another lean construction year. I worked on several jobs. I was going home one afternoon in my pickup when a fellow passed me going in the opposite direction. He started honking as though he had just spotted his long lost brother. I caught a glimpse of him as he went by and thought it looked like Phil Gray.

Phil had been flying co-pilot for Bill Johnson, and later Bob Rice, on the DC-3 flying out of Barrow for Interior Airways during the early days of the DEW line construction. He was flying for Wien, stationed at Kotzebue, the last I knew. We had become rather well acquainted, but I thought he was getting a little over excited just seeing me on the street.

A couple days later the riddle was solved. Phil, and his wife Madeline, dropped by the house one evening. He had a Grumman TBM, a Navy surplus torpedo bomber he had outfitted to extinguish forest fires, and wanted me to fly it. After his presentation, I succumbed to his wishes.

Those were years of such uncertainty. We had not yet achieved Statehood and it wasn't really very clear to me what the advantages would be if we did enjoy such status. I had been doing a little flying under the old Pilot Owner certification, but very little. I wasn't sure if I wanted to continue battling bureaucracy. Actually construction work was slowed to five eight hour shifts a week on many jobs, and the jobs were seasonal. Decisions, decisions. This would give me a chance to make a little money while I tried to think out the next move. I became the first Alaskan Aerial Fire Fighter.

After flying that TBM for a while, I really gained a lot of respect for the Navy pilots who flew them during the war. I would fly that thing along imagining there were Japanese Zeros in the area and think to myself how ridiculous I would feel trying to evade one of them. The TBM was carved right out of a block of solid aluminum from the way it felt, and handled. It was powered with the R-2600 Wright engine and had an enormous capacity for armament. Their speed and maneuverability was very disappointing when I was flying along mentally trying to evade a Zero attack.

Bill Northy, a local flight instructor and ex-navy pilot who had flown them off a carrier deck during the war, told me on his first enemy encounter, he found himself trying to hide behind the control stick. Realistically foolish, but then realistically, so is aerial combat.

Bill was another of my friends who was killed in an aircraft accident. The accident occurred off the eastern end of Phillips Field in Fairbanks, about where Spenard Builders Supply show room and warehouses now stand.

Some people question whether or not dropping retardant on forest fires from airplanes is a viable way to combat forest or brush fires. I can assure you, used properly, it can be very effective.

After seeing many errors committed by the fire bosses and control officers, it seemed to me if I just played dumb and put the retardant where it would do the most good, we would all look better—especially if it rained and the fires went out. I had borrowed a manual from Fred Varney so I could study the science of fire control. The book was about an inch thick and the size of a sheet of typing paper. I learned enough to figure out that if the fire bosses and control officers had passed their courses using that manual, it had been a long time ago and they had forgotten most, if not all of it.

It was easy for me to see the fire crews were afraid the airplanes may deprive them of their livelihood. It was obvious the fire bosses were not asking for assistance from the air drops until the fires were hopelessly out of control. The whole thing reminded me of the time the carpenters at Amchitka wanted to strike to prevent the use of skill saws because they would put so many carpenters out of work.

One fire, late in the fall, was near the village of Minto. There was a real threat to a very nice stand of large timber, as well as to the village itself. A call was sent in for retardant. I cranked up the TBM and headed out to drop in front of the fire, as we had been instructed. The smoke was so low and thick when approaching the fire at the dropping height the actual fire line was not visible. At what I judged to be the proper moment, I opened the gates, and immediately saw I was lined up to hit the blaze directly down the fire line, instead of ahead, as they seemed to think best. There was absolutely no way the airplane could be redirected to move the drop to one side at that low altitude and I could not close the gates for another try. I never looked back. I dashed home, filled the drop tanks again, returned as fast as possible. I could hardly find the fire. The first drop had completely extinguished the rolling flames. There was nothing left but small tendrils of smoke the ground crew successfully terminated with their hand-held pressure tanks of water.

That was the last fire of the year and the next spring the BLM would not use that TBM because they did not like the tanks. Some of the higher echelon managers evidently had seen some more modern arrangements in Montana and California during the winter and didn't wish to appear unsophisticated. It was a rather crude system but it also extinguished fires. Their attitude was something like the home crowd booing the quarterback because the receiver dropped a pass.

Phil Gray notified me he had some twin engine fighter aircraft being converted to fire bombers and hoped I would be ready and able to fly one of them as soon as the modifications were completed. I had much familiarity with twin engine aircraft but I did not have the rating. I took steps to rectify that as soon as the weather turned nice. Hawley Evans, a flight instructor with many, many hours to his credit, gave me a couple hours dual and a recommendation ride. I contacted an FAA inspector for the actual check ride. That was an interesting experience.

The F7F's

✈

For some reason many of the FAA inspectors, especially those with little experience or self confidence, seemed to harbor the notion we, as pilots, were all trying to get ourselves killed just to spite them. No space will be allotted to them, but their mention makes the dignity of the more competent come into a better focus. It seems most all professions have their good, bad, and ugly. Maybe we should say professional, acceptable, and mediocre.

One of the first FAA flight inspectors I encountered who really had some knowledge and experience to contribute was Mel Derry. He was a person who displayed self confidence and ability. He gave me the check ride for my multi-engine rating. We flew a "Bamboo Bomber," a twin Cessna, which left a little something to be desired if a person really experienced an engine failure. I loaded the aircraft to full gross weight and cautioned him it would not fly on one engine in a critical condition, so he shouldn't chop an engine on me in a situation that was in any way questionable if he wanted to be home for supper. Mel assured me he was a past master in the twin Cessna and he would not put me into any position from which the aircraft was incapable of recovering, especially on take-off.

He was true to his word until we had done all the necessary work, then told me to go ahead and take-off from Fairbanks International and return to Phillips Field. On take-off, after we were all cleaned up (flaps and landing gear up and locked), he chopped an engine and of course we had sufficient speed and altitude to handle the situation. I always felt he did it just to show me I could really handle it if necessary—maybe as a confidence builder.

181

It might also be interesting to here relate that Johnny Lynn, flying for Northern Consolidated Airlines, managed to stretch a glide for about twenty-five miles to reach a nice gravel bar on the Yukon River, downstream from Tanana. He had lost one engine on a scheduled mail trip in an airplane exactly like the one we were flying. His judgment told him he would not reach the airport at Tanana, so he thanked his lucky stars for a low water condition and used one of the big, beautiful gravel bars so conveniently scattered along the Yukon River.

After we returned and parked the aircraft, Mel spent considerable time imparting knowledge he had acquired over the years. I appreciated that.

One humorous thing that happened while Mel and I were doing air work in simulated single engine configuration will cause all multi-engine pilots to chuckle. Just the design of the twin Cessna makes full rudder trim and full throw of the rudder pedal necessary to hold the aircraft in a straight-ahead flight path. I had right rudder pushed all the way and my leg out straight with my knee joint locked. I thought I was about through. Having completed the maneuver to his satisfaction I was looking forward to the opportunity to relax my leg.

"OK, now take it up two hundred feet," Mel said.

"OK, but please help me on the rudder," I replied.

He jammed his foot on the rudder pedal on his side, "It's all in now."

"Yes, I know," I said, "but then so am I."

He got a big laugh out of that and helped me hold the rudder until the altitude was gained and we could increase the airspeed. He then gave me back the engine, still laughing.

Early in the spring, we had the Grumman F7F Tigercats in buildup, but problems kept arising and they were not ready as soon as we had been promised. The entire country was burning in May, unusually early, but the BLM stubbornly refused to use the TBM with the undesirable tanks, even until the arrival of the F7F's. We pulled out all stops to get the F7F's on sight at the earliest possible date.

Phil Gray was ramrodding the conversion of the F7F's and as soon as possible, he sent for me to come to Hayward, California, to fly one back to Fairbanks. I had been fortunate enough to get my hands on an operators manual so I was familiar with all the flight characteristics and power settings before I ever saw one of the airplanes. I sat in the seat of one of them and taught myself where everything was, using the blind-fold method of orientation. It was good practice and came in handy on the very first take-off.

Phil was flying a D-18 Beechcraft, which would cruise about as fast as the F7F's when we had them slowed down to the lowest economy cruise settings. Sam Steel, an old crop duster, who had been a crew chief on B-29's during the War, and I, flew the F7F's. We left Hayward, had the normal problems and made the normal mistakes, but eventually arrived at Fairbanks. I had a good laugh when the customs official finished inspecting my airplane after landing in Fairbanks and after having flown non-stop from Whitehorse, Yukon Territory, Canada. We couldn't even get out of the airplanes until he arrived. He was so non-communicative he was abruptly successful at establishing an atmosphere of "us and them," right from the start. He searched the wheel wells, the cockpit area, (which was devoid of anyplace to cache anything, even a notebook) and all the inspection doors he could find. As he was leaving, I opened one of the huge ammunition lockers in the wing and started handing my daughters (who had been watching through the doors of the terminal building) bags of oranges from California, which he had totally overlooked. He pretended to not notice.

The big laugh was in Penticton, British Columbia. Sam and I were both just beginning to feel comfortable in the seat when we landed at Penticton. The weather had been good and the flight was smooth—so far.

We spent the night in Penticton after fueling and preparing the airplanes for an early departure. After breakfast the next morning, I didn't like the looks of the weather. There was blue sky showing but there was considerable low fog in the canyons also, and besides, I didn't have a radio or a map. The radio in Sam's airplane hadn't worked since we left Hayward. Phil insisted we give it a try so we took off. Immediately, it was apparent to Sam and I that we could not stay under the fog and make the bends in those canyons, so we went on top, which wasn't too bad at first. We kept going, for we knew the fog would eventually burn off. Before reaching a place that gave us any comfort where continuing to any place in particular was concerned, our fuel was about half exhausted so we turned back.

Upon arriving back at Penticton, I made a circle to allow Sam to land first. He had taken off first and was probably lower than I on fuel. Completing a rather large circle, I figured Sam would be on the ground and clear of the runway, but I couldn't see him. I really couldn't spend a lot of time looking either, so I lowered flaps and landing gear and was coming over the fence when I realized there were workmen all over the airport. No wonder I couldn't see Sam taxiing to the fuel ramp. I pulled up, made a circle and another approach, while watching over my shoulder for Sam, but no one had moved from the airport surface. I was too low on fuel to play games while they diligently plied their various trades. I figured the natural instinct of self-preservation would predominate over stubbornness. I closed the throttles and landed right in their midst. The shovels, picks, and lunch buckets were everywhere. Men were running like crazy while shaking their fists at me, but once I was on the ground we could take time to argue, if that was the order of the day.

I had just called for fuel when Sam came back and landed down wind on the other end of the airport. Then here came a pickup rounding the corners on two wheels. The driver skidded to a stop, jumped out, leaving the door open, ran into the Airport Managers office, and was immediately told to not even say it. That Airport Manager was a politician—not only did he know we were out of fuel and had to land, but he had just acquired two customers who would purchase, and pay American cash for four hundred dollars worth of fuel in the next thirty minutes.

After a good lunch and checking all weather ahead, Sam and I decided to climb to eight thousand feet and head straight for Fort St. John. We were there fueling when Phil arrived. He was forced to land on a small airport in one of those canyons and wait several hours himself. The rest of the trip was normal except maybe the leg after the next stop, Fort Nelson to Whitehorse.

We left Fort Nelson as soon as we were fueled, thinking we could make it to Whitehorse for the night. The weather didn't seem too bad but Sam had the only map, so naturally he took the lead. Everything went fine for a few minutes, but as we started up a creek that would take us to a divide which would eventually drop us into the Liard River valley, the ceiling kept creeping down. It was just about as tight as I was willing to fly, but since Sam had the only map, I figured I'd better stay with him or I wouldn't know where Whitehorse was. I was squirting along about one hundred seventy knots, just as slow as I could get that thing and keep my engines running. As it was, they were both periodically coughing because we weren't pulling enough power to keep them sufficiently warm.

The ceiling kept creeping down. Finally the thought came to me, this canyon was getting a little too narrow for two F7F's, going in opposite directions. Since it was still wide enough for me to turn around I had better do so while it could still be done with dignity. I had a good laugh the next day when Sam told me how badly he wanted to turn around but all he could think of was me coming up that narrow canyon behind him at one hundred seventy knots.

Sam was able to slip over the divide into the Liard Valley and I went back to Fort Nelson. I refueled, spent the night, and caught Sam and Phil in Whitehorse the next morning.

Upon arrival with the Tigercats at Fairbanks, we flew a couple of practice runs with plain water while all our friends, the BLM "brass," CAA inspectors, news reporters, and interested spectators watched. We then prepared for the more serious business of extinguishing fires. There was no shortage of that commodity during the summer.

We were fortunate enough to have a few smaller fires out in the flats, near town, where we could get a little practice approaching and leaving the fire area with safety. Flying with so much weight and power in such a new and unconventional manner, simply required some unconventional approaches— we needed a little practice. One problem we needed to overcome was the tendency for the nose of the aircraft to pitch up as soon as the gates were opened to drop the retardant. It developed that the greater the speed, the greater the problem. The idea was to leave some of the retardant on the ground, not floating on the breeze. Actually, the problem appeared to be more than the expected rise which always accompanies dropping a load and suddenly the weight is no longer suspended by the lift of the wings. The nose of the F7F's actually pitched up.

In a twin engine aircraft, maintaining speed, at or above that required to control the aircraft with only one engine in the event of an engine loss, is quite naturally a number one priority. The operators manual of the aircraft said one hundred twenty knots was adequate to maintain control with one engine. In actual practice, I determined it was necessary to be reading one hundred thirty knots, with the tanks mounted as they were and filled with one thousand gallons of retardant. Twelve thousand pounds was an overload, but the tanks would hold that much and the aircraft handled the load well. If a person carrying the heaviest load shut one engine down at one hundred twenty knots, he could still save the aircraft using the remaining engine, if he had fifty feet he could safely sacrifice. They were beautiful airplanes.

In an attempt to overcome the tendency of the nose of the aircraft to pitch up when retardant was dropped, I did some experimenting. Since I was the only one of the crew with prior retardant dropping experience, they all had a tendency to look to me for instruction. Noticing the tendency increased proportionally with the increase of speed, I tried reducing speed to see if that would alleviate the problem, or at least diminish it.

Since the aircraft ballooned so badly when the gates were opened, the fire bosses decided where possible, dropping up hill would be an ideal answer to the problem. A fire developed on the Chena River, above Chena Hot Springs, east of Fairbanks. I was first in line and felt dropping up that long ridge, which rose in altitude about six hundred feet from bottom to top, would require a little extra airspeed at the beginning. Sometimes a good education comes slowly, at other times, rather abruptly.

I circled the fire on top of the ridge, figuring out all the ways to get out of any possible adverse situation I may find myself entertaining. After carefully checking the gyro headings to use in case smoke should restrict my visibility, I started my drop at about thirty feet above the trees with an airspeed of one hundred thirty five knots. When I opened those gates, both at once, the airplane took off toward the heavens as though a swarm of Zeros were in the near vicinity. Pushing forward on the control stick until hitting the stop did absolutely nothing but those two beautiful engines responded to the plea and we cleared the ridge top with plenty to spare. The fire boss called me on the radio and started chewing me out for such a sloppy drop, wasting an hour's flying time, a thousand gallons of borate, etc.

When he finally closed his mike key, I told him to "Shut up and listen, and do not interrupt!"

I told him, most emphatically, to not allow anyone to drop uphill under any condition, until I had a chance to talk to all of them on the ground. I also insisted he repeat what I had told him, thus I knew he realized the danger involved.

Before the day was over, I had made several other trips and discovered by slowing the aircraft way down and setting the power to hold level flight with the load, then push the control forward as the gates were opened, or slightly before, the operator could control the drop to within ten feet. The only real danger was in allowing the aircraft to fall below single engine control speed. That was a trade-off.

After the flying for the day was all done, I called the crew together and told them what I had discovered and cautioned them to set up the drops just like a landing. Any self-respecting pilot will land with the fuel selector on the tank he feels the most reliable, set the mixture, boost pumps, props, and flaps, all in take-off configuration. They would have to experiment with the airspeed and pushing the control forward, until they developed their own feel for the maneuver. The decision to slow below single engine control speed to gain the ability to control the tendency to pitch up when the load was released, was up to the individual. I had only told them what worked for me.

The Tigercat was the most forgiving airplane it has been my privilege to fly. One could actually slow fly that aircraft with a full load at sixty knots by using plenty of power and flaps. One could actually maneuver and, with care, safely climb.

The take-off performance was also impressive. I would taxi to the "elephant ear" or engine run-up area, wait my turn for the take-off, line up on the runway, feed the power in to take-off power and at the second taxi way, we would be off the ground with the landing gear coming up. A couple of years later, it was my privilege to fly one of the B-25's that had, by then, became fairly prominent on the aerial fire fighting scene. On my first take-off, when we passed the fourth taxi way and were still not in the air, I began to wonder if those things were built to fly. To think that Jimmy Doolittle flew them off a carrier deck. He told me it was no big deal at all! The F7F was a beautiful airplane.

Those aircraft were manufactured to be a carrier based fighter for the Marine Corps. They made their debut just at the very end of World War II and actually saw very little, if any, combat. Their use in the Korean War was practically nil. The early models of the jet fighters were crowding the previous reciprocating engine powered aircraft out of popularity.

As a result of the aircraft having lost a place in the scheme of air superiority, our aircraft were all practically new, service wise. They had the very reliable Pratt & Whitney R-2800-34W engines, with two stage superchargers. The "W" designated water injection, which was used during times of combat when excessive power was drawn from the engines to allow a pilot to extricate himself from a situation which could very likely be more serious than the loss of an engine on the way home. The manufacturer realizing that in such a situation a pilot would use that extra power to save himself and hope the engine would not fail, at least not yet, created the water injection feature to make it possible to use that extra power briefly and still not damage a good powerplant. Of course, it was not necessary for us to use that feature in the manner we used the aircraft. However, without water injection being used, the engine would still deliver all the power a sane person could hope for under conditions controlled by the operator.

H. A. "Bogy" Bogenrife, the instructor that helped me get my float rating in the forties, taught me one of the most important basics of my bag of do's and don'ts. "Always use a procedure for everything and remember, *IT IS TOO LATE TO BE A HERO.*"

A huge fire developed up the Chena River, about seventy five miles east of Fairbanks. We were all called out to drop borate. We had been joined by Ed Thorsrud, of Missoula, Montana. He was flying his own TBM with a much more efficient tank setup than we had on ours. This fire was just a couple days after the lesson about never dropping going uphill.

We finally reasoned the cause for the aircraft pitching up so badly was that the borate all came out of the front of the tanks first. This shifted the weight aft, and the wind held the remainder of the borate in the rear of the tanks longer. We could cure that by slowing down and pushing down slightly on the control just as the gates came open. If we coordinated that move properly, the fact there was only a two degree down travel on the elevator was not a problem.

Going back to Bogy and the lesson on procedure, now was a time if there ever was one, to employ that lesson. I looked the whole area over, considered the height of the hills and the breadth of the valley, and mapped out a plan for the next drop. Should I happen to get caught in the smoke and not be able to see where I was going, I'd immediately take up a heading of eighty-five degrees for one and one half minutes, turn to the heading of one hundred seventy-five degrees for forty-five seconds, then to the heading of two hundred sixty-five degrees, and hold that until I either came out of the smoke or climbed above it. During the maneuvering, maximum climb power and rate of climb would be employed. The smoke in the area was extremely dense and experience told me it would get worse with each trip.

It was obvious to me if the BLM fire control officers would just tell the borate pilots where they needed the retardant and get out of the way, allowing them to make their drops in the best manner they could devise, the operation would go much smoother. After a couple of seasons, the BLM management came to the same conclusion and efficiency of the retardant drops improved dramatically.

On this particular fire, the spotter, of course, was not a pilot. He knew nothing about how to set up for a drop, considering wind, departure, maneuvering area, etc. He was an excitable person, who when excited, would shout into the microphone, exceeding the range of his radio and making himself completely unreadable. An attempt on my part to quietly ask him to speak more slowly and not so loud, only made matters worse. I had no idea what he wanted, so I tried to put the drop where it would do the most good to assist the crew on the ground.

The heat of the fire made a draft which fanned the flames and created a tremendous amount of smoke, normally not too serious, but it was extremely thick from the ground up to about fifteen hundred feet. The fire line itself was quite visible.

I had been practicing slow flight, single engine procedures, with landing gear both down, and up; virtually every configuration there was any likelihood to encounter under adverse conditions. My sentiments were that approaching a fire below single engine control speed was far less likely to be a problem, than trying to contend with the tendency of the aircraft to pitch up so badly as the load was released.

Checking the sweep second hand on the clock just as I approached the fire, I hit the money handles to drop, pushed the nose down slightly to counteract the pitch up tendency, but nothing happened. I cycled the system again, and still nothing happened. OK, now we are solid instruments in the smoke, with twelve thousand pounds of borate that was supposed to have been spread out on the fire line, and our airspeed down to seventy-five knots.

I only added climb power as this was not a dire emergency—yet. Climb power should get us out of here. I had my procedure well in mind and was sure the aircraft would do the rest. Naturally, the airspeed was allowed to build back up to climb speed and the heading held for the full one and one half minutes, then the right turn, then another right turn. I was just rolling out of the last turn when I emerged from the smoke. With that problem behind me, I moved on to the real problem, a complete loss of hydraulic pressure.

The operators' manual, which I had studied diligently, said that considerable pumping on the emergency hydraulic system was required to lower the landing gear. It did not, however, say it took one hundred thirty two strokes just to open the nose wheel door! When that door finally opened, it ushered in huge quantities of encouragement. The pumping routine was continued until three green lights were staring me in the eye indicating all three landing gears were down and locked. By then we were almost back to Fairbanks. It was a good thing I figured it was more dignified to fly an extra few miles with the landing gear hanging down than to ask the tower to hold up other traffic while I anxiously pumped in the traffic pattern.

Under normal conditions one would never land with that load. It is programmed to be dispensed before returning. Since I had no other choice, I made the smoothest landing of my career.

On the trip from California, our first landing was at Redmond, Oregon. As Sam landed, his left engine quit. It was then that he discovered the hydraulic pump on the right engine was not functioning. Since the entire country around Fairbanks was either burning or in danger of it, there was considerable pressure to get those F7F's on the scene. We had no time to really check them out and make adjustments, so it was just up to Sam to figure out a quick emergency procedure and employ it immediately. By pumping vigorously on the hand pump he saved the day, so I knew it could be done.

Knowing that I was landing vastly over gross weight and would be using up that ten thousand foot runway at the rate of ten thousand feet a minute when I came over the fence, I had best use breaks and hand pump judiciously. I knew Sam had been successful, so I didn't alert the tower of a problem. I dislike fire engines on the runway when I'm landing—it makes me nervous. I got onto the brakes and continued vigorously pumping and was able to decelerate enough that no heroics were necessary returning to the parking area.

We found bits of rubber in the hydraulic system. They were the residue from the plumbing done with aeroquip hoses during installation of the tanks and dropping mechanism.

Later that fall, Sam had to land that same airplane with the landing gear up, due to the same cause—a chunk of rubber under the unloader valve. They got all the debris out of the system that time and the airplane functioned normally for years.

The rest of the summer went fairly well, only the normal small problems and routine maintenance. Both airplanes and engines functioned beautifully. We wore out a pair of tires every two days because the rubber was so old and had been out in the desert sun too long. They were twenty ply nylon, so we changed them early and had them recapped that winter. With the new rubber one pair of tires lasted all the next summer.

Flying fires was really a lot of fun. We were able to fly some beautiful airplanes, but it was paramount one never lose sight of the seriousness of the enterprise. Sometimes, after dropping retardant on the big fire all day, clouds would move in and after a night of rain the fires would go out. It was very easy for a person to convince himself he was really the one responsible for, almost single-handedly, extinguishing that fire.

Reality dictated we look a little further down the road. In the early part of perfecting the technique of controlling fires with retardant dropped from airplanes, the fire crews on the ground were afraid if we were too successful, their livelihood would be in jeopardy. We had no guarantee for minimum pay, so in my case it was hard to pass up a good construction year to collect *any* hourly dollar amount, with no guarantee of a minimum number of hours. The season could also be cut quite short if no fires were prevalent after August. Nobody likes to be on the unemployed list late in the fall of the year in Alaska.

As the years went by, the problems were worked out, guarantees were given and a person could know generally how much money he could make, minimum, and be as big an optimist as he pleased. However, by then I had made my changes and was off in another direction.

The Decision

!

While flying the fire retardant airplanes it was necessary to be on call at all times. Of course, if there were no fires by five o'clock in the afternoon, there probably would be no calls before ten the next morning. Sam and I stayed fairly close together. We told each other lies about what we had done this far in life, discussed the possibilities of becoming tycoons before our fortieth birthday, and what business enterprises would be a sure success.

Sam Steel, an ex-air force crew chief on a B-29, with a world of experience crop dusting and aircraft rebuilding, was a nice person to be around. He was bordering on being a mechanical genius and was always ready to work on the airplanes if necessary. Our twins were about six years old and he enjoyed playing with them. We held picnics in our large yard so we could avoid the discomfort of cooking in the house in such warm weather. I had a radio that would pick up the BLM radio frequency. If someone called to report a fire we could respond immediately without anyone having to locate us.

Sam had a good sense of humor, was a good, clear thinker, and a good pilot who did not approve of taking unnecessary chances. He had a clear picture of things as they were, not just the way it would be nice to have them. I described my idea of having a trading post on the Yukon and flying trappers as well as any other travelers who were tired of walking. He was more than a little impressed. I told him how I had taken fish as pay for flying done, brought the fish to town, sold it, bought groceries in Fairbanks and taken it back to the Yukon to trade for more fish, and other such stories. He allowed I was already in the trading business. He made a very good sounding board off which I bounced my ideas. My decision was made, my ideas formulated. I needed a little more money to make the move and to establish the location for the trading post.

First things first. I needed to make the money so I decided to do no more flying with the BLM. It was too uncertain. Though I was doing so rapidly, my main goal in life was not to just get old. Actually being the world's richest man was not my goal. I did wish to be in a position making it unnecessary for my children to have to take care of me in my old age. I also enjoyed using my knowledge and ability to help others. I went back to work for Bachner's Aircraft that winter and declined to fly borate bombers the next summer.

I'm not sure what all were the deciding factors but when the airplanes were returned to California that fall to help keep San Francisco from burning down. Politics entered the scene. In order to get any work in California, Phil had to declare the operation a California enterprise and not go back and forth to and from Alaska. It appeared to me that to the BLM, the real goal was building the pyramid, extinguishing fires was secondary.

One afternoon, late in the year, Phil Gray and his co-pilot came into the hangar to visit for a few minutes. He told me he was flying a PBY for Stanford University. The PBY was a twin-engined, military surplus, very long distance, "patrol boat," used for search and rescue work during the war, as well as patrolling in search of enemy vessels of any kind. They were a slow, durable, amphibian, built by Consolidated Aircraft. Phil said they were doing some sort of research that required a mountain of electronic gear. It was a rather easy job with one exception. They were having trouble with one engine. While Burris Smith, who was along as his crew chief, and Bill Laws, who ran a local repair shop, were trying to make the engine behave, they were visiting and watching the weather over their intended route to Juneau.

A few days later, we heard the ominous news. A PBY, owned by Stanford University and doing some research work in Alaska, was missing on a flight into Juneau. They last reported approaching Annette, picking up considerable ice, and one engine had failed.

The Decision

Phil Gray was a very competent instrument pilot. He had a handsome "baby face" and an infectious smile. His dancing blue eyes emanated confidence and optimism. He was a good mechanic. He was a good instructor. Actually he was quite experienced in all facets of the aviation industry, but he suffered from one very serious weakness.

He knew weather well enough to analyze the reports and make a good, logical, sensible decision, but he only had the patience to wait about so long. He would then go anyway, even though the weather had not actually improved.

While in Fairbanks, Phil told me they had actually completed their work, and were returning to California. They had experienced engine problems before, but upon leaving Fairbanks it was running sufficiently well, they figured they could get it back to California. Then if necessary, they could make a complete engine change.

On the flight to Juneau, severe icing conditions and foul weather were encountered. The bad engine quit. The airplane would not carry the ice with only one engine. Their last radio broadcast placed them something like twenty-six miles from the station, inbound. The search was intensive, but unsuccessful. Months later, the aircraft was found just three miles from where they had placed themselves on the last position report. It was on a small island among dense, tall, spruce trees, making it very difficult to see. They had no chance of survival. There were three of them on board, Phil, Burris Smith, a mechanic who at one time had worked for early day aviation pioneer Harold Gillam when he was operating out of Fairbanks, and the co-pilot whom I had met, but do not recall his name.

The lesson to be extracted from this unfortunate situation is: make your go, no-go decisions based on available information about conditions. If conditions do not change, neither should your decision. Above all, never attempt to battle bad weather and a bad engine at the same time. One at a time, a person may take a calculated risk and win, but not many would be so bold as to try to fly two bad engines, so why fly foul weather, with one bad engine?

Far be it from me to criticize pilots who "bought the farm" and cannot defend the actions that led to the tragedy, but I do hope to learn something of value from each of the sad experiences of which I become aware. Hopefully I will learn enough to be able to continue writing stories, instead of "buying the farm."

That summer, Ron Eberhart and I set up a sports fishing and sight seeing venture at Paxson Lodge in the Alaska Range. We had a fairly new Cessna 180 with very credible floats. The engine was good, but the combined performance was dismal. I never figured out what the problem was until after we sold the airplane. Had it not been for a few emergencies and a trip to the Kuskokwim for a load of king salmon, we may have found it necessary to take our collective family to the bread line.

Good things always come to those who are willing to wait patiently. An acquaintance of Ron's wanted to trade a PA-18 Super Cub, with floats, for our C-180. Since we were not making any money and prospects didn't look good, Ron and I decided he would keep the Cub, I would dissolve my interest in the venture and look for a job.

I finished the season shaping the cooling ponds for the power plants at Clear Air Force Station, came to town long enough to go on a successful moose hunt, then back to Clear for the winter as a heavy duty mechanic.

There seems to be a humorous twist to almost everything a person does if he will look for it. I walked into the Union hall after the moose hunt and asked if they had a job for a couple or three weeks—before winter set in for good. The business agent told me he might have a job for a blade operator out at Paxson—he would let me know. I had just come from that area and knew there was no activity out there so I said, "Look, either you have a job or you don't. If you have a job I'll take it, but if you don't, say so and I'll go get myself a starvation job as an A&E mechanic for the winter."

"Oh, mechanic, mechanic—we need a heavy duty mechanic at Clear. Can you do heavy duty mechanics work?" he asked.

It was my turn to squirm a little, I said, "We-e-ll, I think I can probably handle the job, just what does it entail?"

The Decision

"They just called in for a heavy duty mechanic, can you do the work, or can't you?" he asked.

"It isn't the work," I said, "I can do the work, it is the tools. I carried a set of heavy duty tools for twelve years and never opened the box once so just last June I gave all my heavy duty tools to a friend of mine."

He then asked, "Do you have up to an inch and one-eighth? The company is supposed to furnish everything over an inch and one-eighth."

"In that case I'm home free, I'll take the job," I told him.

When I got to the job site, the foreman put me to keeping the Herman Nelson heaters running. Those heaters were used to start cold equipment and keep the unheated working areas warm for the men. That was a blessing in disguise. I had overhauled about three hundred of them for Bachner's, in the past couple of years, where we did all the overhaul for the military.

After working about three days and discovering there were no parts, I made up a parts order and gave it to the foreman. I told him if he could get those parts, I could keep almost all the engines running, instead of about thirty per cent of them. He asked me three times where I obtained that parts list. I kept telling him I had made it up. He finally asked me specifically where I had obtained the part numbers. I then understood his confusion. He just couldn't believe anyone could come into the shop with no parts book and be able to order parts, complete with numbers. I told him I knew every part number in that engine by heart. He then expressed concern about being able to get the parts from the regular supplier. I told him to forget that supplier and order them from Bachner's Aircraft, they were the Continental engine distributors anyway. I added a couple parts books to the order. We got our parts and kept all the engines running. Heavy duty mechanic! I could carry an engine in each hand. I didn't use any heavy duty tools on that job either.

That was a good job. As work was completed, more buildings were kept warm from their own heating systems. About the first of December, I was made field mechanic. Part of my job was to arise at four o'clock in the morning, take Bob

Huggins, a heavy duty mechanic with whom I had worked at Donnelly in 1946, and jump-start equipment with my pickup, which had a huge battery installed. We started all the busses, truck-cranes, emergency, and supervisors equipment. Everything was ready to go when the shift began at seven o'clock. The weather turned warm soon after we were assigned that duty and we did little except make money for the next two months.

Early one morning I got a call from my wife, just as the day shift was beginning. She told me she was calling Mike Agbaba, an old-time dog musher turned cab driver, to come and take her to the hospital. Today was the day. Late that afternoon another call informing me Zoanne Elaine had arrived on time, and all was well. Little Granny was on the job again caring for the other little ones. By the time the job was completed and we moved the equipment back to town, it was almost time to start thinking seriously about the next construction season.

I was slowly getting closer to the trading post, financially at least. I still had to make a decision about a location. I had several places in mind, and the one I thought best was the location of old Kokrines, above Ruby, on the Yukon.

Peger Road

①

The early sixties provided quite a number of opportunities to both further my financial position and work on a definite location for a trading post. My idea was to get a good location, homestead, and build a trading post. The Kokrines area still looked quite promising as there were warm springs, the location was on a high bank of the Yukon, and on the south slope of the hills. I hoped to get a number of solid, hard-working, progressive families to move into the area, work the soil to produce numerous crops known to flourish in that vicinity, and whenever possible, work on forest firefighting jobs or construction. I could conduct a flying business from there.

I approached the Bureau of Indian Affairs (BIA) and proposed they buy some farming equipment for the people and I could see it was properly utilized, maintained, and kept repaired. In this manner, the BIA could help the people provide for themselves in a changing economy and I could advance my venture; each being an aid to the other.

I was given a curt, "Go on down there, establish your farms, trading post, and flying business. If in a couple of years it seems worthy of our support, then we will be more willing to talk of giving assistance."

Thanks a lot! If I can keep my head above water for two years, I'm not going to need any help. I should have known where the BIA was concerned building pyramids took precedence over assisting the natives.

I had discussed the idea with a number of the more progressive families and they all thought it would be a good move. I even suggested the men, after the crops were planted, could go work on a job in construction, firefighting, on the river boats, or whatever presented itself as an opportunity for them. They could have their pay, minus enough for personal expenses, sent to the store, thus insuring the fact there would be sufficient money to make the big spring and fall orders necessary to carry on a trading operation. The idea was to have sufficient cash available to have a good stock of supplies. The women could come into the store, buy the things needed to keep the family going and charge that against the money the head of the house had contributed. Either a co-op type of operation or a corporation could be organized. Still just ideas, as yet not quite jelled. Among the people, the suggestion had good support.

Bill Carlo and I were working on the Peger-Van Horn Road at Fairbanks. We were doing whatever needed done. Al Wright and Buck Allen were the primary chain of authority. Al was like most of the rest of us — he could do about anything that needed doing, and he was well-liked. Buck had worked on the other projects at Soldotna and Tyonek, also a well liked supervisor. Bill and I both ran about all the equipment, were mechanics, and both had been foreman on a number of jobs. Working together was not new to us. Walt Minano, an Eskimo from Nenana, was working with us as a mechanic. Walt reveled in accomplishing something engineers thought was too complicated for man to understand. His pet remark was, "We sure fooled them engineers that time." Every day was a circus, but we moved lots of dirt and kept the equipment running. We were making money and were enjoying what we were doing. We discussed trading posts a lot.

One evening after work, Bill and I jumped into my airplane, a PA-18 Cub with tundra tires, and went over to the Gold King area looking for moose. Those were the days when it was still legal to shoot the same day a person was airborne. We shot and butchered a moose, placed the meat up on heavy brush to hold it off the ground allowing the circulation of cooling air, and were able to get off the ground before dark.

The next day, the weather had deteriorated some, but we felt we could still accomplish the task of retrieving our meat. We were mistaken. Late fall fog had lowered just enough to cover the hill top on which we had butchered our moose. The same situation persisted for three days and precipitated a laugh from Al Wright.

"That just tickles me pink," he said, "I thought I was the only one things like that always happened to." The fourth day we made it but bears had also been there. There was not a morsel left. Al got a good laugh out of that one also.

The story that got us the most mileage though, was another moose hunt. Yes, you guessed it, we didn't bring home any meat that time either. We were flying the Cub with the big tires again. We saw a moose out in a large swamp, feeding under water, so we landed on a nearby gravel bar on the Totatlanika River. We waited until things were nice and quiet again, then started calling the moose.

The reader will not be burdened with excuses nor detailed descriptions of the things we did wrong, but we decided we'd best head for home, meatless. Just as we turned to start the take-off run, we pulled a valve stem out of an innertube, and the right tire went abruptly flat. Oh boy!

We had no tools, but we did have numerous ideas. One of which was that we may be able to disassemble the wheel with our bare hands. Persistence prevailed and we were successful. Those valve stems were made in two pieces. The larger piece was the stem attached to a plate that was forced through a hole in the innertube. Another plate and a nut slid over the stem and was screwed down to hold the stem in place, creating the necessary compression to assure no leakage. This we accomplished quite easily with our bare hands, but we had no tools to tighten the nut sufficiently so we did the next best thing, we hoped. We removed the valve core from the stem and I blew all the pressure I possibly could. I then instantly installed the valve cap which held the pressure I had been able to create with my face. Two pounds is about the maximum a person can blow, but will actually suffice, providing everything else is almost perfect. It wasn't.

We moved forward about fifteen feet to avoid a particularly rough area before starting the take-off run. The tire went flat again. We repeated the drill, except this time we employed a small hatchet as a hammer, and a rock as an anvil. Bill managed to complete almost another full turn by tapping on

201

the nut. If this did not work we had planned to put sand, willows, grass, or something in the tire to keep it round long enough to take-off. Fortunately our last try was successful. We took off and were almost completing the landing roll at Fairbanks before the tire went flat again.

We pushed the airplane off the runway, ran down to the hangar, grabbed my pickup and came back to the airplane. We had the small, mounted tires in the back of the pickup. We jerked the flat tundra tire off the airplane and replaced it with a small one. Bill taxied the airplane into the tie-down area and we went home.

The next morning when Bill and I appeared at work, Walt Minano asked us what had caused one of the wheels to shrink during the night. He knew enough about airplanes to know what had happened, but always enjoyed a good joke and the story that was bound to go with it.

Bill was running the D-9 bulldozer and the grader operator did not show up that morning, so I was running the grader, leaving Walt in the shop alone. Being Saturday, FAA inspectors were out nosing around on their week end surveillance, when one noticed the Cub with the two different sized tires. He came over to the shop and asked Walt if he knew who owned the Cub across the runway with the two different sized wheels. Walt assured him he did.

The inspector asked him if he would tell the owner he would have to change one of the tires. Walt asked him which one. Of course the inspector said he couldn't determine exactly until he had a look at the log book to see which one was legally installed and the logbook was not in the airplane. Walt told him he thought we had been landing on a side-hill and had installed the small tire just to level the airplane up on landing and take-off. Walt was a master at looking serious and playing dumb, so the inspector told him to just forget it, he would leave a note on the airplane. Walt, trying hard to be helpful, thoughtfully suggested he could leave the note in my pickup, parked just outside the door, if he wanted to. Of course, the flat tire and the other mounted small tire were obvious when he stepped to the pickup to leave the note.

Soon afterward, Bill had to go back to Tyonek to finish up a job. In that area, close to the coast, the dirt work could continue much later in the season than around Fairbanks, due to a much later freezeup. Before leaving, Bill told me he had bought a Cub, as-is, where-is, from Bachner. A fellow had rented the airplane then damaged a landing gear on take-off and the airplane was at the base of the Alaska Range, about eight miles south of Grubstake airport. Jesse Bachner had looked the airplane over from the ground and it wasn't too badly hurt. Bill wanted me to get it out of the hills for him while he was gone.

Harold Esmailka and I had both finished up our construction season so we gathered our gear together to resurrect the Cub for Bill[1].

On a beautiful day, we headed toward the Alaska Range to keep our promise to Bill. Trying hard to cover all bets, we took plenty of gasoline, a pair of aircraft skis tied to the wing struts, an extra propeller, an eight foot 2x4 to use as a lifting device while replacing the landing gear, and Mr. Browning's wonderful invention, a twelve gauge, automatic shotgun.

By the time we got to Grubstake, about eight miles from the downed plane, it was obvious we weren't going to retrieve any cripples that day. The wind was blowing so hard, we sat right over the airport for two minutes and could hardly detect any forward movement. The closer we got to the hills the higher the wind velocity became, so a decision was forced upon us. The only noble alternative was to cancel the resurrection detail and search for a moose kill. We went wolf hunting.

We had the necessary licenses and permits required in the days before aerial wolf hunting was banned in Alaska.

We dropped quite low and started back in the general direction of Fairbanks. Halfway home we crossed fresh wolf tracks in the snow. It looked like a pack of six or seven. We dropped down even lower to determine the direction the wolves were traveling, then followed the trail to the animals.

---

[1] This story appeared in Alaska Magazine as "Resurrecting the Cripple."

When we approached them, it was obvious they had just fed on a recently killed moose. They were somewhat lethargic, but not yet to the drowsy stage. It was a young pack with the exception of one old female.

They were in the tall trees so we flew over them and Harold shot straight down into the trees. That moved them into the open where I could make a low pass over them, lining up three in a row. Harold attempted to shoot but the shotgun wouldn't fire. We decided it had badly worn friction rings which caused it to not clear the empty case from the breech so a fresh round could be chambered. The gun belonged to Bill so we were not aware of the trait until too late. We had to operate it like a manual loader instead of an automatic.

The airplane was so loaded, both inside and out, it made maneuvering ticklish. Safety demanded time and space.

After going around and lining up two more wolves, Harold was able to down one, but the gun and its tricks got to us again. We finally got home with two nice wolf pelts which we gave to Marie Woods, a local lady who sewed a lot of natural skin products. At least we brightened her day.

Bill finished the job at Tyonek and Soldotna and returned just as the weather turned beautiful. It wasn't easy to convince him we had earnestly tried, in his absence, to salvage his latest purchase. Standing there in gorgeous weather, viewing the beautiful one hundred mile distant mountains where the Cub was resting, it was hard to even visualize bad weather.

Bill and I had known each other for years, worked together, and visited on many occasions. We could communicate with a minimum of lost time and a maximum of forward motion. We again got our tools and paraphernalia together and set out on another attempt. The day was clear and calm; the snow just deep enough to make ski operation possible. The broken airplane was on a fairly steep hillside and we didn't consider it a very good place from which to operate. We landed a short distance away and carried or pulled our supplies to the downed craft.

The aircraft had suffered a broken landing gear and bent propeller in the initial accident, but Mother Nature had then taken a hand, dumping the little plane unceremoniously on its back, breaking the windshield and spilling the fuel.

Our first task was to right the ship. I had some steel concrete-reinforcing rods, and a set of rope blocks. We drove the rods into the hillside and set about righting the Cub in reverse to the way it had suffered such embarrassment in the first place. We had installed the new landing gear while the craft lay on its back.

Everything worked fine until the airplane would rise almost to the point of success, then it would slide up the hill on the snow, instead of continuing to turn over onto the landing gear. Finally, we got it just as far as we could before it started to slide. I ran down and lifted for all I was worth on the tail while Bill took up slack on the rope blocks. That did the trick. We gained just enough that with both of us pulling on the rope blocks, the airplane continued to rotate over the prop onto the landing gear and eventually the upright position.

It was getting late and we had to work fast. We poured fuel into the tanks and cut up the gas cans to use as patching for the broken windshield. Then came a disappointing discovery. The fuel tank selector valve was frozen. A small amount of water in the gasculator had apparently run to the selector valve, then frozen, while the airplane was on its back. I got the selector to move, but couldn't get a flow of fuel through the ice in the line.

We had no choice but to leave the plane on the hillside and go for more equipment and some alcohol to run through the fuel lines to clear out the ice.

We returned the next day and got everything almost ready to go, ran alcohol through the lines repeatedly, filtering it each time, then I glanced at the mountain top. We were appalled. From the top of the mountain a streak of snow, looking like the point of an anvil, was blowing straight out for about a quarter of a mile, pointing in our direction. I told Bill we had to go right now, ready or not, or both airplanes would be on their backs in twenty minutes or less. He agreed.

205

He hurriedly made the last few stitches with safety wire in the tin-plexiglass windshield repair, then we taxied both planes up the hill into take-off position.

I helped Bill get his plane off by shoving his wing struts and getting him moving. By then the wind was getting strong and squirrely. I couldn't get my skis to slide. It seems unbelievable now. I was using full power and facing down hill into a good wind. I had Bill's old, metal-bottomed skis on my airplane, which had enabled us to carry my lighter, fiberglass skis on the wing struts as we flew to the downed craft. Those metal skis simply wouldn't slide. (A common problem with those old, metal bottoms.)

I was nearly frantic. My only recourse was to get out and push with the throttle wide open with no one at the controls. I have done that on many occasions when I was stuck in deep snow, but then I had time to tie a rope to the throttle and once the skis started moving, I'd pull the rope to close the throttle, slowing down or bringing the plane to a stop. On this occasion, I didn't have time to do that. The wind was increasing so rapidly, I knew I was down to a margin of perhaps two minutes or less.

Literally throwing caution to the wind, I opened the throttle all the way and standing on the ground, gave a mighty heave on the wing struts—it had to go.

As the plane began to move, I jumped onto the ski and began to climb into the seat. Going downhill, empty, into such a wind, we were off the ground before I even got my feet inside. I didn't yet have the door closed or my seat belt fastened. I was still sitting crosswise in the seat, my feet and legs were actually still hanging out the door as the airplane came off the ground. I was really flying it with only the control stick and still trying desperately to get properly into the seat. It is hard to have the necessary room to move the stick enough to fly the airplane and crawl around it to get properly into the seat at the same time.

A large boulder lay ahead, almost directly in line with the right ski. The airplane seemed drawn to that monster like a magnet. We were passing over it by about five feet when a wind gust slammed the airplane back to earth. I couldn't prevent the right ski from striking the top of that boulder, severely bending the right landing gear. Fortunately, it didn't look too bad from where I sat. I closed the door, fastened my belt, and headed for home.

At Fairbanks, I carefully landed on the good landing gear, and slowly allowed the weight to ease gently onto the bent one—it held. Inspection proved it to be sound, just bent.

I couldn't find Bill. He had left at least five minutes ahead of me. Where was Bill? No one at the hangar had seen or heard anything. Where was Bill?

Darkness was falling and still he hadn't arrive. I had watched carefully for him all the way home, but hadn't seen him once. Nor did I see him at the little private airport we often used. I had about decided I would wait a little longer, let it get good and dark, then go back looking for a fire.

Finally, about five minutes after dark he came staggering in, flying slow, frozen half stiff, his battered airplane still intact but leaking air badly around our hastily built, tin windshield. He had become so chilled he had to land and build a fire to thaw out in order to endure the remainder of the trip.

Bill rebuilt the cub and installed floats. The airplane served him well for a number of years, until a fellow pilot obliterated it when he flew his Cherokee Six right through it as it was parked on the float dolly in front of Bachner's hangar.

I made a trip to Minto Village, about twenty minutes west of Fairbanks, to help Paul Haggland, a pilot with whom I worked at Fairbanks Air Service. We repaired a Navion he had bought after it was damaged. It only took a short while to have it ready to go, so I walked into the village. I wanted to see if I could find a girl willing to come to town, live with us a few weeks, and help out when the new baby was born. That is how Mary Ann Frank became a part of our family.

One evening, I took my wife to the hospital and within a couple hours she had presented me with a new daughter, we named her Myrna Lee. We now had eight children, all but seven of them were boys. Little Granny soon came from Akiak for the winter, Mary Ann went back to Minto, and Myrna grew up to be left-handed!

The Last Year

•

The beginning of January 1963 was much like any other new year. It was cold, very cold. The most important issue at the time was keeping everything running until warmer weather made it pleasant to do so. I was following my usual procedure of working as an aircraft mechanic or flying during the winter and keeping the union dues paid so I could grab a good job in construction, should one surface, come springtime. This was my second winter with Fairbanks Air Service.

One beautiful, spring day, we were working with the hangar doors open. We were enjoying the sunshine and health we were receiving, free for nothing. A young fellow came up to me and said he had lost both mags at the same time and his airplane was sitting on Beaver Creek, about thirty minutes north of Fairbanks. Could I help him?

Things usually aren't that simple and suspecting a broken cam shaft, I told him he hadn't lost both mags at the same time, there had to be something else. He gave me the exact procedure he had used to trouble shoot the problem and I began to suspect he may be right. He said when he turned the engine over he could hear the impulse coupling snap so that eliminated the broken cam shaft. I suspected the mag switch, but we could circumvent that. We would go tomorrow, Saturday.

I gathered up a couple of good mags, jumped into my little Cub, glad to be able to get out on a beautiful spring day such as this. We headed over the hill to Beaver Creek with several hours of a warm day left. We thought we could resurrect that cripple in about thirty minutes. No matter how many times a person performs a task, he will sometimes forget something.

I knew as soon as we approached the little Aeronca, we had a problem. The engine was a "C" series Continental with what is called a dash 12 crankshaft, which is tapered. A dash 8 is a flanged shaft and the mags turn in opposite directions from the dash 12. We had brought mags set up for a dash 8, and the engine in the Aeronca was a dash 12. By making a change on the impulse coupling in the mag, I could correct the problem, but they do *not* change with a dzus fastener.

By the time I had one alteration completed and the mag timed to the engine, the sun was going below the horizon and quite frankly, my fingers were getting cold. I was more than a little soft after a winter inside a warm hangar. I asked him if he felt any trepidation about flying back on one mag. He told me, if I thought it safe, he was willing.

After we arrived at Fairbanks, he told me the engine turned up better on the one mag than it previously had on both. I then broke the awful truth to him. He could hardly believe he had been flying all over the country on one bad mag, he said he always checked them before take-off.

I explained he must have a bad mag switch, which meant he was not actually checking mags at the end of the runway. He had been merely turning the switch to different positions and accomplishing nothing. I explained he should turn his switch completely off and back on as he was taxiing out, once each day. He should do it quickly and listen to see if the engine actually stopped firing briefly. He would then know the switch was actually grounding both mags.

He seemed to understand all this. I then told him I couldn't work on his airplane to finish the job as we just didn't have the available time to work on outside aircraft. My main obligation was to the operator for whom I was working and his principal interest was in flying. He wanted me available to work on his equipment at a moment's notice. It wouldn't be fair to him, or my employer, to take his job and be a week completing it. Time for the resurrection just happened to be an available bonus.

I suggested he take the work up to Bachner's Monday morning, and tell them about the switch so they could check it with a meter. Marvin Jones changed the switch for him, converted and installed the other mag, and he was ecstatic. It ran so well, he thought he had just added another cylinder to the engine.

In the late fifties, the Cessna factory produced a new airplane they called the Cessna 175. It was very similar to the four-place Cessna 172, but did have more horsepower and some modification of the empennage. In order to boost to one hundred seventy five horsepower the basic one hundred forty five horsepower engine, it was turned much faster. In order to prevent the propeller tips from traveling too fast and being in danger of departing due to excessive centrifugal force, a reduction gear had been installed in the nose section. The whole design was so ill conceived that each bad decision made, demanded another. The installation of the reduction gears caused the propeller to turn backward. This was serious, it could dictate a special propeller would have to be cast just for that one engine and it used on only one airplane at that time. To overcome that problem, the direction of rotation of the entire engine was reversed. That made usable a normal propeller of the proper length and pitch. The only other difficulty was, now the magnetos would have to be reversed in their rotation also. Not a big problem.

Enters the Case farm tractor engineers. To overcome the magneto problem, Case submitted a design for what they called a Slick magneto. They were a good, hot mag, when they were brand new. The installation was enough different that a mechanic had to sit down with the first one he saw and learn their idiosyncrasies, the least of which was definitely not the way to time one. Also, the mechanic as well as the aircraft owner, had to be prepared to throw them away when the engine came in for overhaul. One mag just would not last two runs of the engine.

Once the engine was overhauled and new mags replaced the old ones, there was fair assurance the engine would start, and the mags would last the life of the overhaul, but no other superlatives could possibly apply. We called them throw away mags.

Not long after the resurrection of the Aeronca a stranger came into the hangar and asked me if I could time a Slick mag. I told him I thought I could and asked where the airplane was. He told me it was over at Fairbanks International Airport, but he could fly it over on the one good mag, as the problem was in the non-impulse mag. I suggested he just turn the bad mag off for the flight, if it should fire intermittently, especially if it happened to be out of time, the result would be non productive or downright frightening. We both thought the mag was out of time.

Upon his arrival I walked out, removed the cowling, removed the mag, set the engine up properly, replaced the mag and told him to try it. He was dumfounded. The fellows who had been taking his money beforehand were making a project out of it and refusing to consult a book. After all, they had timed numerous mags on Cessna 170's and 172's, they knew how to time a mag. Not that I was necessarily so smart or even experienced, I had overhauled one of those engines and knew the reasons why everything worked backward. In order to have it come out right, the mechanic had to also think and work backward, where that engine was concerned.

The owner took the airplane and would occasionally come back to the hangar asking questions. He never really bothered me or held me up so I visited with him and answered his questions.

Finally one day, out of a clear blue sky, he said, "You know, you must be nuts."

Now it was my turn to be dumbfounded. "Why is that?"

"I've noticed your boss keeps coming out here and asking you questions concerning things about which he should be making the decisions instead of asking you," he said. "He should be working for you instead of you working for him."

He was a painting contractor and seemed to have things well enough in hand, he didn't feel he needed to be right on hand all the time and he made money. People had asked my opinion so much, I didn't see it as being as unusual as he was able to observe. I did some real serious thinking that summer and actually only worked one more job, an emergency dike job at Galena, for GHEMM Co., of Fairbanks. Even they put me in charge of the night shift for the short job.

That wasn't really much of a compliment though, since they gave me the best crew one could possibly assemble. All I had to do was tell them which piece of equipment to run and get out of the way. On the crew were Charlie, Frank, and Bill Carlo.

I had known Frank Carlo for years. He was an old time cat skinner, the oldest of the brothers. About all one had to do was designate the piece of equipment and the pile he wanted moved. Frank would do the rest in a time conserving manner and a smooth job was the result. He was running the big bulldozer.

Charlie had worked for years in the NC Co. store in Ruby, but was no stranger to heavy equipment. He was running the smaller bulldozer, spreading dirt on the fill.

Bill could do anything a person wanted done. He was an exceptional loader operator, so he was running the machine loading trucks off the dirt pile.

There were a few truck drivers who had been with the company for some time and knew what they were doing. I also had Robert Thurmond, from Galena, who surprised me one night.

When we went to work his truck was in the shop with the differential removed. We had no mechanic on the night shift. I told him to go on home and I'd see he got paid half a shift, but be here again tomorrow.

"Why don't you let me put the truck together and drive tonight?" he asked. I asked him if he knew what he was doing and he said yes, so I told him to go ahead. I knew those Thurmond boys when they were on the trapline. I supposed since I'd last seen him he must have been in the Army or somewhere and learned something I didn't know about but I did know he would not lie to me. If he said he could do it, he could do it. I was really surprised when he came driving into the dump area in about two hours, with a load of dirt. I expected it to take him longer. The truck completed the job with no further trouble and the superintendant never mentioned it.

One serious problem surfaced after the temperature hit about twenty degrees below zero. We were filling dirt behind the existing dike around the Galena Air Force Station. We were strengthening it in the most likely problem area, preparing for the spring flood waters sure to come. The dirt we were hauling was warm and damp. When dumped into the cold, steel dump boxes on the trucks, it froze to the boxes. If they were not cleaned each trip, the amount of dirt left in the box increased with each trip. Soon a driver would be hauling back and forth more dirt than he was leaving in the fill.

One morning at the end of the shift, I asked the job superintendent to order a roll of four mill plastic. If a person stepped onto a piece of plastic on the ground and was not a rather athletic individual, he may need help to regain a standing position. Surely that same plastic could remedy our problem if the boxes were simply lined with it before loading. The result was phenomenal. We used that system for the remainder of the job. One driver, just to see what he could do, managed to save his plastic and reuse it for thirteen trips.

This had been a good, hurry-up job, and we all made money. We were allowed to work all the overtime we wanted, so we worked twelve-hour shifts for the last couple of weeks. When it was completed, we were all in good financial shape for the winter.

I had a good airplane, a Cessna 180 with wheel skis. With the stake we made working much overtime on that dike job, I was able to again get the flying business off the ground. Of course the first step in the right direction was to get the state required insurance. Next came the operating certificate.

I had made my application as Yukon Air Service for the state certificate in June, but had heard nothing. At one time, the old Pilot Owner Certificate the Federal Government issued during Territorial days could be simply replaced by an Alaska State Certificate. I had waited too long to apply. My presumption for the delay was that they had no real grounds to disapprove my application, but were probably deluged with applications. They did not want to approve any that lacked the appearance of serious intent, or lacked persistence. I persisted.

When the operators whose business may be affected by my operation were notified, Cliff Fairchild called me. He asked if I could change the name. Yukon Air Service was a little close to Fort Yukon Air Service, which he operated out of Fort Yukon. I asked him to not object and after receiving the certificate I would not use the name but would wait a reasonable amount of time, then change the name. Those were the days when two friends could make an agreement and both uphold their part of it, without a long, expensive legal document on file.

I called the Alaska State Public Service Commission, Department of Air Commerce, on the telephone, and asked about the status of my application. I assured them I had the insurance and it was imperative I get to work immediately in order to feed my wife and children. I was advised there were no objections and the certificate would be forwarded to me, post haste, as Glenn R. Gregory, dba Yukon Air Service, with headquarters at Ruby. The next summer I changed the name to Gregory Flying Service, with headquarters at Tanana, and everyone was happy.

There seems to be humor dripping from every move I make, totally unintentional, but I am glad I was endowed with the necessary disposition to enjoy it. When filling out the application for the certificate, all the necessary assets were listed and under liabilities, I entered "one wife and eight hungry kids." I didn't owe anything and had no contract payments.

I forgot all about that statement until several years later a state employee, representing the Department of Air Commerce, was giving a seminar in Fairbanks to help prospective operators fill out their applications so they could be processed without two or three trips back and forth in the mail. He asked if I was in the group and of course I was not. He then read off the statements I had put into my application. Naturally, I got a lot of kidding about my wife and eight hungry kids.

My first trips were down the Yukon to Ruby, Galena, Koyukuk, Nulato, and Kaltag. I was right back into the trading groceries for fish, buying fish, taking fish for flying and anything else I could accomplish to increase the flying. I took out a number of trappers and established almost a schedule to Ruby.

A few years before, when the NC Co. decided to sell the store in Ruby, Johnny May, who had lived in Ruby since the end of the war, bought it. He had been running it by himself for a number of years and, being exhausted, was about ready to sell. I was really interested in buying, but Johnny was so busy he couldn't get down to figuring out a legitimate price, before inventory. I could see we could string things out for a long time, so I set a date and told Johnny if he couldn't come up with a price I could consider by then, I'd have to look for something else, maybe in Tanana.

Johnny was so overworked I could see he could hardly entertain a new thought, even briefly. By the date I had set for a deadline, Johnny hadn't yet come up with a price. I had made my brag about looking in Tanana, so when I took Emmitt Peters and his dogs, who later won the Iditarod race in 1975, to Tanana for the dog races, I spent a little time looking around and talking to different individuals.

I located a building and made a tentative deal with the owner to use it if I could get the rest of my plans in order. A strange occurrence came into play regarding what I was trying to accomplish.

Years before, I had been stuck in Tanana over the fourth of July, due to heavy smoke conditions from forest fires. I had a float plane tied up in front of the NC Co. store. As I walked to the river to check the airplane, I would pass a huge, old house, with a glassed in front porch. The glassed-in area extended about five feet in front of the outside walls. Windows ran the full length of the house. I felt the strangest premonition that someday I would be running a store in that building. I never really seriously considered the feeling, but also never forgot the sensation.

While eating lunch, I asked Paula Eller, who was running a little cafe near the old house, if there were any houses available for rent. I had made tentative arrangements for a store building, but still needed a place to live. She suggested I go see "old Louie." Imagine, sixteen years after sensing a likelihood of future acquaintance with the old building, Paula was sending me to that very place to talk to Louie Kalloch about renting living quarters.

Louie was one of the old timers that had entered the country over Chilkoot Pass in search of gold and just stayed. When I asked Louie if I could rent some space, he told me he couldn't rent to me but he would sell me the property. I asked how much he wanted. He thought for a while, screwed up his face and started to name a price and almost said it twice, then dropped it a thousand dollars and said, "And I want cash and I won't jew a penny."

I, of course, had to look professional, so I said, "Well, let's look around, see what you have, then we can talk seriously." Naturally, for the price and the scarcity of buildings available in Tanana, I didn't need to look any further, but at least the look around told me this building would serve both purposes, store building and living quarters.

I told Louie I would pay his price, in cash, but I did want an insured title. He agreed. Before I left, he told me he wanted to move to Fairbanks and asked me if I could look around for a small cabin he could buy in town. I agreed.

Trying to arrange for title insurance was a little difficult. Doris Loennig wanted to see the Commissioners records before she would write insurance and even though I could fly her down and back, keeping lost time to a minimum, she never could seem to keep an appointment. I finally asked her to tell me where to look for any possible liens and I'd look for them. It took me approximately fifteen minutes to establish there indeed was a lien on the property. It was obvious there would be, since Louie had been on welfare for twenty years. Doris knew that.

I started back to Fairbanks and was about twenty minutes out of Tanana, feeling quite dejected, when I conceived a brilliant idea. I turned around and went right back to talk to Louie. I asked him if he would approve transferring the lien to the new property in Fairbanks, if I could persuade the state to condone it. He was agreeable.

In an effort to be as fair and impartial as possible, I located three pieces of property in Fairbanks I thought would satisfy his needs, brought him to town and had Kitty Harwood,

217

an old friend of his from **Rampart** and **Tanana**, take him around to look at the different cabins to make his own choice. I explained to Kitty that I didn't want to even suggest one over the other, but I would buy the one he wanted and pay him cash difference in exchange for the property in Tanana. We had our attorney, Warren Taylor, who was still in the legislature at the time, make the legal arrangements with the State.

The deal went off quite smoothly. At last, we could move to Tanana and set about establishing the trading post to supplement the flying business so the flying business could supplement the trading post. It sounded good.

Focusing on only one common goal, we could cease casting around for the most likely move to establish a viable business enterprise to provide a living, summer and winter, and grow annually. We concentrated on continuing the flying business to make a living, while we planned and executed a move of family, home, and business.

The Move to Tanana

There are many pieces of a puzzle that must be put properly into place before a picture is complete. If we follow a similar pattern in the changes we organize in our lives, things will go much more smoothly. To get a trading post operating, many things were necessary. Organizing the move of just the household was not a simple task. Thirteen years of marriage and being a natural junk collector made for an unusual amount of furniture, goods, and airplane parts. What can we do without? What do we simply have to keep?

The flying business was keeping me busy. We were trying to get our present home into condition to be attractive enough to sell easily and there was the daily living that occupied a certain amount of time. Naturally, little things kept surfacing to cause consternation and slow down the flow of progress.

I was getting considerable business from the BIA and the regular trips down the Yukon were keeping the fuel bills paid. One day I dropped the BIA realty officer, and an assistant at Rampart and went to Tanana, then to Manley Hot Springs and on into Fairbanks. When we landed at Manley Hot Springs someone called to my attention, the engine seemed to be smoking more than normal. I checked compression and figured we had either a broken ring or a bad valve. My overhaul experience with Continental engines told me I had probably already ruined a cylinder if it was a ring, but I was sure it would get us to town.

Upon arrival at Fairbanks, it was necessary to make arrangements for another airplane to go back to Rampart to get the BIA customers I had left there in the forenoon. It was quite late when we arrived back in Fairbanks but the customers were happy, especially in light of what had happened. They scheduled for me to pick them up at Fort Yukon at six A.M., Sunday morning. This was Friday evening.

That evening, I took off all the cylinders and the next morning, took them over to Bachner's Aircraft to have them reground. Eldred Quam, the engine overhaul mechanic with whom I had worked for several years, did the work. He called me about four-thirty Saturday to tell me the cylinders were ready. That is service! My wife and I finished the replacement at one o'clock Sunday morning. I took off and flew until the cylinder head temperature stopped rising, then decreased slightly, then stabilized. I knew I could do nothing more. I landed, topped off the oil and fuel, and went to bed. Up again at four to go to Fort Yukon, then down to Ruby and back to Fairbanks, with no oil consumption. From then on, I never ran another engine on the ground after overhaul. I flew them all, saved a lot of time, and had nothing but positive results.

I contacted Weaver Bros. Barge Lines about shipping to Tanana. We started getting things packed: keep the encyclopedias, leave the study for the Devils Canyon Dam on the Susitna River (a decision I regretted many times), keep the children's books, leave the westerns, keep all the reference books, leave the magazines. Oh heck, let the wife pack that stuff! Load the piano into the pickup, tie it well, then just drive the pickup onto the barge. I called Lew Applegate and left all my old Stinson and Cessna airplane parts with him. Being in the aircraft repair business, he was much more apt to need them than I — I hoped.

Naturally a certain amount of recreation was necessary to keep minds on an even keel. We decided to all go fishing to Pasco Creek. There was myself, my wife and the kids. Usually I didn't file a flight plan with the FAA. I would call George Thiele, Al Wright or someone upon whom I could depend to use good judgment as well as a clock and calendar, to check to see if I ever made it home. For some reason none of them was home or I couldn't reach them so I called FAA to file a flight plan.

220

I knew all the communicators—except the one on duty. He asked the number of people on board, so I told him, "There is my wife, myself, and my kids." That certainly should be plain enough for anyone.

He called back and asked, "What is the number of people on board?"

I again appraised him there was just my wife and me, and our family.

He still wasn't satisfied for some strange reason, and asked, "Please, what is the total number of people on board the aircraft?"

Well, I felt I had dug that hole myself, I replied, "Total number on board —is ten." (In a four-place airplane.)

"Roger, copied total on board is ten," he calmly replied.

The part that caused the entire countryside to hear about my hauling ten people in a four-place airplane wasn't my transmission over the air, although that was what I was trying to avoid, it was the fact that Fred McGuire was standing right beside the communicator. He knew what I was trying to tell him without saying it over the radio. He was having too much fun to tell the communicator, who was new and didn't know me. We didn't catch any fish either.

Not one to accept defeat easily, my wife and I and Myrna, the baby, went back up the Salcha River fishing again about a week later. It was a Saturday evening and I don't even know the name of the little strip where we landed. It was about eight hundred feet long, but down in very tall spruce trees. Not a problem for us with the Super Cub. About a half hour before we were ready to leave, a Stinson Voyager landed. I could hear the engine working quite hard, but didn't think too much about it.

As we were gathering up our gear and putting out the fire, a lady walked over and told us that on landing they had blown a tire. She was quite distressed when I told her I could not bring them a tire that night—it was almost dark then. I told them I'd send one out in the morning. I sized up the situation and came to the conclusion the blown tire was the best piece of luck they had experienced all day.

Upon returning to Fairbanks I called Lew Applegate and gave him the name of the pilot and asked him to fix him up a tire and wheel, enough to at least get them back to town. I then called George Thiele and asked him to use my Cub and take the tire out to them. I also suggested he insist the lady ride in with him. George has the ability to convince or persuade people and I knew that Stinson would not clear the trees with the full load they had brought in. George has a lot of experience in Stinsons and was of the same opinion I was, so he cautioned them that the tire wasn't too reliable, she better ride with him. He told me later they hardly cleared the trees without her as a passenger and most assuredly would not have had she been on board.

Back to loading barges and moving people to Tanana. When we were ready to take possession of the buildings, my wife, little Granny, and all the younger kids made the big move. The twins stayed with me in Fairbanks to get the house cleaned, cupboards painted, and what ever else they could accomplish while I was flying. Those little girls were twelve years old. When we were established in Tanana, they immediately began taking their turns in the store. Today the child labor laws would put me into jail for doing such a thing. Those girls have come back and thanked me for providing them the opportunity to develop responsibility and confidence and to learn the dignity of work at such an early age.

I received a letter from the State of Alaska, Department of Labor, telling me I had not properly registered all my employees with the Department of Labor. I just ignored the letter, but when I got a second letter marked "second notice," I wrote back and advised them I owned all my employees. I heard nothing more.

Before we moved anyone to Tanana, a night out for dinner was in order. We went out to the Club Eleven, eleven miles out the Richardson Highway from Fairbanks. We had a fabulous meal and that was the first time I had seen a "doggie" bag employed. Being from the old school and quite conservative, little Granny couldn't bear the thought of leaving all that good chicken which she could not eat. She remembered that dinner with great fondness.

The author's family of ten.

Little Granny was Eskimo and there was only one other Eskimo lady in Tanana, but she was soon a sought-after guest at the houses of all the older ladies. She invited them to our house for "tea and crumpets" quite frequently.

I was certainly glad I had gone in to see Bill Stroecker, president of the First National Bank of Fairbanks, the fall before. I told him I needed a new car. "We are having a sale tomorrow. We had to repossess Chrysler City and will have the entire inventory on the lot until they are all sold," he calmly said.

I went up and picked out a little green Dodge station wagon that turned out to be one of the most reliable cars we ever owned. We used it for twenty years. All of the kids learned to drive it and when it gave up, that was done with dignity also. I used it dozens of times to "jump start" airplanes for myself and others.

By the time the Yukon was frozen, we had the move completed, the house in town sold, all the bills paid, the trading post stocked, and more business than we could handle — almost. As soon as the transfer of headquarters for the flying business from Ruby to Tanana was a reality, things smoothed out considerably.

A competitor started spreading the word that we would be bankrupt by spring, so no one need take us seriously. I didn't say a word to correct any of the rumors. Let them think what they would. If competitors thought we were not to be taken seriously, they would not work so hard to try to depose us. By springtime, we would be solidly situated.

True to the plan, we had a good, smooth flying operation, all property and equipment paid for, and the trading post gaining in volume each month. Everything had worked out just as we had planned. Reilly had nothing on us. Look out future, here come the Gregorys!

Getting Organized

※

One of the things Eldred Quam taught me, while working with him in the engine overhaul shop, was to get all your materials, parts, tools, and anything you may need, assemble them or know where you can procure them with no loss of time or forward motion, then move ahead. Incorporating that procedure in everything I did was to be very valuable assistance in organizing the trading post and flying business and making them work smoothly together.

The layout of the property provided many possibilities and it was our intention to take the fullest possible advantage of each. There was an old woodshed out back which was about thirty feet long and twenty feet wide, with a loft from the back to about the center of the building. We split and stacked considerable firewood in the lower part, but used the loft for paper products such as paper towels, toilet paper, and other large, light products that would not be bothered by freezing. These were not likely to be high theft items, so having them behind locked doors was not crucial. In future years, we were to learn theft in Tanana was not a major problem.

The original house had been built around the turn of the century; a two-story structure, log on the lower story, frame on the upper. There were adequate safety flues for installing wood burning stoves to keep the entire building warm, but it was quite a task carrying and feeding wood into those stoves. We installed a new, reliable, oil-burning stove in the store. We couldn't chance forgetting to awaken and feed the stove, thus allowing merchandise to freeze, especially produce. The building was so old and the logs had shrunk to the degree that cold seeped between them with little resistance.

The frame part had no insulation between outer and inner shell. Originally, sail cloth had been stretched across the studs on the inside and painted to help slow the wind as it came through. The effect was minimal, especially after damage had been rendered in places. The place was cold. It was provident we had many girls who could cuddle up close to each other to share body heat. Stephen was impervious to cold. I had my little wife to salvage me. She is somewhat of a cross between a hot plate and a frog stomach, depending on what part of her anatomy one happens to touch. I tried diligently to avoid her feet.

We made it through the first winter but before entering another, I had our back door neighbor, Walter Nicholia, insulate every crack he could find, inside and out. It made a world of difference. Walter was a very good helper, worked independently and always kept busy. He lived immediately behind us, so he was always handy.

On the down river end of the house, was an added cabin which was not part of the original structure. A closed-in hallway connected the two. It was newer and much tighter than the original house. That cabin had been fitted with bars and for years, used as a jail. Old Louie gained a little income from renting that and feeding and housing a jailer and his prisoner when necessary. We turned the jail cabin into the store. It was small but served the purpose for the first couple of years. We built shelves from wooden gasoline boxes, the same furniture seen in many trapping cabins. Looking ahead, we intended to build completely new, so investing in expensive furnishings was not in our best interest unless the furnishings could be moved and utilized in the new structure when it was completed. Our competition was the Northern Commercial Co. which had been established in the country since the late eighteen hundreds. Their furnishings were not too different. There was no pressure on us to be just as good as the competition.

Our first encounter with a health inspector was humorous. I was not in the store when he first entered, so he had time to assemble a considerable list before my appearance. It was sixty degrees below zero and I was not flying that day which translates to the fact that neither was he. I was upstairs plumbing and not aware of his presence until my wife called me down to answer some questions.

His first question was, "What do you intend to do about the large cracks in the floor and ceiling?"

Not wanting to begin by asking if he had asked the competition the same question, but wondering if he had, I simply said, "We don't propose doing anything about it."

The shock registered on his face was exactly the reaction I had hoped for. I then continued by stating we had plans for a new building as soon as the weather moderated to the point we could prepare the proper base for footings and a basement. He was elated and gave us many pointers about regulations to check before beginning to insure compliance with code. He was really helpful and we appreciated his reaction.

We entered the trading business right at the end of the 'old ways'. For decades, traders like the NC Co. had operated by allowing the customers to run up a considerable amount of credit, knowing they were going nowhere and would eventually pay. A good example of how credit was viewed when we first started was that some of the wholesale grocery companies would extend credit, not demanding full pay immediately, but expecting the previous order to be paid in full by the time a new order was placed. Times and attitudes were changing. We had to be very careful about allowing credit simply because we couldn't replace the stock. Credit had doomed many otherwise well-run enterprises. Many of the older people didn't understand that paying off their credit, some indefinite time in the future, was not a viable procedure for the newer traders. We were approaching the point where most of our suppliers wanted their money now.

One source of humor was the brand of a product. As an example: the NC Co. sold a Centennial Pancake Mix. It was a good pancake mix that we had sold and used at home for a number of years but a salesman persuaded me to try some Krusteaz. We liked it much better so we stocked it in the store along with Centennial. When the time came, we didn't reorder any Centennial. Some people wouldn't buy the Krusteaz. One day I told Harold Woods, one of our regulars who insisted on

227

Centennial, I'd make him a deal. I would give him a box of Krusteaz but if he liked it he was to tell others about it. He bit and we sold Krusteaz by the gross. After that, we would take a new product, open a case, remove and hide about half of it, then set the case where people could see it. They would think others were buying, so they would also. We had much fun. After a few years, most of them were no longer skeptical of new products. We entered the scene just at the end of the old ways and the beginning of the modern system was fascinating.

One of our strongest advantages was the combination store and flying business. Before our debut no one even tried to supply fresh produce and fruit. My first load of lettuce, celery, and tomatoes was a trial run, and we were really surprised at the reception. The first lady into the store called her neighbor on the telephone and she called her neighbor and soon we had nothing left. From then on, we regularly carried produce. We also had good meat — cut, wrapped, and priced. People would pick up a steak or a roast, look at the price, then ask, "How much more for freight?" When told that was the total price, we were instantly successful meat suppliers.

For years I had carried a little notebook in my shirt pocket to list the special items people wanted from town—items not available in the village trading post. Before we moved to Tanana, I would turn those special orders over to my wife

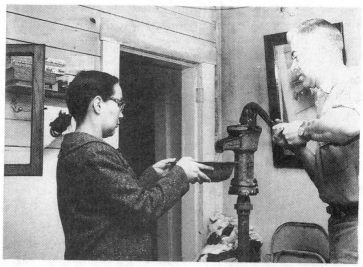

We had "running water" in the house when we first moved to Tanana.

who would do the purchasing while I was flying. The next trip, I would have their purchases. That system endeared many customers to the service of the older flying businesses. I always got a warm feeling in my heart by seeing the look of appreciation on the face of those ladies unable to buy for themselves.

We continued to pick-up special items through the store at Tanana. I would charge the customer one dollar for picking up the special order. Sometimes I felt like a thief accepting a dollar for picking up a one dollar skein of yarn, but it involved time and on occasions, a parking ticket, plus the gasoline for driving around town. It sometimes took several stops. By the time we started hiring regular pilots, the pick-up had increased to two dollars. I asked one lady if she really thought it was worth it. She gave me an emphatic yes, so I told the pilots to make the pick-ups if they wanted to, but not to feel it part of the job obligation. If they wanted to do the pick-ups, they could keep the pick-up charge. Everyone was happy. I felt the small amount of extra gasoline it cost us was returned in good will.

Another tremendous advantage of the combined flying business and store, was my opportunity to see any new fad that hit the streets of Fairbanks, buy a couple of cases and stock it in Tanana. By the time the NC Co. could order and receive the same product through their cumbersome ordering system, the fad would have run its course and they would have a non moving product. We had fun.

It is asking much of your family to leave a home with all the modern conveniences and move to a locality not even having running water. So as soon as possible we mounted a concerted effort to rectify that problem.

I called John R. Swenson and Walter Nicholia over to the back yard one evening before freeze-up and showed them where I wanted to dig a septic drain ditch. When I came home the next day, that job was completed—what workers! I had those two do hundreds of hours of work for us in the future— usually available, always going full throttle. They dug right through the rhubarb patch and the next spring we had rhubarb growing everywhere. We got the septic system and drain line installed and covered up before the ground froze. We could connect it from within the building later. We had a well with a hand pump right in the middle of the kitchen, so we installed a sink under the kitchen window and a bathtub in the upper story.

I felt I could always sleep in the garage if necessary, but I couldn't get the car under the bed so next comes a garage for the car. John R. rounded up some logs and I told him to lay them all butt end to the front and use the normal system of swapping ends across the front and rear. In so doing, there was about a ten inch drop from the front to the rear of the roof. We installed a flat roof. Wind was strong and regular enough we only found it necessary to shovel the snow off the roof about twice. We kept the newly acquired Dodge Dart Station Wagon in the garage and it wasn't even necessary to build a fire in the stove as long as we used the car every day and put it away late. If we didn't use it, we started it first thing in the morning, warmed the engine, and repeated the performance before bedtime. It always started.

Our new home and store building. We built an octoagonal building of logs.
The walls were 20' inside each wall. Part store/part home.

The first time the temperature dropped to sixty below zero and all prudent pilots were home playing with the kids, Walter and I got out our well-driving tools and started to sink the well a little deeper so we could develop a reservoir, or pocket, within the gravel formation to create enough water reserve to utilize an electric pump. We drove until we could hardly determine any progress, then installed the electric pump, primed it and pumped away for about fifteen or twenty minutes. No water was discharged. We unscrewed the union and removed the pump. I saw water about six inches below the top of the pipe. We allowed it all to drain back down, hoping it would help flush free of clay the screen at the bottom of the pipe. We replaced the pump, turned it on, and a trickle of water came from the discharge. It worked. We let it run all night. The next morning, we had a nice flow of very good water. We had running water in the house! I think we were one of half a dozen houses in Tanana able to make that boast.

When a person moves into a small community and is trying to get properly organized to be able to conduct a smooth, profitable business, it is necessary to try to associate with all facets of the community. One need not indulge in practices not of his liking, but he does need to allow those who wish to indulge, the privilege to do so. For instance, I actively supported dog mushing with special rates and outright gifts, but never really participated myself. Some of our kids loved to participate. I couldn't get Vicky into the same room with a prime marten skin, but she loved mushing dogs.

The combined trading post and flying business, a very positive relationship, had some drawbacks. The most dramatic was the necessity to answer the call when EMERGENCY was shouted. It was most commonly shouted on Sundays, Thanksgiving, and Christmas. Usually just as we sat down to a nice turkey dinner or at three o'clock in the morning.

231

Moments You Don't Forget
✈

When we first moved to Tanana, some days it was necessary to make as many as three trips in one day, to Fairbanks and back to Tanana. Naturally it was easy to monitor the changes in the weather with only an hour or two transpiring between trips. At times, a person will try a little harder to squeeze over the hills under low clouds when he knows the visibility and ceiling are flyable on the other side. At other times, a person may be prone to fly on top of broken clouds simply because the sun shines bright up there and the ride is so much more smooth and pleasant. One can always go down through a hole in the overcast as he gets near his destination.

One day, on the third trip in the late afternoon, upon approaching the eastern edge of Minto Flats and crossing the hills into Goldstream Valley, I elected to go down through a hole to the railroad tracks which were visible below. I had throttled back, extended full flaps, then increased power to keep the engine warm in case full power was needed in the near future. Pulling the Cessna 180 into a tight spiral and going down through a small hole made it possible to descend without losing sight of the ground.

The fact that I could see the tracks before starting down was the good news. The fact that after getting clear to the bottom of the hole it became apparent there was nothing but bottom, absolutely no visibility up or down the valley, was the bad news. Oh boy!

Often a person hears about a situation someone got himself into through his own lack of planning, forethought, or knowledge, but occasionally situations just develop. When they begin to compound, we call it snowballing. That is what this situation became.

To begin with, we always fueled in Fairbanks as the supply was there and the price was better. It is also easier to fuel from a metered pump than a fifty-five gallon drum using a hand pump and funnel. I was low on fuel. I had made the previous trip two hours before and the weather was not a serious concern at that time. My transmitter had also been working on the previous trip, but I could no longer get anyone to talk to me. The receiver worked normally.

At the bottom of the hole, it was apparent that it was essential to utilize instrument assistance and the full power being held in reserve. I had to climb back out on top and head back down over Minto Flats to let down again. Without a transmitter I could not request an approach clearance. Fifteen hundred feet would clear the ridge between the tracks and Minto Flats, so I would just ease the flaps up and climb. With an empty airplane, fifteen hundred feet was nothing, except why wouldn't those flaps come up, trying again, they still wouldn't come up—what the heck? I decided to forget the flaps, just get to fifteen hundred feet. Suddenly I was there. I then turned back out over Minto Flats, held the heading five minutes, turned south and let down. Boy is was good to see the ground, but why would those flaps not come up? I had to forget the flaps, I was in no position to do anything about them. By concentrating on what I did have going for me, I could get home, then repair the flaps.

It was inventory time. I had adequate fuel, but flying with the flaps all the way down required about ten to fifteen minutes more flying time. I could fly in this weather but without a transmitter I had to establish my own separation from other aircraft. About the only way to do that for sure was to be where it was inconceivable anyone else would be. There was a head wind which could add five or ten minutes to the flying time.

Considering the known flying time from present position to the airport, plus the added time required by the undesirable events then harassing me, I had about the exact amount of fuel required to do the job. Conservation measures were now a priority.

Admitting the fact I was not going anyplace very fast with full flaps down, diminishing power would not adversely affect the performance to a noticeable degree. It would, however, save fuel, considerably extending the time I could remain in the air, which translated to covering more ground before a mandatory stop.

By throttling back until the engine was no longer working to propel the airplane, then adding back just enough power to be able to hear the engine actually pick up the load to stay in the air, then leaning the mixture until shame told me *that's enough*, the time in air available was extended. Crossing the Tanana River and cutting straight across the flats where it was totally inconceivable to encounter another damphool staggering along in the weather would see me to the end of Peger Road, which led straight in to the end of Wright's Field, the closest one I could reach, somewhat legally.

Once again, everything worked—I think. I'm fairly sure I stayed out of the control zone for Fairbanks International Airport, but if not, I am sure no one saw me to recognize me. If Wright's Field is slightly inside the control zone, I didn't know it, and I'm not going to be foolish enough to ask.

About the gremlins, that antenna wire was broken right where it passes through the skin of the aircraft, thus making the transmitter totally non-functional for the time. The flaps—a mechanic could hardly believe a little piece of .016 aluminum, three-eighths of an inch wide, could exert enough resistance to overcome the leverage of that long flap handle. There are no unimportant parts.

The FAA issued a new regulation requiring all commercial operators carrying passengers for hire at night to have a valid, current instrument rating. I was caught in somewhat of a bind when that happened. I had passed my written examination years before. Having been furloughed from Wien, the rating was not a pressing matter. Before the grace period expired,

235

between passing the written examination and actually taking the flight examination, I had abruptly worn out my Stinson and had nothing to fly for a flight examination. As individual operators, we were not required to hold the instrument rating, so many of us got caught without the rating when the requirement suddenly descended upon us. There was just no way I could break loose and concentrate on completing that requirement and keep the operation going. I was studying all the time, but taking the examination takes both time and coordination. That first winter it was necessary to be careful and actually I had to turn down some business to keep from deliberately being illegal.

I did have an ace in the hole though. I studied the regulations which stated: No pilot shall carry passengers, for hire, at night, without a valid, current instrument rating. The key was, "at night". Another regulation described the hours of darkness to be that time when the sun was six degrees below the horizon or in Alaska, that time when an unlighted object cannot be recognized at three miles. My position was that Mt. McKinley was an unlighted object, more than three miles away, and if I didn't fly into it, obviously I could recognize it. Anyway, I got away with it for that winter, but the next fall, even with a crew working full time on the new building for the house and store, I was compelled to yell for help. I contacted my old no-nonsense instructor, Bogy, to do the flying in my absence. I headed for Portland to get that rating far enough advanced to be legal. The weather got so bad at Portland I was forced to finish up in Fairbanks, but the written was done, the rest was easy. Just work it in.

I flew a recommendation ride with Ron Klemm, a local instrument flight instructor. Don Jonz passed me for an instrument rating. I was now legal to do what I'd been doing for the last fifteen years.

The first two years after moving to Tanana, the winter weather was about normal but the summers were constant fog and rain. Really not much fun. In September of 1965, the weather moderated enough to look like a good moose season in the offing. That is what Steve and Arlee thought also.

Flying out of Tanana in the sixties and seventies, with the hospital just a few hundred feet downstream, made a full night of sleep something to be hoped for but not always experienced. We were awakened one morning about one o'clock by Arlee Charlie, the maintenance mechanic for the Public Health Service hospital, repeatedly calling to us—there was an emergency. My wife opened the window, asked him what the emergency was, then advised me it would be best if I got dressed and went down to talk to Arlee.

Since it was September, darkness was creeping back to the northland, and evenings were cool, even crisp. The ducks and geese were beginning to flock up for the long trek southward. Most of the people had 'snagged' their winter supply of wood from the Yukon during high water. Some of the fish camps were shut down with the catch in the fish house for the winter. Moose season was open and all who could get time off the job were out to see what could be done about supplementing the fish supply with a nice, fat, bull moose.

Steve Matthew, head cook at the PHS hospital, furnished the boat and motor for a several party venture up the Yukon looking for their winter meat. They casually cruised up as far as Rampart where they visited for awhile, then began to drift back down the river, keeping an eye on both banks for a moose coming to the river edge.

They drifted until almost dark when Steve decided to take a snooze and curled up on his sleeping bag while the rest of the crew handled the boat. When it became too dark to see to shoot, they started paddling toward shore. They planned to make camp and continue at dawn. When the water became so shallow the paddles were hitting bottom and the depth of the water was determined to be about a foot. One of the paddlers tossed his paddle into the boat, planning to step out and handle the boat by hand by walking on the gravel bottom. As he dropped the paddle, there was a terrific explosion.

The battery had no cover and as the boat was all metal construction it served as ground for the electrical system. Unfortunately, the paddle which was also metal, simultaneously touched the positive terminal of the battery and a metal fuel can which served as a grounding device. The paddle caused a direct short to ground, burned a hole in the fuel can, which

237

caused sparks that ignited the fumes in the can. Steve actually had to jump into the river to extinguish the flames on his clothes. The worst part, though, were the flash burns caused by the initial explosion.

I went to the hospital with Arlee as he was filling me in on what had happened. The doctor also had to be apprised in order to know what to take with him. As luck would have it, Valerie, Steve's wife, was the registered nurse on duty at the hospital that night. Never have I seen anyone more calm or efficient in preparing the kit for the doctor to take on an emergency, even when their own loved ones were not involved.

I told the doctor to come on out when he was ready and I'd meet him at the airplane. I filled the airplane completely full of fuel so we could fly to Fairbanks, and back, if necessary. Having had some experience with flash burns, I was afraid of what we may find when we got to Rampart.

As the story unfolds, the hunters were not too far below Rampart when the accident occurred, so they elected to return to Rampart and try to contact us at Tanana on the high frequency radio, thus saving much time. The women at Rampart could make Steve more comfortable while waiting for an airplane. They had also lost some of their fuel as a result of the accident.

A problem surfaced upon their arrival at Rampart. All stations they had thought to contact were closed and no radio contact could be established. The next logical move was to run the boat back to Tanana. Their only error was taking someone else at their word concerning the amount of fuel necessary for the trip. They ran out and had to drift for the last couple of hours before reaching Tanana.

Darkness still hung over the valley and canyons when the doctor arrived at the airplane, ready to depart. I told him I had filled the airplane with enough fuel to go to Fairbanks if he decided to do so.

"Why would I want to do that?" he asked me.

All I could think of was flash burns I had seen during the war, but I just said, "You may not want him down here, after you see him."

The weather was clear but there was no moon and upon arrival at Rampart, the entire village was undetectable with the exception of the few lights twinkling in the windows of those still up attending Steve. The Village and runway both lie close to the river bank. The hill immediately south rises abruptly to an elevation of about two thousand feet. We felt it cast a shadow over the most important piece of real estate in the country.

I utilized every trick I knew trying to get lined up with the runway and shine my landing lights upon the end of it, allowing me both time enough to get properly lined up and land, and still get stopped before running off the far end. The stars gave enough light to see the runway from five or six hundred feet altitude, headed toward the river, but we could not get turned around and still see it. I tried getting low over the river but there were enough trees between the edge of the water and the end of the runway it could not be seen from the altitude and direction we had to look. Landing toward the river was out of the question as the birch covered hills were too high on the upper end to be able to position the aircraft low enough to prevent using all the runway, and wishing for more.

Finally one of the women attending to Steve came out of the cabin and asked what that airplane was doing up there. One of the fellows told her it had been up there circling around for about forty-five minutes. She told him to get out there with some lights so the pilot could see to land. In another half hour, we may have been able to see from the first morning light, but that wasn't really the idea of the extra fuel.

When the fellows ran out to the airport to shine their lights on the runway, it was really amusing. Their dim glimmer did tell us where the end of the runway was and that was all we needed. With that knowledge we could shed enough altitude with safety, knowing there was no standing cord-wood between us and a location where our own landing light would illuminate the runway ahead.

The doctor took considerable time before he announced we would be taking Steve to Fairbanks. He had given him a shot but as Steve was so talkative I queried the doctor about

239

it. He explained, with the shot he had given him, he would still feel pain but his brain would tell him it didn't hurt and he would still be talkative.

We called ahead on the radio to have St. Joseph's Hospital, in Fairbanks, notified of our estimated time of arrival. A doctor was waiting with the ambulance and took all the information from Dr. Thompson so we returned to Tanana. I mentioned to Dr. Thompson that I assumed he was glad we had put extra fuel on board. He candidly admitted he really wouldn't be too surprised if Steve didn't make it—then on second thought, immediately swore me to secrecy. I didn't even mention it to my wife. Steve spent quite some time in recovery but eventually was back on his feet and resumed his cooking.

There is no substitute for extra fuel.

With flights of that nature so common, a telephone ringing at four o'clock in the morning was bound to spell the end of sleep for the night. I never dreamed I would one day actually appreciate a call at four o'clock in the morning which turned out to be a wrong number. As the years went by, we became extremely adept at getting into bed early in order to be prepared for that five o'clock emergency we knew was coming. In fact, a ritual was eventually established going something like: The phone rings, the wife answers the phone, gets pertinent information and comes back into the bedroom, looks in the clothes closet, under the bed, in the shower stall, until she finally finds me and gives me the news. There is an emergency at Allakaket, Hughes, Stevens Village, Galena or wherever— from then on it isn't so bad. The night of sleep has been ruined, so we may as well stoically go about the mercy mission as though it is a regular trip. Never mind it is snowing pitchforks, it is still pitch dark, the runway at the destination has neither lights or communication, nor has the airport been plowed of snow. "You chose your profession, now live with it." Just don't forget, it's Too Late To Be A Hero.

The problems were not all in the area of the flying business, we still had a trading business to operate.

Supplies
✈

The supplies for trading posts on the Yukon and associated rivers historically came on the first spring and last fall barges of the year. Freight rates had been set at the turn of the century, considering St. Michael the staging area and starting point for the Yukon. A deep water port that could accommodate sea going vessels was necessary to make possible a transfer of freight from the sea going vessels to the river barges. The freight rates set at the turn of the century continued to prevail proportionally without restructuring even after completion of the Alaska Railroad, which, at this setting, owned tugs and barges operating on the Yukon. The starting point was now Nenana, at the railhead, instead of St. Michael at the beginning of the Yukon River. It was strange to receive fuel from the bulk plant at Nenana, then fly three hundred seventy five miles down the river to Holy Cross and pay less for fuel than you paid in Nenana—especially knowing that to get there, it had been freighted right by your front door!

We had a lot of things to learn but we tried to run the operation close enough to the vest to be able to survive the little mistakes and still continue to remain solvent. We tried to utilize the barge lines to ship groceries and other needed supplies, but we also flew our produce and meat, along with some of the more staple supplies, with our own airplanes. We operated right out of the cash register. My wife would make a bank deposit every day and I would deplete it almost daily.

We kept the flying and trading accounts separate, but were not too precise where those accounts were concerned. For instance, I would bring in a sack of potatoes, the freight was six cents a pound, so we would add the freight to the cost of the potatoes and collect it in the store. We were not too

241

articulate about paying that six cents to the flying operation, it was more of a problem than it was important. There was no tax problem as far as the IRS was concerned, so we didn't allow ourselves to become concerned. The important point was, we could save the store money by bringing a load of *something* whenever we found ourselves in Fairbanks with an empty airplane or even just one empty seat.

Several problems raised their ugly heads in relation to unloading freight from the barges. First, the barge seemed to always arrive at Tanana about midnight. If we had freight, it was necessary to get a crew organized for unloading, then round up a couple of trucks. We would get one truck load of groceries immediately, then nothing more until about six the next morning. Of course we were paying a standby crew all that time and accomplishing nothing. After that happened several times we realized it was the plan causing the situation, rather than a poor loading or unloading technique. Also, we had considerably more damage and theft than I thought was normal for a well run freighting enterprise. The barge line didn't really want to handle anything other than fuel in the barges, but by law they were obligated to accommodate the deck freight in order to hold their certificate. By making it disagreeable, the traders would find other means of moving their freight, leaving the barges free to devote their tonnage and time to fuel which could simply be pumped.

One fall, we had an order of groceries scheduled to meet the last barge of the season from Nenana. The barge lines had dutifully sent us a letter advising the cut-off date was August 21st for receiving freight for the last run. All was going according to schedule when the dock workers in Seattle went on strike. That would make our freight two days late arriving at Nenana. I called the barge lines to advise them the freight was coming, would be a couple days late, and why. It had already been shipped. I was advised the freight had to be physically on the docks on the 21st of August or they could not take it.

OK, now let's think for a while. I contacted Alaska Railroad to continue the freight on to Fairbanks where I made arrangements with Cliff Everts, a local entrepreneur who owned several airplanes. I leased a Curtiss C-46, an old, reliable cargo airplane. All arrangements were made and a date was set. I brought a crew of men from Tanana to Fairbanks in the Cessna 180. If things went well we should be able to whip this out in a day, easily. "The best laid plans of mice and men!"

The C-46 hadn't been swept clean of snow and it had rained, then turned cold. We had about an inch and one half of crusted ice to remove from the entire airplane before we could even fly it over to the International airport to commence loading. The aircraft was parked at Metro Field, a small, quite nice airport, adequate for empty operation but we didn't wish to try to fly off that field with a load. By the time we had the C-46 de-iced, it was too late in the day to get a van spotted for loading.

Cliff arranged for a captain with a C-46 type rating to fly the airplane. I had not flown a C-46 for about twenty years, and then not as a captain, but I was capable of flying as his co-pilot. I knew that airplane inside and out from working on them as a mechanic. When Cliff brought Bob, the pilot, over and introduced us, a little red flag popped up immediately. He was congenial and I couldn't remember where I had seen him before but the little red flag would not retract. We finally got the airplane cleaned up and running about nine o'clock that night, so we all went to a hotel, or home, to bed.

After eating supper, I couldn't get that red flag out of my peripheral vision, so I called three of my friends, all of whom were C-46 type rated. Bob Rice was stuck in Gulkana in freezing rain, George Thiele was on vacation in the lower forty-eight states, and the other fellow, after hearing my concern that I may not be able to depend on Bob, assured me he could help me any time, just yell. OK, with that base covered, I could go to bed and enjoy a relaxed sleep.

The next morning, we reheated the engines and flew the airplane to Fairbanks International Airport. Naturally, the first order of the day was to call the freight line and have them spot the van for unloading. It was still dark and as we were walking from the aircraft to the terminal building, a black car drove up beside us and the driver barked, "OK, get in." Bob went around to the opposite side and climbed into the back seat. I just kept walking. The driver pulled up beside me and again barked, "Get in." I just ignored him and kept walking, so he asked, "Didn't you hear me, I said to get in?"

I politely but firmly told him I didn't want to get in and besides, I had to make a phone call. He slightly lowered his threshold of authority and said to go ahead and make the call, then come into the coffee shop, he wanted to talk to me.

After making my calls and making sure the crew was located, I told them to go ahead and order breakfast and bring me the bill. I then went over to the table where the two fellows and Bob were drinking coffee. I didn't even sit down. The fellow who had elected himself spokesman told me to order a cup of coffee, he wanted to talk to me. I advised him I didn't drink coffee, and didn't particularly want to talk either, I had things to do. He then asked me if I knew who he was.

Well, I had a pretty good idea who he was but I didn't like the set of his jib and I wanted to keep him on the defensive as much as possible. He asked me to show him my pilots license and latest flight physical examination report. I asked him, "Just why should I show you anything?"

He was a little taken aback by that comeback so he told me, with great emphasis, that he was an FAA inspector, **and** he wanted to see my credentials. I calmly told him I would just have a look at **his** credentials before I showed him anything. He gave me that steely-eyed look he had perfected somewhere along the line, and asked if I really wanted to fly that airplane today. I just steely-eyed him right back and told him to have no fear, I would have my groceries in Tanana by nightfall. He capitulated and showed his credentials so I politely showed him mine. I think the fact slowly dawned upon him I may just be aware he couldn't file any violations until *after* I flew the airplane. So far we had only flown an empty airplane from Metro Field to Fairbanks International Airport.

All was in order so he then asked about the airplane. I assured him it was all legal and up-to-date with a signed contract. He then told me to go get the contract, he wanted to see it also. I told him to go jump into the lake. He emphatically stated he was entitled to see that contract and he intended to do so. Again I politely told him I hadn't the slightest question about him being entitled to see the contract but it stated right on said contract, it would not be taken from the aircraft until the job was completed. If he wanted to see it he most certainly could but he was going to be obliged to scrutinize it in the aircraft. The fact that it was twenty degrees below zero with no heat in the airplane and no light, other than a dim flashlight, probably dictated his quick approval of the contract. He just said, "It looks to me as everything is in order, you can go if you have the proper insurance."

I looked him right in the eye and said, "Thank you for your approval, and since insurance is completely outside your jurisdiction, I will just ignore that last remark."

He just smiled and left. He was one of the blue ribbon team that kept popping up in unexpected places to hassle people who were striving diligently to conduct a profitable, safe operation, in order to pay the taxes which paid his salary. That was not my last encounter with him but I won them all.

Bob Hupprich, a Sealand Service Inc. driver, spotted the van for us. We procured a fork lift to handle the pallets of groceries and loaded the airplane. I showed the boys how to tie the load and went to find Bob to tell him we were ready to go. He knew about when we should be finished loading.

I looked in the terminal, called his home, called Cliff. No Bob. Now I am beginning to understand why the little red flag was so insistent, so I called my friend. I told him I couldn't find Bob and couldn't wait all night as we were going to have to make another trip after this one. Could he come right over?

"Oh no, I talked to Bob at the employment office. He told me the Feds were right there to meet you guys when you landed at International, besides I am overdue for my flight physical and they cost thirty dollars and it isn't likely I'll get any more flying before the physical expires again. But any other time I sure would help you."

"OK, thanks anyway, I do appreciate your willingness to help—some other time."

For a brief, fleeting moment I considered having Harold Woods act as my co-pilot and flying the C-46 myself, but even if I had experience of a recent date, that would not have been fair to Harold nor Cliff. I was afraid to think on it too long or I may have started to argue with myself, and won. As I was walking back to the airplane, wondering what in the world I was going to do since I had used up my repertoire of C-46 captains, a light went on. Paul Haggland, my direct competitor, was qualified in a C-46. I turned right around and went back to the telephone which was outside on a pole, in a box made to protect it, and called Paul.

Paul came to the phone and whispered, "Hello, this is Paul, what can I do for you?"

"Paul, I have a problem," I said. Then explained the situation.

"I'll be right over," he whispered.

Paul explained the whisper, he had a problem with his throat that didn't bother him other than being unable to make himself heard. Flying was no problem. He later learned he had a touch of pneumonia and pleurisy, but nothing serious!

Twenty minutes later, we were in the air. We went to Tanana, unloaded and returned to Fairbanks. Paul went home and said to call him about half an hour in advance of completing the loading. We made the second trip and the job was completed. When your competition is that classy, who needs friends?

I learned something about handling freight through that experience. If you fly it, your loss and damage is much lower, practically nil, and the freight all comes at once. Everyone involved is concentrating on the same thing.

From then on, we flew all our freight in either Northern Air Cargo DC-6's, C-82 Boxcars, or Interior Airways Hercules aircraft. The entire operation was much nicer.

The wife and kids were able to take inventory right during the unloading process, and everything was placed where it would be stored until used. A much more efficient operation.

About the little red flag — I thought about that many times. Why would I feel I could not rely on Bob? I could not remember where I had seen him. I knew I had never flown with him. A person looks much different in a parka and winter gear than in summer clothes, maybe I had encountered him in the summertime. Suddenly one day, it came to me.

I had been the crew chief over some C-46's when a small, non-scheduled operator bid on some contract flying one spring. We agreed to do their turnaround and maintenance for a couple of weeks. One day we received a call from the FAA, one of the C-46's was returning on one engine. He landed and taxied to the parking ramp without assistance. He and the co-pilot were in a high state of excitement and, of course, an FAA inspector was Johnny on the spot to try to determine the problem.

It was impossible to get any good information from either pilot or co-pilot, so I told the inspector to take one of them off alone and I would take the other. We would see if we could establish a place to start in looking for a problem. Neither of them could give an inkling of a cause for the problem. Those beautiful Pratt & Whitney engines don't quit out of contrariness, there has to be a reason and it is usually quite obvious. So far we had established nothing. I asked the inspector to keep the pilots around while we looked at the engine. They told us the right engine had suddenly quit after take-off at Hughes.

We removed the cowling, pulled all the screens, looked at the intake pipes, the fuel lines. In short, we eliminated everything that could have caused a problem. I went up to the cockpit to run the engine and as I was preparing to start the engine, noticed the firewall shutoff valve was pulled.

In case of an engine failure, the firewall shutoff valve will, with the pull of one lever, close all valves that could possibly feed any kind of fuel to a fire in the engine. The co-pilot didn't even know what the firewall shutoff valve was and Bob said he was satisfied with the prop, throttle, and mixture being placed in closed position when the prop was feathered. He was cagey enough to avoid admitting he also didn't understand the firewall shutoff valve. That dim memory, way back in the dusty corners of my sub-conscious mind, must have triggered the raising of the little red flag.

Meanwhile, back at the trading post.

Fur

♠

The fur trade has settled more of the world than any other commodity. Gold has historically stolen the headlines, but the mainstay of the early explorers was fur. They could wear fur, they could trade fur, they could gather fur from almost any country through which they were traveling. In many cases, they also chose to subsist off the carcasses from which the fur was gathered. Beaver and lynx were a mainstay and considered a delicacy.

One of the first people we encountered in Tanana, after we purchased the property from "old Louie," was a young man who had grown to adulthood on the trapline with his parents. He had seen some traps in one of the buildings prior to our purchase and wanted to make a deal with me for those traps. I told Lee "Buzzy" Edwin to take the traps and bring me one lynx for payment. At that time twelve dollars was a good price for lynx. He took four traps. I never got the lynx.

Buying fur was not one of my better developed talents. I had watched Dominic Vernetti, the trader at Koyukuk, as he bought fur but it is difficult to watch those wise, old foxes and learn anything. Jimmy Huntington tried for fifteen minutes to show me how to spot a "singed" otter but I didn't know for what I was looking. One day I discovered it for myself but lost money on several purchases before I got wise. Sometimes it works that way.

Selling fur after acquiring it was another point that was very important in the process of remaining solvent. It was not possible to remain aloof as a fur buyer. Many of the customers who supported the store brought in fur to sell in order to have money to buy. It was a foregone conclusion, in the minds of the trappers, that the trader would buy fur, they all did. It was essential that I learn to buy fur. All I needed was a system.

One thing I learned in a hurry, the fur sheets sent out by the various fur buying establishments in Seattle, Kansas City, and points east, were designed to excite the trapper, not guide the trader in buying fur. If anyone ever got top price, as posted, for a piece of fur, regardless of size or quality, it was never brought to my attention.

Most competitors compared fairly closely in their quotes for low, middle, and top prices, but I found it advisable to consider the middle quoted price as absolutely top price any of the fur houses would ever pay. I found it easiest to work with the Seattle Fur Exchange.

I finally developed a procedure for furthering my education. I would sell fur to one of the fur buyers, who established themselves in Fairbanks or came around to the villages each spring, only if they would explain in each case, exactly why they paid less for one piece of fur than another, that to me, looked exactly alike.

Early one morning I got a call from a fur buyer announcing he would be in Tanana at ten o'clock to buy fur and he would like to look at mine, could I wait for him? There was absolutely no way I could wait on such short notice as I was scheduled to fly in about forty-five minutes. I told him he could talk to my wife who would be in the store all day. (Had he chartered me, instead of a competitor, to fly him down, maybe I could have found time to wait.)

I had the fur in the basement. It was mostly beaver, all separated according to size. Several piles of each size. All he had to do was count them. I told my wife what he would probably offer but if she could get him to give her my figure, to accept. I was willing to take less than the expected Seattle Fur Exchange price if I didn't have to bother sacking and shipping them. I gave my wife a reasonable figure. He measured every beaver pelt! I had missed his figure only fifty dollars on four hundred fifty beaver, but she couldn't get him to raise his price one bit. We got the expected price from Seattle Fur Exchange. I was learning.

Fur

One spring day during the dog races at Tanana, Pete Shepherd, a Wildlife Protection Officer from McGrath, dropped in to see us. He asked me if I had any beaver that needed to be sealed. All string-tagged pelts were later sealed by a protection officer, then they could be separated and sold individually. After sealing all the beaver, he asked if we had any wolves or wolverine to be sealed. I told him I was unaware they needed to be sealed. He then asked if I ever read the regulations. That gave me a good opening. My wife had been trying all winter to get some new regulation booklets, but to no avail. I told him I would read them if I could get a copy, but my wife, who was the tagging officer, wasn't even having any luck getting them. About two days after he returned to McGrath, we had plenty of new regulation booklets.

When all the sealing was completed, I asked him if he was going from Tanana to Hughes and he assured me he was. I asked if he would take a package over for me and he readily agreed to do so. I brought him a case of 12 gauge shotgun shells addressed to Bill Williams. He showed no surprise or facial expression of any kind and assured me they would be delivered tomorrow.

Bob Magnuson, a local pilot who operated from McGrath, who was flying and helping Pete, had to hide behind one of the huge spruce supports in the basement to keep Pete from seeing him laugh. He knew full well those shotgun shells were for springtime goose hunting and he knew Pete knew it too. Just a good Alaska-style joke.

The shells were delivered as promised.

The Cherokees

✈

efore we moved to Tanana, we lived not far from some
friends named Olsen, John, Rosalie, Terry, Kent, Dee,
Randy, and Chris. The oldest Olsen boy, Terry, for-
mally known as "Jigger," had flown for Fairbanks Air
Service while I was their chief of maintenance. Our family relationship was such that I was welcomed into their home for
an overnight stay whenever I was forced to spend a night in
Fairbanks. We enjoyed visiting. Many of our friends were mu-
tual acquaintances. This was back during the days when young
men were still drafted for a couple of years military duty. Jigger was soon to be discharged, so he contacted Fairbanks Air
Service about returning to work for them when his military
duty was completed. Upon learning he had continued to up-
grade his qualifications during his absence, he was rehired upon
his return. He had also taken a wife and now had the beginning
of his own family.

The name Don Jonz will ring a bell with most people
who have spent much time associated with aviation in interior
Alaska during the fifties, sixties, and seventies. He was an excellent instructor and supported himself in that manner while
attending the University of Alaska in Fairbanks. His experience with various airplanes and flying in various parts of the
world with pilots who themselves had lived a colorful career
helped qualify him as an instructor with something of value to
impart.

He was absent from the Fairbanks scene for a few years
while gaining most of that experience but for various and sun-
dry reasons he returned and took up right where he had left
off. He eventually flew for almost all the operators in the area.

253

He had the knowledge and experience to handle the many jobs which would spring up occasionally, but are not part of the daily routine. A qualified pilot available to make the odd trip is truly a valuable acquaintance, especially when an operator cannot afford and does not have enough work to employ another full-time pilot.

Don was an instrument instructor. That is where I had my first close contact with him, even though we had known each other for many years. He had worked out an agreement with the management of Interior Airways, who held the Piper Aircraft dealership at the time, to do some flying and sell airplanes.

Since my operation and home were in Tanana it was unusual for me to spend a night in Fairbanks. However, one night, for some reason, I was spending the night in town and Don called Rosalie Olsen on the phone and asked to talk to me. He wanted to come over and talk. I agreed.

The summer before he had given me the opportunity to fly a new Piper Cherokee Six-260 with all the bright lights, whistles, and colorful knobs to embellish the appearance and function of the aircraft. There were five of us in the aircraft for that flight. I was the smallest one of the crowd, the fuel tanks were full, and the performance was good. The loading arrangement that could be utilized for passengers and freight was impressive, especially the front baggage compartment. After the flight, Don asked me what I thought of it. I frankly told him when they came out with more horsepower in the engine to come back and see me. I'd probably make some serious talk.

Don was a little surprised and questioned why I even thought they may add to the available horsepower. I mentioned that, at some time, all airplanes are under powered and a brief look at the history of the Piper line would tell volumes. The Super Cub started out at forty horsepower and grew until the now standard engine was one hundred fifty. The Clipper was one hundred fifteen, then they added flaps, put the one hundred twenty-five Lycoming in it and eventually had it up to one hundred fifty and called it a Pacer. The Comanche was born with a one hundred eighty Lycoming, then they added the two hundred fifty option. I readily agreed the performance was good but I wanted excellent performance for the type of situations I knew we would encounter. "When they put in more power, come see me."

Upon his arrival at the house and all the introductions and social amenities were properly observed, Don said, "You told me when Piper Aircraft came out with more horsepower I should come see you. So here I am."

He continued, explaining the options, the new engine, which was three hundred horsepower and equipped with fuel injection. I wasn't impressed with the fuel injection part as experience with the Cessna 185's had given me some anxious moments, but they were still using them. Not too many pilots were forced to don the snowshoes because of them. Later I was to find the injected Lycoming had no equal for starting dependability and faithful operation. I never had a problem with the Lycoming pooling fuel in a cylinder, as the Continentals did. The most impressive initial love affair was that carburetor ice was a thing of the past.

The conclusion of his visit was to leave Don with an order for a new Cherokee Six-300 with seventh seat and cargo door, the first sold in Alaska. After ordering the new Cherokee Six, I began considering making an offer to Jigger that he go to work for me, keeping one airplane in Fairbanks, the other in Tanana, with daily phone conferences to coordinate our work. I had yet said nothing to anyone and was still studying things out in my mind, when one evening, on the return to Tanana, I heard a report of an overdue aircraft. I called Wien on the HF radio and asked if they knew who the pilot was— Terry Olsen.

My Cessna 180 was on wheel-skis, so I called John, Terry's father, and told him to meet me at the Fairbanks Air Service hangar the next morning and we would search. The next morning when I went out to the airplane, I had a flat tire. I threw a two by four under the ski and pumped the skis down, which served as a jack so I could remove the wheel. I dashed home, quickly installed a new innertube, returned and replaced the wheel, headed for Fairbanks and fueled up. John and I were still the first ones in the air on the search. We were given a search area it was inconceivable Jigger would be within, but if we were going to conduct a coordinated search, we had to cover it just in case he may be there. After completing that grid we moved over to the area where we thought he was more likely to be, but darkness and shortage of fuel only allowed us a few minutes more search time. The next day a Wien pilot discovered the wreckage right where we thought it would be. There were no survivors.

Soon after taking delivery of the new aircraft, the 1967 flood descended upon Fairbanks and outlying areas. During that week of weather down to the tree tops, I had my first stretcher emergency, from Huslia to Tanana, then on to Anchorage the next day. I'd counted tree tops and railroad ties all the way, but was fairly impressed with the airplane. Later I was to learn the airplane was an excellent instrument platform. It felt just like a big, stable machine. The ice carrying capacity of that airplane was enough to make an old Boing 247 Captain, or DC-3 enthusiast, doff his hat in honest respect.

I also learned the loading configuration of the aircraft was far superior to what I had originally envisioned. I could put the two rear seats in the rear baggage compartment, then place a couple cases of bread right on the seats, thus not exceeding the weight limit of the rear compartment. That left a huge space for cased goods in the area originally occupied by the two seats. The three center seats could be placed in the

My favorite airplane, a Piper Cherokee Six, on a gravel bar on Nowitna River.

front baggage compartment when necessary. It was possible to have three passengers in seats and a full stretcher, plus having the other three seats in the front baggage compartment. This made it easy to deliver a stretcher case, then bring home a full passenger load, all in legal seats.

The airplane cost almost the same as a Cessna 180, cruised about the same speed, used about the same amount of fuel per hour, and handled almost twice the load. It was a money- making machine and a pleasure to fly. With the "black box," or auto-pilot, engaged, it would fly hands off, so I could catch up on my reading, a habit not all my passengers fully appreciated.

About that time I developed an itch problem for which the doctors, who rode with me occasionally, were giving me benadryl. I didn't know I wasn't supposed to be driving if taking benadryl. In fact, I didn't even know what I was taking. It came in a special pharmacist container which explained that I was to take them in such and such a manner. I did, however, wonder why I was always so sleepy on the way home every day. It got so bad, I would sleep about fifteen or twenty minutes every afternoon on the way home. I felt it was because I had eaten lunch, was flying into the sun, and the drone of the engine had a hypnotic effect. Years earlier, I had developed the ability to run caterpillars and sleep on the haul road, waking in time to make all the turns, and never had a problem. Flying could be a little more serious, but I did have a system.

In order to insure safety, I would set up the auto-pilot, get it all trimmed out, place my right foot on the top of the cable tunnel between the two seats, rest my chin in my hand, brace my elbow on my knee and open one eye occasionally. If an instrument was even slightly off center, I would abruptly come fully awake. On days when I was extremely sleepy, I would hold my microphone in my hand. If I dropped it, I would immediately be wide awake. Any loss of altitude causing a change in the sound of the engine would also awaken me.

Once while still getting comfortable in the Cherokee Six, we were approaching to land at Huslia, which lies on the bank of the Koyukuk River among many lakes and sloughs. The time was early September, and thousands of ducks and geese were gathering in preparation to begin their annual, southerly migration. We came down over a lake full of waterfowl a little lower and faster than was actually necessary. The geese flew off the water in every direction. We did not pull up—just stayed low over the lake. What an exhilarating thrill! Birds in every direction. They were so good at getting out of the way— or always had been in the past.

On board was a Public Health Service doctor from the East coast who never quite thoroughly understood anything one tried to explain to him. Also on board was a State of Alaska nurse that needed an explanation for nothing. Suddenly THUMP—oh,oh! I was afraid to even look. The windshield was intact. The prop seemed OK as everything was still running as smooth as a Singer sewing machine. The engine instruments told me nothing. I couldn't see the undercarriage but — I wondered — I hoped, then I cautiously slid my left eye along the leading edge of the left wing and could hardly believe what I saw.

That wing was caved in clear to the spar just inboard of the tip fuel tank. All I could see was torn and crumpled aluminum. Goose grease and feathers were sliding back toward the trailing edge of the wing, moved along by the slip stream. There was very little blood, just goose fat, down, and a few small feathers.

Of course, after we landed at Huslia, there were numerous people on the field, there always are, and they were all laughing. They needed no explanation. The doctor walked around the airplane, looked at the mess and asked what had happened. I casually told him that one of the geese was too clumsy to get out of the way. He shook his head seriously and said, "My goodness, I'm certainly thankful it wasn't a condor." I swore them both to secrecy ... yeah, you bet!

The doctor and nurse stayed in Huslia. I stopped in Ruby on the return to Tanana, only to be lectured for forty-five minutes by an old fellow who had read a book about aviation and things that contribute to accidents. He was appalled that I would even consider flying back to Tanana before performing major surgery and a skin graft on the wing. Admitting I realized it would not heal by itself, I tried to reason with him that it got me into Huslia after the impact, it got me to Ruby after the landing at Huslia, and I was willing to take the calculated risk it would get me on to Tanana. It did too, but he was still shaking his head in disbelief as I was taking off at Ruby. I'm sure he would have made an excellent FAA inspector. That wing even got me on into Fairbanks where we completed the permanent repairs the next day, but the moral of the story is—**DON'T HORSE AROUND**. A few months later, I hit an eagle at three thousand feet.

On one trip to Bettles, from Nenana, the weather was quite low over the Yukon but good at Bettles. We elected to fly instruments and during the climb we encountered a little ice. Being sure we would get out of the ice before long, we continued to climb. When we leveled off at cruising altitude, the propeller governor control would not move when we attempted to adjust power for cruise. The only thing we could do was continue at climb RPM until we landed at Bettles. Upon examination, it was easy to determine the problem was ice on the control cable. The next time I stopped at the hangar in Fairbanks, I fashioned a small piece of aluminum angle to fit onto the bolts of the prop governor base. It would collect the ice instead of allowing it to freeze on the control cable. It was so satisfactory I put them on all the Cherokees in the future and never again experienced a problem.

Pete and Chuck Garden, visitors from Wisconsin, and Cherokee Six's.

The alternators on the Cherokee Six's had a capacitor installed thereon to quell radio noise caused by the alternator. I heard Al Wright had a problem that burned out several gauges and a radio. I got to wondering what could have caused his problem. The best theory I could dream up was that the capacitor, which was mounted directly on the alternator, had failed mechanically. If that capacitor should fail mechanically, it would cause a direct, internal short to ground. The regulator would call for full output of the alternator. When something burned in two or just broke contact within the shorted area, the entire surge of full alternator output would immediately go through every electrical device activated in the system, probably destroying them all. To preclude this ever happening, we installed a fuse holder between the capacitor and ground. We inserted a very low value fuse which would function beautifully to bleed off all radio noise. It would burn out immediately in case of a higher load being placed upon it by any mechanical failure of the capacitor. Through the years, we had several of those fuses blow and the pilot would know it immediately as the radio noise would increase dramatically. All that was necessary to correct the problem was to replace the three dollar capacitor and fuse and we were again on our way, minus the radio noise. Later the FAA came out with an AD note requiring an overvoltage relay be placed in the line at a cost of seventy-five dollars, plus installation. Subsequent new airplanes had them installed at the factory.

When flying off gravel airports, the stabilizers of all airplanes took quite a beating as a result of flying gravel. The Cherokee Six was especially vulnerable. The stabilator, a combination stabilizer and elevator, was built of aluminum and had a blunt leading edge. The spray of gravel caused as the wheels touched down was particularly devastating. Through trial and error we discovered the best way to land the aircraft was to touch all three wheels at the same time, as smoothly as possible. Larger tires helped. Paul Hoysington, a very approachable FAA inspector, suggested a spray rail on the wheel pants. That worked extremely well except for the fact the wheel pants were very difficult to remove and replace and they were not conducive to all operations. They were actually dangerous on fields with tall grass. They also accentuated any tendency there may be for a nose wheel shimmy.

The final modification to prevent the destruction of the leading edge of the stabilator caused quite a stir around the halls of the Fairbanks Aviation Safety Office. I was talking about making a cover to protect the leading edge when Tony Shultz, who was one of the old time Alaska bush pilots with about twice my acquired flying time to his credit, suggested I make it of stainless steel. Due to the very toughness of the stainless, I liked the idea, so I made a pattern and had Bob Gamble make up a couple in his sheet metal shop. Once the holes were drilled and blind nuts installed, the cuffs were easily installed and removed for any future maintenance that may be necessary.

They worked beautifully, but how do you go about getting something like that approved by the FAA? The best approach we could contrive was to keep our mouths closed and play dumb. It finally caught up to us and one of the young, more exuberant inspectors, put out the word he was going to make us take those cuffs off or ground the airplanes. Nothing that makes a more efficient or better airplane could be tolerated by the FAA without their prior permission and nods of wisdom.

OK, now we have a dilemma, and a challenge. We are not going to remove the cuffs. They are the most efficient and cost effective method yet devised to maintain the integrity of the stabilator, plus they shed ice so fast we had never had ice on the tail when we landed, even when there was still three quarters of an inch on the leading edge of the wings, prop spinner, antennas, etc. We didn't know why, that was just the way it was, and we liked the idea. So how do we get these things approved?

One day I saw Paul Hoysington at Bachner's hangar on Phillips Field. I called him over to look at the installation. I told him that in my experience, I never had any problem when working with someone who had some background and experience, but I could never seem to achieve good results talking to someone who had spent all his time studying books and attending KGB[1] schools.

Paul assured me I had a nice idea, a good clean installation, but the problem with stabilators, historically, had been balancing them. Anything that may disrupt the balance was very critical. I agreed with him and showed him the lead strips used to insure proper balance. I explained the strange fact of ice not tenaciously adhering to the stainless steel and bringing up the point that ice too, could cause an imbalance. I was discreet enough to not mention the body putty many people used to fill the dents of a damaged leading edge, which definitely disrupted the balance and was just a shoddy repair, at best. I knew he must be aware some were making that type of repair.

After looking the entire modification over and asking me many questions about how I had established the balance, he told me to make him a drawing, complete with weights of the stainless cuffs and lead strips and he would give me a field approval. From then on we put them on all the Cherokees. The beauty of the installation was when they did suffer dents they could be removed and the dents tapped out from the inside and replaced in a few minutes, making them look like new again.

The real positive side effect was that we had again foxed one of the new breed of inspectors who had a stock answer for every good modification, and that was **no**!

---

[1] FAA inspector.

The Cessna 180

✈

One day on a charter in the Cessna 180, split between the Alaska State Troopers and a State Health Nurse, we were returning to Tanana from Bettles. We were almost within reach of the airport, but couldn't raise anyone on the radio, when the engine quit. I didn't think we could make it to the airport so we turned around and landed on a very narrow, steep road, that accessed the White Alice sight on top of a hill, north of Tanana. The White Alice sight was a communications repeater station. A tie-in with the DEW line.

I always operated the 180 with the fuel selector turned onto both tanks, making fuel management simple, but it also helped keep the fuel in the tanks level. A wing-heavy problem, from burning all the fuel from one side, never occurred. On occasion, if the airplane was parked with one wheel low, the fuel would run from the high side to the lower one. I noticed my fuel was almost exhausted in the right tank, but the selector was turned onto both. There was plenty of fuel in the left tank, there should have been no problem.

As we came in for a landing, the road was much steeper than it looked from a few feet in the air, making it necessary for me to flare abruptly, but still we hit hard. I jammed the control forward to hold the wheels on the road. I did not want to bounce. The road was so narrow two ground vehicles couldn't pass and I needed brakes to steer to stay on the road. After we stopped, the engine was still idling, so I added power and parked on one of the turn out areas made specifically so any vehicle coming down hill could pull off the road allowing the loaded water truck, moving uphill, to continue.

I called my wife on the HF radio asking her to send one of the girls up with ten gallons of fuel. While waiting for the fuel I removed the gasculator, or fuel screen, to see if there was any obstruction in the line. I was surprised to see almost an entire bee, in pieces, come from the screen. My deduction was: a bee had flown into the end of the hose at the refueling tank and been overcome by the fumes, then pumped into the tank. After disintegrating, the bee passed down the fuel line to the selector valve and the pieces lodged there. The fuel exhausted from the right tank and the left could not flow. When we made the hard landing the weight of the fuel, plus the force of the hard landing, had forced the bee down the line into the strainer where I found it. Fuel was thus allowed to flow, refilling the carburetor and the engine continued running on the ground. The next day I fashioned a cap for the fueling hose to prevent a reoccurrence.

My daughter took the passengers back to Tanana in the car. I taxied to the top of the hill where there was a little airstrip which I used for take-off, and flew back to the airport.

Of course there was a big inquiry and after talking to everyone else in the country, the KGB finally came to me for an explanation concerning the problem. I simply told him exactly what had happened, with no apologies. The inspector almost bowled me over with his next statement. "I understand you make it a habit of sleeping while you are flying."

There was no point in denying it. I knew by the way he made the statement he had already persuaded someone to give him a written, signed statement, affirming the fact, so I just said, "So?"

For a minute he was speechless, then said, "W-e-l-l, with all the accidents we have been having, don't you think it's a good idea to stay awake while you are flying?"

Knowing I was caught red-handed, I felt I may as well enjoy this while I could, so I said, "Well, I guess that just proves a point, doesn't it?"

"And just exactly what is the point that it proves?" he asked.

"That I can do a better job of flying in my sleep than some guys can wide awake," I answered casually.

In spite of himself he laughed right out loud and dropped the subject.

A couple of weeks later, flying the same airplane, I took Angus Roberts into Stevens Village. He made an annual trip in a boat up the Yukon as far as Tanana, then I flew him as far as Fort Yukon gathering information on subsistence fishing for the Department of Fish and Game.

We saw the schoolteacher with a wheelbarrow moving his winter supply of foodstuff, from a mound stacked on the airport, to his quarters. He was a little overweight and probably feeling the effects, so he stopped to talk for a minute. He made some mention of the airplane and I told him I had landed it, with a dead engine, on a very narrow road a couple of weeks ago.

"Yes," he said, "I know the feeling, I once landed a B-17 on a narrow road in Germany. I did pretty good too, until I came to that right angle corner."

It's Too Late to be a Hero.

Upon arriving home one afternoon, a call came from the hospital asking if they could get an immediate flight to Anchorage. They had two small boys who had gotten into the iron pills their mother was taking and no one knew how many they had actually swallowed. A nurse would accompany them—could I go right away? I assured them I could and as the Cherokee chartered for thirty dollars an hour more than the C-180, I assumed they wanted me to take the C-180. Later I learned they would have been happy with the Cherokee and it would have made me very happy about an hour into the flight.

About the time we crossed the upper Kantishna River, the clouds were forcing us down and I really didn't relish the idea of following the railroad tracks all the way into the Susitna Valley. I had done that about a week before in the Cherokee. More realistically, we were still quite a few miles from the railroad tracks. I noticed the fog was not extending clear to the mountain side. The ceiling was consistent, but there was about a two or three hundred foot column of clear air right up the side of the mountain, clear up to blue sky. I knew the only thing that could hold fog away from the mountain in that manner was a strong updraft, so we nestled up to the side of the mountain, and sure enough, the elevator ride began.

I reasoned if we got up there by using the updraft, it was just as likely, once we started to move away from the effects, we may get a down draft that would pull us back down into the clouds. The only real worry was that the C-180, unlike the Cherokee Six, wouldn't carry enough ice to qualify as a good morning frost. Occasionally we, as pilots in general, swap judgment for luck, but try to have all we can going for us before making the final decision. I knew if we could achieve eleven thousand feet we could maintain at least eight thousand until we were fifteen miles from the mountain, then we would have plenty of clearance over the tops of the highest points around Talkeetna.

As it turned out our elevator ride took us up to thirteen thousand feet and then we were barely on top, but feeling that was enough we turned and headed for Talkeetna. Just as I had figured, we started losing altitude down to eleven thousand five hundred and were picking up ice. We had three good radios. The best T-30 Lear HF (high frequency) in the state, a brand new Bendix ADF (automatic direction finder), and a new King KX 150 B, a VHF (very high frequency) radio which contained the Omni navigation system, which was fairly new in Alaska at that time but many transmitter sights were in place fulfilling the needs of the military and Air Carriers. The Omni needle pointed to the bearing the pilot selected making following a course as simple as keeping the needle centered, which was accomplished by slightly altering the heading of the aircraft. All three radios were receivers and the HF and the VHF were also transmitters.

After computing our exact position, I called the Control Center and requested an instrument clearance from present position to Anchorage. I gave them my position as two hundred forty degrees from the Talkeetna VOR (the station sending the signal for the Omni), and while waiting for a reply to my request I did all my math again. I realized I had mistakenly given them the wrong radial, plus the ADF had just ceased to point. I called them and corrected the radial to three hundred forty degrees from Talkeetna and reported the problem with the ADF. The controller asked me if I would accept a clearance at thirteen thousand on top. I told him no, if we could maintain thirteen thousand we would still be there. We had no problems, we still had plenty of radios to do what we wanted to do but we would like to have a slot so someone else, bigger and faster than we were, didn't ruffle our feathers from behind while we were stuffing this thing through a cloud at a much slower speed. We forgot to mention we were picking up ice.

I realized by telling him the ADF needle had ceased to point and making a correction on the radial, he surely thought I was confused and didn't really know where we were. I tried to assure him we had no problems at all, just give us a slot. About that time the Omni ceased to function also. The VHF transmitter and receiver both still worked. We could tool right down the old Low Frequency Range, just give us a slot, please. I didn't think a wise person would mention the ice just yet; the temperature was such that with a little more loss of altitude the ice would melt anyway.

An Air Force Globemaster called in and the controller wanted me to transmit so he could get a strobe on us and give him a fix. I told him we didn't have UHF (ultra high frequency) and I knew where I was, just give me a slot to keep others out of my immediate vicinity. I gave him my position, my heading, which was a converging course to pickup the Summit range leg, and my altitude. We were still talking and we hadn't yet received our clearance when we picked up the range leg, so we made a turn to maintain course on the range leg. We reported the new heading. After about ten minutes, he asked me to change course to a new heading, two minutes later to change course again and happy day, *he* had found us!!

He then gave me my clearance, complete with permission to descend to five thousand feet. The ceiling at Talkeetna was fifty-five hundred so we canceled instruments and landed to get more fuel. I had also neglected to tell Center we were a little short on fuel. Upon fueling at Anchorage it was determined we would have made it without stopping at Talkeetna to add fuel but I don't like to cut it that close. I also couldn't forget the necessity of crossing Cook Inlet. We had used full power extensively and were cruising much slower, due to ice on the wings, so we had used more than a normal amount of fuel.

We were cleaning up the airplane at Merrill Field when the nurse told me that before leaving Tanana they had given the boys something to make them vomit and make their bowels move. Thanks a lot. A week later the boys were back in Tanana striving diligently to imitate the Katzenjammer Kids.

While at Merrill Field, I asked about a good radio repairman and was given the name of one Andreason. I forget his front name but he could surely fix a radio. I wrote him a note telling him the radio had almost kilt me and would really appreciate it if he could correct the bad habits. He got quite a kick out of my note. The radio worked about two weeks and quit again so that time I sent it to Seattle along with a note detailing the history of the past month. The repairman happened to be a fellow I had flown to several camps while he was working out of Barrow for the contractors during construction of the DEW Line. He wrote me a note telling me there was something in the airplane making contact with the back of the radio and shorting out a transistor. Sure enough I found a broken support to the radio bracket, corrected that and the radio kept functioning normally for many days.

I wrote the Bendix Corp. about the problem with the new ADF and all they could tell me was I had experienced a problem they hadn't yet overcome on the type installation we were using on the C-180. The problem was simple. Rain water was forced under the loop and drained into the cable connections shorting them out. It seemed this only occurred on the top mounts. We simply cleaned out the connection well and filled them full of Dow Corning DC-4 compound, placed a large "O" ring around the hole where the connection was made at the skin of the airplane and bolted the loop back down. We never had another problem. I told the Bendix Company what corrections we had made. I hope we were somewhat instrumental in making that unit a success as they were really a good ADF and popular for a long time. They are still in use today, with updates of course.

One of the beauties of those ADF's was their ability to "read" stations from great distances and point accurately. I have climbed to seven thousand feet on a flight from Fairbanks to Tanana, tuned in San Francisco and it would point. Quite consistently, on trips from Anuktuvik Pass to Fairbanks, I could "read" Fairbanks from eight thousand feet, making it possible to fly direct and clear all obstacles.

After the twins moved to Fairbanks to attend high school, I made it a policy to listen to the news on the ADF each morning on the way to town. Often I would meet with one of the girls for lunch, or just to visit, and we could discuss current events and be up-to-date.

High School

📖

When we arrived at Tanana, a move was underway to establish a full four-year high school program. Nevertheless, for several reasons we felt it best to send the twins, Dolly and Robin, who were the oldest, to Fairbanks for their last two years.

My wife had found it necessary to leave home at an early age to make further education possible. I had gone overseas during the war at age eighteen. We were both aware of the trauma inflicted by an abrupt, complete break away from the home environment. We planned for all the children to go to college if it be their desire and had decided to send them to Brigham Young University, in Provo, Utah, if possible. A long way from home and no contact with family while there.

We decided sending the twins to Fairbanks would be a good plan as they still had a number of friends with whom they had attended classes in their younger years. I was in town every week day. If they found it necessary, or desirable, to see me it only involved a telephone call and establishing a time and place. That worked well with the twins so when Vicky finished her second year of high school in Tanana, she also moved to Fairbanks for her last two years.

Parents plan, make sacrifices, establish goals, budget for the financing of each and sometimes they actually come to fruition but again, "the best laid plans of mice and men, will often go awry." The part about allowing them to break away from home gradually worked quite well. The twins graduated and went on to enroll at BYU. If they suffered from the lonesomes, they never complained.

Vicky was staying with Bud and Margaret Bozeman who were our 'across the street' neighbors when we lived in Fairbanks. They had a large house and insisted I come stay with them when spending a night in Fairbanks. By accepting their offer, I could visit with Vicky. Bud and I had a lot in common so our visits were always enjoyable. The last six months of her senior year, I began to notice a change in Vicky, a maturing effect.

One day Margaret confided in me that I shouldn't be too surprised if I should acquire a son-in-law in the near future. I told her I had begun to suspect something of that nature.

One evening I found it necessary to delay departure back to Tanana so I called Vicky and asked if she wanted to go to dinner. When I arrived to pick her up, her boyfriend, Jack Phipps, was there. (I still don't know if she quickly called him or he just happened to drop around before my arrival.)

"No problem, we can all go out to eat," I said.

We had hardly been seated when the conversation became serious. Vicky excused herself and Jack and I continued the discussion. It was agreed Vicky would come home for the summer and work in the store while plans were made for a BIG wedding. Parents only get to do that once for their little girls, so they wish to make her as happy as is within their means. Margaret was the prime mover in making arrangements and the wedding was all Vicky had wished for. I was proud of her when I learned that before they started down the Alaska Highway on their honeymoon, Vicky had written and mailed all her thank you notes for the nice wedding gifts they had received— even the washboard given her by Jim Ebenal.

We tried to not think about having six more girls who would be coming up with disturbing regularity in the next few years. While we paid our girls for their assistance in the store, we knew we were losing some of the best trained and most conscientious help we would ever enjoy. We started them at a very young age and insisted they make decisions and choices. They have appreciated that early training. While we made those demands out of necessity, we will not tell them it was other than wise parentage. Maybe they will never figure it out. It all still comes under the heading of education.

Lolita was the one who inhaled books. She could have easily graduated from high school in three years and we thought she planned to do so. For that reason, we did not send her to Fairbanks for her last two years. For reasons of her own, she elected to go the full four years before graduation.

Then comes Marquita who did opt to graduate in three years. Albert Guthrie and Lolita were classmates. Al graduated in three years but did not enter college the next fall. I thought his reasons were sound—they just didn't have the classes he wanted to take. When Marquita, who incidentally had twenty-two credits, asked to graduate in three years, she was not denied the privilege but also was not told she could. She was kept in suspense right up to the end of the term. The only reason given for not making a decision, was that Al had not gone on to college after graduating in three years, as if that made a difference. In the meantime, she had been accepted to three different colleges.

One evening she was acting quite nervous and distracted. She told me she was to meet with the principal and superintendent again. I told her we both knew that Al's actions were a ridiculous excuse for indecision so to consider the source and ignore their position on the matter. I advised her to go to the meeting, being as courteous as possible. When they refused to make a decision allowing her to graduate, tell them that she had already been accepted to three colleges and really didn't need a high school diploma to enter college this fall but it would be nice to have one.

Of course they were wise enough to realize their ridiculous position and that they had completely lost the argument. They told her they would approve the graduation though not issue the diploma until the following year with her regular graduating class. The next spring, she completed her finals at college and was back in Tanana in time to speak as valedictorian of her graduating class.

Then came Stephen, the only boy in Tanana who had to account for his whereabouts and time. I knew how tough it was on him, but also had to uphold my own principles. I had to pretend to be unaware of some of his activities to keep from appearing to condone them or else try to put a stop to his hunting activities which were slightly outside the strict letter of the

273

law. The migratory waterfowl laws were so unfair it was ridiculous. They still are. Most years, by the time the legal season opened, the birds were all gone but people in Canada, the lower U.S., and Mexico could hunt all winter. Trying to change the law would be laughable.

I went over to the school each year to help Stephen make out his schedule and was very sure he was taking subjects that would get him graduated in three years but I never mentioned it to him. The latter part of his third year it became evident to me he would never finish another year. If he started the year, I knew he would quit as soon as basketball season was over so I urged him to graduate that spring, in three years. He did.

Our youngsters always did well in school. They all liked to read and we had one entire wall shelved for books, including many reference books. The older ones helped the younger ones learn to read.

Lynne Gallagher, daughter of an Episcopal Minister at Tanana, and Zoanne were the same age and spent much time together. When they entered school both were immediately welcomed to the third reading level. Our girls played well together and were not a problem when their mother was in the store. During rush hours, the older girls and Stephen were home to help. Both Zoanne and Myrna, the youngest, worked in the store when they still needed a stepstool to reach the cash register.

Both Myrna and Zoanne graduated from high schools in the lower states after we left Tanana. Only a couple of times did anyone try to take advantage of them due to their youthfulness. In both cases one of the local men who happened to be in the store really straightened out the young punks, leaving no question about what they thought of their attempt. Both were from another village.

Myrna was the one who always wanted to run the boat or drive the snow machine. She helped considerably in the store; enough that she easily found employment later as a result of her experience. However, during school hours it was becoming necessary to have help due to increased volume of trade. We hired local girls who did a nice job for us.

For entertainment we liked to open our house to the locals and have an old fashioned sing along. We posted a *'no smoking'* sign. No one objected in the least. We had an old piano which we tried to keep in tune and Elaine Mitchell, whose husband Bob was a White Alice mechanic, would play while we sang up a storm. We all loved it. Diversion in the bush is essential.

We always held Sunday School in the living room on Sundays if there was no emergency causing me to have to fly. Sometimes there was only our family, but occasionally we would have twelve to fifteen adults present. We had one State Trooper whose wife was a member of our church. Another State Trooper was also a member.

Fred Otte, one of our pilots, was a member who contributed much to the Sunday School lessons. He was a good instructor and always prepared a good lesson when it was his turn. One doctor and his wife were members. Later the hospital administrator and his wife were members of our church. They were both good sports and she joined me having some fun with one of our Yukon River characters.

A Night at Rampart

✈

There are some things in life which seem to always go together whenever an opportunity is presented. For instance, if you leave your hip boots home it is a foregone conclusion, whatever your conveyance, you will find yourself mired and it will be necessary to wade in the mire to free the conveyance. Early-day cowhands sang a song about leaving the slicker in the wagon, and rain, being synonymous. I had a customer whose appearance was a sure sign of bad weather, regardless of the weather report or present condition of the sky.

At the time, our flight operation had two Cherokee Six's, both of which were approved for instrument flying. They both had about the same instruments and radios with the exception that 8942N had one more Narco Radio. That translates to one more needle telling you what you need to know. In instrument work that always comes in handy. On this day I was flying that airplane.

When the client and I departed Tanana for Galena, Nulato, and Kaltag, the weather was quite good and the forecast indicated we could expect the same upon our return. The doctor who chartered the flight was an ear specialist for the Public Health Service Hospital in Anchorage. He was checking all children under twelve years of age who had a history of ear problems. The ones he felt needed immediate attention were brought along with us and they were to go with him back to Anchorage for surgery.

The children were so small we didn't bother to count them. It was easy to put two into one seat, have a safety belt over both and still be way under the weight limit. I don't recall how many we had on board, but we had a whole covey of them by the time we left Galena for Tanana.

As we neared Tanana, the weather was deteriorating rapidly. Surprisingly, a call from the Tanana Flight Service Station was unreadable. This situation was quite common with the old low frequency system, but not much of a problem with the new very high frequency radios. Also my navigation receivers did not seem to be functioning very well. We got very close to Tanana, but couldn't quite make visual contact with the ground in order to be able to pursue a safe approach to the airport. It was also getting late. Those radios were too erratic for me to feel comfortable asking center for an approach clearance. Communication frequencies were so unreadable it would have been a good opportunity for miscommunication.

We went out south of the airport about fifteen miles where I knew the hills were not very high and let down as far as was safe. We could see the ground but not well enough to justify further decent and it was fast getting dark. I had been caught on that maneuver before and tonight wasn't the time to push our luck. The last report was good weather in Fairbanks. In desperation, we headed for Fairbanks. The ADF pointed well on the commercial radio stations.

I told the doctor we were going to divert to Fairbanks.

"What are we going to do with all these little kids?" he asked, very concerned.

"The first thing we are going to do is get them safely on the ground, then we will make further decisions," I told him.

By then we could see the beacon at Nenana, about seventy miles away, so we were not bothered with weather concerns at that time. The kids were all asleep and if we didn't borrow too much trouble, this could still turn out to be a good day. I decided to save time by stopping at Nenana for fuel, then we could still go on into Fairbanks if necessary.

After landing and refueling at Nenana, I called the Tanana Flight Service Station on the telephone. They told me about ten minutes after we had passed Tanana the weather cleared up beautifully, but they could not raise me on the radio.

Naturally we cranked up and returned to Tanana without even having to awaken any of the little tots before arriving there. To the doctor's great relief, the nurses at Tanana took good care of them.

The next morning when I went out to ready the airplane to go to Fairbanks I noticed one of the "rabbit ear" antennas was broken off. That was what had caused our inability to navigate with the radios the night before. While I was replacing the antenna, I discovered a poor connection in the lead-in line to the communications radio so was able to correct two problems at once. Now we could navigate, ask for weather conditions, and hear what they said, all at the same time.

A month or so later, the same doctor was making rounds to the villages to check on the progress of those who had undergone surgery on their ears. It was so much easier to check on them at home, since most of them were doing well and there was no need to disrupt their schooling or other activities if they had no problems. He also didn't want them flying yet if it could be avoided. Most of the surgery had been eardrum repair and altitude changes were to be avoided if at all possible.

On this trip we were flying 5242S, the other Cherokee, my favorite of all my airplanes. About two o'clock in the afternoon we arrived over Venetie to find the runway in a horrible condition. There was about eight inches of new snow on top of whatever was originally there, but we could not determine what that was. Neither of us had any hankering to walk all the way back to Fort Yukon, so we decided the reasonable thing to do was bypass that village.

The doctor was really not too disturbed as he had no particular anxiety about any of the patients at Venetie. We felt this may turn out to be a real good conclusion We should be able to arrive in Tanana in time for him to, yet that day, make arrangements for a flight into Fairbanks and on to Anchorage.

279

As we departed the vicinity of Venetie I called Fort Yukon to revise my flight plan, give an estimate for a time of arrival at Tanana, and check weather. About fifteen minutes after leaving the Venetie area we encountered a light snowfall. The country is very flat so ceiling was no problem and the low visibility really only contributed to the monotony of the flight. A person couldn't see much and the feeling prevailed that we were suspended in place—time stood still.

We took a heading that should conduct us to the Yukon River just a short distance above Stevens Village. Error would cause us no problem for if we drifted a little to the left we would simply hit the Yukon above Stevens Village, but if we drifted to the right we would come to the Ray River which would also lead us to the Yukon. Once on the Yukon it was a simple trick to follow the river on into Tanana.

We pressed our noses against the windshield hoping the Yukon River was still there. The doctor developed a splitting headache. I tried to assure him that was my department but he insisted on taking a couple of my aspirin for good measure. He even took them dry.

He was feeling better by the time we passed the village of Rampart. We were over the Yukon and could see where we were going. The weather didn't appear so bad. I asked him if he had met Trader Ike at Rampart and he told me he hadn't (I assured him his education had been neglected.)

By the time we arrived at the upper end of the rapids, where the hills come very close together, squeezing the river down to less than half the previous width, the weather was fast deteriorating. Turbulance increased as we approached the rapids. Visibility was dropping and the temperature, which had been rising, was about thirty-one degrees. That was a dangerous situation.

If the temperature should rise one more degree we would be in an icing condition, possibly serious. I had the utmost of confidence in the ability of that Cherokee to carry ice, but this, to me, had all the earmarks of becoming freezing rain with the temperature rising as fast, as it had been. Freezing rain could build ice so fast an aircraft may not be able to carry more than a few minutes' exposure. Considering that fog was putting in an appearance, along with the other less than encouraging ingredients, I felt there was no better time than the present for the doctor to further his education by becoming acquainted with Trader Ike.

Returning to Rampart we landed, and taxied to a sheltered area to leave the airplane. I didn't put the engine cover on as it was so warm. I was sure it was going to rain and I didn't want to get the engine cover soaked and have to carry it along until I could dry it out. There was little danger of not being able to start the engine at the existing temperature or even with a twenty degree drop.

We walked down to the village and stopped at the trading post where I introduced the doctor to Ira Weisner, or Trader Ike. Ira had written several books about Trader Ike on the Yukon. They were quite amusing and about half of the stories were based on things that had happened, or could have, at Rampart.

We had our own High Frequency radio in Tanana which was operated mostly by my wife. Mr. Weisner also had one so we often heard one another and on occasions called back and forth. He had conversed with my wife considerably over the radio waves but had never met her personally. He allowed me to call my wife to close our flight plan. For me, it was always a thrill to hear her voice on the radio.

Ira was always joking about hiring a blond cook or a blond clerk for the store. One day I took a trip into Rampart for some reason and had extra seats available so I invited Janet Hughes, wife of the hospital administrator, to go along. She was quite nice looking and had waist-length, light blond hair that was very becoming.

Since Ira was always talking about blondes and had never met my wife, we thought it would be a good joke to introduce her to him as my wife. I was an old gray-haired geezer, almost fifty years old, and she was about twenty-three. We agreed on the procedure we would use and the results were quite amusing. One could almost hear him think, "Why does *he* get the blond *I've* been looking for?"

When the doctor and I entered the Trading Post, Liquor Store, and Post Office building, the first person we should see was a quite nice looking lady with pale red, almost blond hair, sitting there as if she owned the place. A little later, Ira made his debut and introductions were made all around. Of course there was no question that we should have to spend the night and he assured us that would be no problem.

Ira invited us to dinner in about half an hour and I had to admit his judgment of cooks, as well as that of his blondes, was most fastidious. The next couple of hours were spent with Ira and me trading lies and spinning yarns. Neither the doctor nor the blond were much for talking but enjoyed the atmosphere.

At bed time, Ira pointed to the stairs and indicated there were a couple of beds up there. When we were ready, the fastest one could make his own choice of which bed to use and the slower person was stuck with the other one. At the end of each such sentence Ira had a deep laugh that sounded rather like hya, hya, hya, but his sense of humor certainly needed no sharpening.

After a final trip to the little house on the prairie, we began our journey to the bedroom. We entertained absolutely no thoughts of being robbed that night. I have never experienced the ascent of a set of stairs that creaked with more volume, consistency, or vigor.

I'm not quite sure what had transpired in the past but a strange odor, akin to a large urinal, or possibly even an outhouse, seemed to pervade the room. Turning the wick up on the kerosene lamp to better orient ourselves, revealed numerous whiskey bottles, mostly nearly full, in various locations around the room. All had been opened, emptied and refilled. No caps or corks were in evidence. It appeared those bottles had saved him many trips down those creaky stairs and to the outhouse in the middle of the night, but he had postponed emptying them. Of course, the need for more empty bottles justified drinking more of the original contents. It appeared extreme care should be exercised. We really didn't want to come into his house and start rearranging things so we carefully maneuvered around the obstacles.

We were up and gone by six o'clock the next morning without disturbing any of his samples, specimens, or what ever they were. The temperature was still so warm the engine started with no problem. The storm had gone by. We were back in Tanana in about thirty minutes. The State snow removal crew was still working on the airport so when they moved off to one side we landed to park at the Flight Service Station until they had the rest of the taxi ways and parking areas cleared. There was over a foot of new snow on the ground.

We were really not surprised at the condition of things at Tanana. The snow had turned to rain as we had feared. There was about two inches of ice on top of all the snow, airplanes, automobiles, etc.

That doctor was one of our best customers and all operators have a high regard for good customers. But why did he always have to bring such weather? To insure competence flying in the type of weather he brought with him made it necessary, every six months, to fly an instrument check ride.

Check Rides
✓✈

In the late sixties, taking a six-month instrument check ride with one of the FAA inspectors with whom I had previously flown, I had an opportunity to return a favor. He had shown me a few shortcuts to a successful approach on a previous check ride. On this day he asked me to file a flight plan from Fairbanks to Tanana, which I did. After we were out of Fairbanks about fifteen or twenty minutes, he told me to cancel the flight plan and divert to Nenana. After complying with his request I gave an estimate of twelve minutes to the Nenana VOR and we hit the estimate right on the minute. He remarked about a good estimate then asked me to request a low frequency range approach.

That struck me as a little odd as the old low frequency range approach was very seldom used and Nenana was one of the last stations in the country that still had one. They had been obsolete in the lower forty-eight states for about ten years. It wasn't very likely a situation would arise to dictate the low frequency range approach as the only available option, but I felt comfortable with the request. This particular inspector was a retired navy pilot who was now working for the FAA.

The weather that day was extremely turbulent but otherwise ceiling and visibility were good. I should point out, a special hood which restricts visibility of the pilot to the interior of the cockpit, is used for instrument check rides. After making my request and flying the approach, during which I allowed the aircraft to descend below the minimum altitude by about twenty feet, the inspector asked me to go out and fly another approach. He made the remark that the approach was fairly well-executed and he realized the turbulence was a little more than one would relish but just so he could say I had flown within all limits, let's do it again. I had to admire him for being exacting. After all, being exacting is what keeps instrument pilots alive. During the second approach, I felt as though I was sitting there petting Hogans goat through the entire procedure. We were crabbing about twenty degrees to be able to maintain a heading on the beam. I did not want to descend through the minimum altitude again. I was feeling badly about flying such a poor approach when he told me to take-off my hood. No one was more surprised than I to see the airport ahead, off to the right of the nose of the airplane about twenty degrees, right where it should have been, considering the wind.

After the flight, he told me how happy he was to see someone who still knew how to shoot a low frequency range approach. He had used it considerably in his younger days and was glad to be able to close out his career with the FAA by giving a check ride using the old system. Only then did I realize this was his last day of work before retirement.

After a pilot receives his instrument rating, he is required to fly a check ride with an inspector every six months to ensure he is remaining current in knowledge and ability. After receiving my instrument rating, the FAA inspectors didn't want to fly the six month check rides. John Hodge, head of the Fairbanks office of the FAA, gladly authorized Don Jonz to do it. Don was already a certified instrument flight inspector, so John reasoned if the FAA would accept the ratings Don issued as valid, they should also accept his approval of a pilot who already held the instrument rating, after flying a six month check ride. I flew my check rides with Don for several years, then John Hodge transferred or retired and another took his position. The new chief was adamant that only the FAA inspectors would give six month check rides.

From then on it was impossible to get the FAA inspectors to honor the appointments they made. They couldn't be bothered flying check rides with bush operators, but they wouldn't allow Don to do it either.

Early one January the FAA called a meeting of all the bush operators concerning the move to force us all to become scheduled. As the date approached, it was obvious the temperature was going to be forty below zero, or colder. That always means ice fog at Fairbanks. After several requests, the FAA agreed to postpone the meeting for a couple of weeks. Well, you guessed it, the weather warmed up only to drop down to forty below zero again as the date approached and they refused to again delay the meeting. When I learned this, I called Tom Olson, (no relation to John Olsen), one of the owners of Fort Yukon Air Service, who lived in Fairbanks. I asked if he would represent me and he agreed. I gave Tom all the information I wanted him to present, as far as accidents and safety were concerned. When he asked me, I assured him I could document everything I was asking him to present.

The FAA, like the school system, has their patented approach for pushing through the programs they want. The school system has an answer for everything, just spend more money. The FAA is a little more subtle. In the interest of safety, we need more regulations. If a person opposes spending money on gold-plated door knobs, he is against education — if he opposes more ridiculous regulations, he is against safety, that simple.

The FAA, in the interest of safety, was going to force all bush operators to become scheduled. Scheduled, defined by the FAA, was: if you made nine trips to a certain place during a three-month period, you were scheduled. You must now comply with all the paperwork and regulations of the Civil Aeronautics Board. It seemed that Webster had nothing to say about the word 'schedule'.

I told Tom to advise them, for me, I was not scheduled, I did not want to be scheduled, and did not intend to become scheduled. I flew across no state lines and flew to no foreign countries. To me, in spite of the FAA definition, scheduled meant departing at exactly the same time, to the same place, on a regular basis. This was set down on paper, published, and called a Schedule for people to read and use to plan their travel. I had no intentions of becoming scheduled. Also, I held no mail contracts and was not subsidized.

The FAA was presenting the argument if we were all scheduled, they would be able to monitor our operations much better thus increasing safety etc., etc. I told Tom to remind them that due to the present procedure of not allowing designated flight inspectors to give us our six month instrument flight checks, I was two and a half years overdue for a check ride. That was their fault, as I had made several appointments, all of which the inspectors had broken. Tom was a little reluctant to make that presentation until I again assured him I could substantiate each appointment I had made, date it, and who had accepted and not honored the appointment.

I further told Tom their argument of safety being the reason for wanting us to go scheduled simply held no water. With the Wien-Consolidated F27 disaster at Illiamna,[1] the fatal crashes were exactly two to one for the past twenty years. Scheduled operators had sustained two accidents for each accident of a non-scheduled operator. It didn't take too much imagination to perceive who took the most passengers to the Happy Hunting Grounds.

As would be expected, I soon received a call from an FAA inspector wanting to know if I could take a six month check ride on Thursday. I assured him I could and by the way, what happened to the scheduled plans?

"Oh, they are still being studied." I never did hear anything more about it. If I should give you three guesses to tell me what happened next, you could easily have two left over.

Two inspectors rented a Cessna 172 and flew to Tanana on Thursday. The weather was quite windy and I was in the Flight Service Station when they called on the radio announcing their arrival over the field and reported the air rather turbulent. They didn't think it too good a day to take a check ride. (But they expected us to fly safely in such weather.) I asked the communicator to advise them the turbulence would be much less of a problem in the Cherokee we would be flying for the check ride. The reply came back, "Yes, I can imagine." They turned around and went back to Fairbanks, without even landing.

About a month later, another couple of Inspector arrived and landed. I had just landed behind them with a load. As soon as I had taken care of my load, I dashed out to the FSS[2].

[1] The pilot of a Fairchild F27 was descending into Illiamna when he hit turbulence and lost a wing. All aboard perished.

[2] Flight Service Station

We all shook hands and introduced ourselves. I was already acquainted with Parker Nation, the maintenance inspector, who checked over and passed on the paper work and the airplane.

As we prepared to depart, I gave the airplane the normal pre-flight inspection, got into my seat and drained the fuel strainer, which is operated from inside the airplane. I asked Parker, who was still standing outside the aircraft, if it had completely stopped flowing and he assured me it had. The flight inspector asked Parker if he was going along and he declined. It seemed to me it was a rather emphatic "No," so up goes the little red flag.

As soon as we had the door latched, seats were adjusted, radios set up, and we were ready to taxi, I turned to the inspector, looked him straight in the eye, and said, "Let's get one thing straight before any confusion can arise. This airplane belongs to me, not to you, the government, the bank, or anyone else. If you want something done, just ask me. I'll do it, but you keep your hands off all controls, both engine and flight, unless it is to save both of us from appearing in the obituaries tomorrow, OK?"

He agreed. He also agreed to no short field landing demonstrations, due to poor visibility.

Some days a pilot taking a check ride can't seem to do anything right, but today everything went beautifully. I was able to deliver a performance I could not have repeated for years.

He finally got me into a horrible position and said, "OK, now just close the throttle and land, you have just lost your power."

The urge to kill surfaced, we were headed in the wrong direction, almost over the end of the airport, too high to land without overshooting half the runway, and too low to make a circle and still reach the runway.

"OK, wise guy," I thought to myself, and lined the aircraft up with the runway, about eight hundred feet too high, lowered the flaps, then pulled the nose up to just a little above stall speed. That Cherokee came down like an elevator, no shudder or rumble, just sank down to about fifty feet, when by dropping the nose down a little and coming back up again we made a nice three-point landing right at the second runway light from the end. I taxied up to the FSS and asked him what else.

"Nothing, this is fine," he said. We got out and he certified me for another six months and they left for Fairbanks.

A few days later in Fairbanks, I saw a Helio Courier with a badly damaged landing gear, parked beside Bachner's hangar at Phillips Field. I asked Ken Johnson, who worked at the hangar, what had happened. He said some fellow was taking a check ride when the inspector chopped the throttle on him on final approach. He didn't quite clear the log across the end of the field. I moseyed into the hangar and asked Mrs. Bachner if she knew the name of the inspector involved in said incident. Guess what? The same inspector with whom I had flown in Tanana a few days before. I also learned he had pulled the same thing on another fellow at Metro Field, with damaging results.

When Morrison-Knudsen Construction Co. were building the Fairbanks International Airport, they were assigned areas from which they could extract gravel for the base material for the runway, taxi ways, and attending areas requiring a gravel base. The contract did not specify how the dragline pits should be left after the gravel was removed. There was a gravel bridge between two of the pits which was used by the construction equipment as a roadway while hauling the material. Had this bridge been removed, as the last of the gravel was removed, there would have been a very nice float pond since the pits had all filled with water.

Because the bridge was not removed, the largest of the two pits was just an adequate float pond for smaller aircraft with loads that were not too heavy. It was also used for float practice and check rides.

I was talking with Al Wright about the damage for which one certain inspector had been responsible when he told me about one of his check rides. On take-off they were just off the water when this same inspector chopped his throttle. Al had been around too long to have a fear of FAA inspectors that would overshadow his respect for the gravel bridge he would certainly hit if he accepted a simulated engine failure. Al politely, but firmly, pushed the throttle back to full power. Holding it there he continued with a normal take-off.

After landing Al asked him, "What if I hadn't had sense enough to push that throttle back in?"

The inspector responded with a simple, "That's what I wanted to find out."

The cost of rebuilding all those airplanes meant nothing to him. In this particular case, he was probably extremely fortunate he was flying with Al Wright, instead of someone with more fear of inspectors and less experience.

The foremost thought in my mind was to thank my mother for endowing me with a good supply of little red flags. Flying and passing check rides gives a competent pilot added confidence to perform his duties in a professional manner.

The FAA Flight Service Station operators would prefer flight plans be filed by telephone rather than called in on the radio. There are undoubtedly good reasons for that preference, but it seems to me it takes the same amount of time to copy a flight plan from a telephone as a radio. I didn't spend a great deal of time trying to determine the reason for the preference, nor to justify my position for almost always filing by radio. One disadvantage of filing by radio is, after copying the flight plan, the FSS operator, or communicator if you prefer, gives you a weather briefing and on some occasions this will alter your intentions. Sometimes even to the extent one may cancel the flight and return to the airport of departure. Many times, since we operated off Phillips Field, we could not get to a telephone to file as the shops were all closed at 5:00 P.M. We always kept a general flight plan on file and the specifics, such as number of people on board, amount of fuel, departure time and estimated time of arrival, and altitude intended to fly, were about all that was necessary to complete and activate a flight plan.

One evening with a load of freight which included a plastic bag of gold fish and a case of ice cream, one of which bore the request, "Please do not freeze" and the other a request, "Do not allow to thaw," we prepared for a flight to Tanana. Eileen Kozevnikoff, the only passenger, had been in town several days for a seminar of some sort and was anxious to get home as it was Friday. I wanted to get home also as my time on the weekends was normally devoted to tasks that had been accumulating all week, but had not been completed.

The weather seemed good at Fairbanks, about a four thousand foot ceiling and good visibility, so we taxied out and took off, called the FSS and filed the flight plan which the communicator acknowledged. He then gave us the weather conditions, which included the report of a Navajo pilot who reported picking up two and a half inches of ice on approach at Tanana. He also gave us a pilot report that ice began at four thousand feet, then the question, "What are your intentions?"

The communicator is not trying to put pressure on the pilot, but he does need to know exactly what the pilot intends to do and if further clearances are necessary, he will submit the request to Center. The pilot must think quickly and clearly to be able to make a commitment and requests consistent with his needs, ability, and the capabilities of the airplane he is flying.

There was only one Navajo in the country at the time. That told me who the pilot was and the reliability of the report. It is almost impossible to pick up two and a half inches of ice, just on approach, in the Interior of Alaska, unless there is freezing rain. If there is, that will be reported. Also, the information that ice begins at four thousand feet tells me we can expect ice clear up to eight thousand feet, but seldom any higher. I had noticed ice forming layers in the Interior almost never exceeds four thousand feet in thickness.

Since the Cherokee Six would carry more ice with dignity, than most of the old ice delivery wagons slowly disappearing from the streets, I wasn't too concerned about performance. We were not loaded too heavily and had an abundance of fuel. The Navajo also handles ice so well I reasoned he had been sitting in ice all the way from Fairbanks to Tanana and didn't realize it. When a person is flying instruments, especially if he likes his cockpit light fairly bright, he may not even notice ice is forming on the windshield unless he looks for it with his flashlight. I felt he had been cleared for and accepted seven thousand feet and was gathering ice all the way without knowing it.

Considering all those factors, I asked for an instrument clearance at nine thousand feet. When the controller read the clearance he gave us seven thousand feet and I refused the clearance. He asked me what was wrong and I reminded him we had requested nine thousand feet. He told me there was no other traffic and seven thousand was all we needed. I then stated if there was no other traffic, I'd still like nine thousand, if I couldn't have nine, I'd accept ten. He cleared us nine thousand feet and I'm sure he didn't have the slightest idea why we had asked for it — pilot idiosyncrasies!

We accepted the clearance to cruise at nine thousand feet and began to climb. The report was accurate for right at four thousand feet we began to pick up ice and as expected, we were on top of the ice forming layer at eight thousand feet, at nine we were shedding ice. We only had about one-half inch and it had dissipated by the time we arrived over Tanana.

When we got our clearance for an approach at Tanana, we let down only to the top of the overcast and upon arrival over the VOR I pulled the nose up, closed the throttle, extended flaps, and brought the power back up to maintain a good rate of altitude loss as well as a little power on the engine for longevity sake. When we landed we had about three-quarters of an inch of ice, a good load for an accumulation on approach, but not two and a half inches.

An instrument pilot is something like a good athlete. If a basketball player is practicing free throws and makes an average of four out of ten, if he plans to really help his team, he will voluntarily stay and practice some more. If his performance is more like six out of ten, if he is tired, he may look around carefully to see if the coach is observing him, then go to the showers. If he shoots eight or more out of ten, he can go to the showers with his head high, making excuses to no one.

An instrument pilot, especially one who has his own operation and is his own taskmaster, will set his own standard of excellence. Professionals do not perform in the near vicinity of one another very long until a degree of respect, consistent with the performance of the individual, is established among his peers. As a result one pilot can evaluate the true conditions described by a pilot report simply by determining who made the report.

In the case of the two and a half inches of ice on approach at Tanana; the report was given by a true professional who was a competent instrument pilot but that is just too fast an accumulation of ice to be consistent with the weather report. Thus my deduction was that the Navajo pilot had inadvertently been sitting in an icing condition longer than he realized, or was willing to admit. He, however, wanted to get the information out to his fellow pilots without bringing too much embarrassment to himself. In case of the controller who gave me a clearance to maintain seven thousand feet, that was the normal assignment for that flight unless there was previously cleared traffic that would conflict. He did not understand my thinking in relation to the icing condition. To protect his own dignity he was able to get me a clearance to "cruise" nine thousand feet. That "cruise" cleared me for any altitude I wished from nine thousand feet down, thus allowing me to get above the ice and still use the normal seven thousand feet if I wished, or could.

Like the professional basketball player shooting free throws, I did not want to fly at eight thousand eight hundred, or nine thousand two hundred feet. I wanted to fly at exactly nine thousand feet, then report out of nine on approach and descend to the top of the overcast but maintain enough altitude to insure no mountains would interfere with future plans. Upon arriving directly over the station, we could plunge down into the overcast knowing we were going to begin picking up ice on the aircraft, but not for long, as we executed a hasty approach, and landed.

As we arrived over the VOR, right at the top of the overcast ready to begin our approach, we were clean of ice, having lost all we accumulated climbing out. We did not pick up the two and a half inches on approach and everything else worked out just as we figured and planned. I guess this puts us into the eight out of ten category—but there is a lesson here also.

All the deductions concerning pilot reports and weather worked out exactly as we had expected them to. The aircraft handled the demands exactly as we had expected it to. In fact, our confidence had been bolstered a little and we now know we are truly among the professionals. Very subtly allow those who will be riding with us in the future to be aware they are flying with one of the best — just make darned sure we don't get to believing it too much ourselves. Therein lies the trap that gets mountains or airports named after the intrepid pilot who almost completed his last flight.

Longevity is also promoted by the approach made toward potential customers, with emphasis on those who think their authority in their own field also extends to the way a pilot exercises judgment in his. A competent pilot will always remember he is a professional too and insist on making his own decisions about weather and the advisability of making the flight.

Be Cautious of John Q.

?

There are situations where one dare not allow John Q. too many privileges. One night in December, we got a call from the hospital asking if I could make an emergency trip to Chalkyitsik, a small village about twenty minutes from Fort Yukon. A man was suffering from a broken leg. It was nine o'clock at night and flying time to Chalkyitsik was about two hours and twenty-five minutes. The trip would take long enough that extra fuel would probably be required to safely complete the trip. Considering all that, I asked the doctor why he didn't have Cliff Fairchild, at Fort Yukon, make the trip. He would be two hours closer to the emergency than I. He informed me he had been contacted but had declined to go because of bad weather. Gee, thanks for the compliment.

After concluding the conversation with the doctor, I checked weather. They were giving a two hundred foot ceiling, one-quarter mile visibility with fog, at Fort Yukon. It was only twenty minutes to Chalkyitsik from Fort Yukon, so it was almost conclusive their weather was similar.

A person absolutely has to make sure of weather, fuel, oil, and mechanical condition, personally. No one else is responsible when you are still ten miles from home and any of the aforementioned conditions are found wanting. I never liked the idea of taking off on an emergency trip and almost successfully completing it.

I was always careful to observe our pilots to make sure they were as conscientious as I was, but I never pushed them to fly in weather I felt it was safe for me. If they flew the trip, they made the decision based on their capabilities, not mine.

One Saturday morning, the 23rd of December, I got a call from a fellow at the hospital asking if I could make a charter to Anchorage. I assured the caller I probably could — after I checked weather enroute. Upon doing so, I learned there was extreme turbulence and severe icing from the ground to thirty thousand feet; right across the area we would have to negotiate on our route to Anchorage. I called the customer and advised him we could not fly in that weather. I could, however, take him to Fairbanks and he could probably catch a jet to Anchorage. He then informed me that he had called me because all the commercial flights from Anchorage to Fairbanks had been canceled because of the weather. He told me he really needed to go as he had confirmed reservations on that evening's Alaska Airlines flight to Seattle and all seats were booked solid until after the first of the year. He asked me if my answer was final. I assured him the day was yet young; I'd check weather each new sequence and if it improved I'd call him. He called me about every half hour for the next three hours. There was no improvement in the weather, but I told him to hang tough, there was still time, if the weather should break.

About three o'clock in the afternoon I heard a friend, Kenny Hughes, who lived in the village of Grayling on the lower Yukon, talking on the high frequency radio. He was going to Grayling from Anchorage and had called in a position report and estimated time of arrival at Grayling. I called Ken on the HF radio and asked him how his weather was, since I had to go right through the area through which he had just flown. Ken called back and told me he was flying an empty airplane, cruising at full throttle and was barely maintaining altitude. His airspeed was about ninety knots instead of the normal one hundred thirty. He said he was getting out of the weather, but I'd be coming right through the worst of it, and he had only hit the edge. I could hardly read his transmission as the turbulence was so severe he couldn't hold the mike still enough to talk into the mouthpiece.

In about fifteen minutes the phone rang. The administrator at the hospital wanted to talk to me. Maybe I just didn't understand the importance of this flight. He just happened to know the man had confirmed reservations on Alaska Airlines to Seattle this evening and the flights were all booked solid until after the beginning of the year. (That sounded familiar.) He really needed to get home for Christmas.

I could visualize, and almost hear, the conversation that had just transpired between he and the fellow wanting to get back to Anchorage. "Just let **me** show you how this is done!"

Using all the self restraint I could muster, I calmly asked him, "Just what affect does all this information have on the safety of the flight?"

"Uh, er, I beg, what?"

"What bearing do those reservations have upon the safety of the desired flight?" I asked again. "The fact that he is willing to pay me to take him from here to where he wants to go is all the incentive I need to make the trip. From then on it all hinges on propriety and safety. It would do him no good, and would be very disturbing to his family at Christmas time, to have an all-out search for me and the head of his family. If the commercial jets refused to fly through that weather, it would probably be prudent for me to decline also!"

I really felt for the poor man who wanted to get home for Christmas. He really did not try to pressure me, just indicated his anxiety, but the administrator did try to use his position to put pressure on me to go against my better judgment. The thing that really irritated me was that he did know better. He was just trying to make himself look important in front of the poor man that was stuck.

My ire had settled and things were fairly tranquil for a time. That all changed with my receipt of a letter from the Public Health Service headquarters in Anchorage. It served to redistribute all the burrs under my blanket.

The text of the letter was about a discussion that had taken place in one of the safety meetings held periodically. Since in the past year, several aircraft accidents in which PHS employees were involved, suggestions for their prevention in the future would be entertained. Several people had suffered injuries of varying degrees but there had also been two fatalities. A suggestion was made that all their people should wear shoulder harnesses and crash helmets while flying with the bush operators. The last sentence was a masterpiece: "We would like to know your thinking and decision."

Since tact is the ability of one person to tell another where to go and leave him looking forward to the trip, I must admit being endowed with a copious amount of tact has not been one of my many virtues. It seems I either have to tell it like it is or get all muddled up and not know myself what I'm saying. I did exercise the good judgment to wait a couple of days before answering the letter.

Essentially, my answer was that in order to install satisfactory shoulder harnesses, an approval would have to be secured from the FAA and that was not an easy matter to pursue. The better your idea, the harder to secure the approval. I suggested they contact Ralph Nader and perhaps the newer airplanes would come out with them already installed. As far as their usefulness was concerned, consider the statistics in fatal automobile accidents. At that time eighty five percent of the fatalities were found sitting on their safety belts, or thrown from the vehicle.

If crash helmets were required in airplanes, people would probably be found at the scene of the accident sitting on their shoulder harness with their crash helmets in their laps. A person couldn't even talk to a seat mate with a helmet on his head, nor reach down to pick up a dropped pencil with the shoulder harness in place. After all we are dealing with people and they do what people do. My suggestion was, since eighty percent of the fatal accidents were weather-oriented, they should pick out the pilot in the area where they intend to fly who has the best reputation for safety and good judgment, then get into the airplane and keep quiet. Allow the pilot to make the decisions. He is a professional too, remember? After all, did they really want a bush pilot standing there during an operation, telling them how to perform major surgery?

A few months later Dr. Lee, one of the more influential doctors at the PHS hospital in Anchorage, came to Tanana and was laughing about that letter. He said it couldn't have come at a more opportune time or been better stated. The very person who had made all the noise, and suggestions, had been in an accident in Bristol Bay just the past summer. Apparently the weather was bad and he wanted to get to King Salmon so he could catch the scheduled flight back to Anchorage on a Friday afternoon. The young bush pilot didn't want to go as the weather was marginal and so was his experience. The doctor told him if he wanted any more flying out of the PHS, he had best get him over to meet that flight. An accident ensued and the doctor wound up with a nasty scar across his nose. He still missed his flight.

I always made it a policy to not accept charters that would keep me away from the home base for too long a time. The folks at home are always there to support the flying business so the flying business should be there to support them. If I was asked to make a charter which would keep me away from home for too long at one time, I would try to 'farm it out' or decline the business entirely.

One day I got a call from the State Department of Education to take a couple of fellows over quite a large area. The entire trip would probably take at least a week. No one likes to turn business down, especially when it originates with a customer who has, in the past, been very steady. I asked for, and was granted, a couple of days to make arrangements.

Don Jonz had handled previous flights for me and I could turn something over to him and forget it. It would be taken care of as though I were there all the time. I called him and asked if he could arrange something. I needed both a pilot and another airplane. It was a slow time of year, after dog races and before breakup, so time and equipment were available. He arranged for a Cessna 180 from Dick McIntyre and agreed to fly it himself. The aircraft he chose was almost new. It was one of the first Cessnas to be equipped with the long range fuel tanks. It would carry close to eight hours cruising fuel. Naturally, that made the aircraft quite heavy even before a load of passengers or freight was added. The end result was that legally one could carry much less freight or fewer passengers, but he could do it for a longer period of time. Since there were only two passengers and they had little baggage, Don elected to leave Fairbanks fully loaded on fuel. One of the most important details of planning a long charter north of the Arctic Circle is to know where you can get fuel and how much it will cost.

Just after take-off at Fairbanks International Airport, the airplane wasn't really climbing with any great amount of enthusiasm. The passenger in the front seat reached over and began to adjust the power settings for Don. Don looked at him and thought, "Shall I hit him now, or wait until we get on the ground where I can get a good swing?" The fellow looked over at Don, smiled, and began to assure him he knew just about all there was to know about these airplanes, and Don need have no fear at all on the trip. If anything went wrong, he could handle it for him. Don thought, OK, I guess it won't hurt to play his little game and assured him it was a real comfort to know that, but since they had so much fuel, it may be wise to use a little more power until they gained their cruising altitude.

It is always wise to be a little suspicious of John Q.

On one trip, flying a Cherokee Six, I had my oil changed at Fairbanks. Upon landing at Tanana, there was oil dripping off everything below the engine, clear to the tail of the airplane. A check of the remaining oil revealed three quarts were left in the system. The operators manual says minimum oil is three quarts, maximum twelve. I still had pressure when landing, so the two quarts I added after tightening the filter another half turn was adequate to see me back to the scene of the crime.

I knew exactly what the fellow who had changed the oil had done. The position of the filter made it easy for the handle of his wrench contact the engine mount. To the inexperienced hand, it felt tight enough to not leak. I showed him the problem and the results. He cleaned the airplane up good, brought the oil level back up to ten quarts, and everyone was happy. He was so embarrassed the best thing to say was nothing and I'm willing to wager he was never again guilty of that error. But it is still wise to not trust anyone too implicitly.

Once after that, also in a Cherokee Six, after departure and climb out from Fairbanks, I noticed the oil pressure indicator was down to the top of the yellow arc. We were just coming up on Big Minto Lake and knowing we could never make it back to the airport, I called the FSS to alert them of the situation. I told them I was sure we could never make it back to the airport, but I would try. In doing so, I would take the long way around by Murphy Dome road, just to keep a road underneath as a second choice, since there really wasn't a first choice anyway.

We had just reached a down wind position as though we intended to land on the road, when the propeller began to hunt (surge), telling me the oil pump had just lost prime, there was no more oil. I pulled the mixture into idle cut-off position, killing the engine, made a one hundred eighty degree turn which set us up nicely for a landing on the Murphy Dome Road. Traffic was very co-operative, there was none. We touched onto a very smooth and level stretch of the road but immediately began an ascent which became quite steep, especially if you are describing an airport instead of a road. When the forward motion ceased, it was impossible to hold the airplane in position with the brakes because the steepness of the road caused the airplane to rock back onto the tail cone. It was necessary to allow the craft to roll backward to keep the nose wheel on the ground. I was trying to steer with brakes, moving backward down hill. The nose bobbed up every time I touched a brake and back down when I released it. All this was done without rear view mirrors, so the reader can imagine the interesting tracks we made on the gravel road bed. I felt as long as I could see the road was straight ahead, the part I could not see must be straight behind.

We had six passengers in the airplane. Alan Starr was asleep in the rear seat. Even after we finally were able to come to a stop he did not awaken. Strange he should be the only one of the entire group to show any degree of hesitation about riding in the airplane after it was cleaned up, and the problem corrected.

I called the FSS and asked them to call Bachner's hangar on the phone, explain the situation, and ask them to send me a mechanic and some oil. I had a roll of paper towel in the airplane, so we removed the top cowling and cleaned everything we could in an attempt to determine from whence cometh the oil. Ed Keith arrived soon with the oil, but didn't understand we had lost it from — who knows where? He had assumed the filler cap had not been replaced, so he brought no tools. I suggested he go a quarter of a mile up the hill to where the White Alice Sight had a heavy duty shop and he could probably borrow some tools from one of the mechanics at the shop.

When Ed returned with the tools, Paul Hoysington, an FAA Inspector with a world of experience, was there. The three of us were all mechanics with considerable experience on this very engine, but we never determined the cause of the problem. Ed had already thought about everything I suggested may have caused the problem and employed preventive measures— before the occurrence.

I was wondering how I could discreetly suggest the original filling was sufficient to get us to Big Minto Lake and almost back to here, so if they would take the passenger in the two cars, I could probably make it back to the airport empty, on a full tank of oil. Paul suggested exactly that proposal, so I let him talk me into it.

While Ed was washing down the machine, one of the Manley Hot Springs passengers, Linda Boa, came up to me and asked, "Mister Gregory, are we going to be able to get home tonight?" I assured her we could, pointing to the other Cherokee sitting a couple parking spaces from the one we were flying. I kidded her that we always kept spares, spare starter, spare alternator, spare prop, spare engine, spare airplane, the works.

After flying back to the airport and washing down the entire engine compartment, windshield, and all other areas contaminated by the oil, the leak appeared to have healed up by itself. It was still full of oil and Ed ran it up hard a couple times with no indication of further leakage. We never did find anything, other than gremlins, to blame for this chapter.

The next problem with oil and a Cherokee Six was a different story. There was a fellow working at the hangar who really concerned me. I didn't like his work and found several things he had done in a dangerous manner. Several times it was necessary for someone else to redo his work. I couldn't see paying for that kind of workmanship. I quietly asked Mrs. Bachner to not let him work on my airplanes in the future. I had implicit faith in the rest of the crew, but didn't have the time or patience to worry about him. If he had seemed to be learning, I could have been a little more patient, but that didn't seem to be the case. That was the only time I ever made such a request.

One day I needed an oil change. They were very busy, so Mrs. Bachner had him change the oil and filter—about as simple a job as a person could be assigned. I had forgotten something and had to return to the airport. While there, I saw him putting the new oil into the engine. When we were ready to depart, I deliberately squelched the impulse to check the oil, thinking, "Good grief Gregory, give the man a little credit." We were also running just a little late. I did check the ground under the engine for leaks to assure myself he had closed the drain cock.

As we departed, darkness was just approaching, but we surely saw all that oil come over the windshield when lowering the nose to build a little airspeed. We went right on around to the left, landed, and came back into the fuel pump where a couple of rolls of paper towel and a few quarts of oil later, we were about ready to leave again. Mrs. Bachner realized I had returned and asked me what had happened. The office was full of customers, so I kept things quiet and short. I just told her, "It's nothing serious, but please don't ever let that guy work on my airplane again."

Just as we were loading up to leave, she came right out to the pump and wanted to know exactly what had happened. I told her I found the dip stick, filler cap combination laying across the cylinders, just as he had left it when he opened the filler tube to replace the oil. He hadn't even checked the oil level after the refill. I even told her why I hadn't checked on him, as I normally would have. The next morning when I came to town, he was no longer working there. I honestly think it was not only a favor to the aviation community, but quite probably to him as well. I guess he was also a representative of John Q.

The Pilots
✈

We enjoyed a special relationship with our pilots. They were all not only very professional in their approach to flying but the type of individuals with whom we enjoyed sharing dinner and an evening. They all had sufficient business acumen that we felt comfortable with their decisions made along the way during their trips. We deliberately kept the operation small in order to maintain closer control but allow pilots to make decisions based upon unforseen opportunities encountered during the day.

We spent very little money repairing even minor damage to aircraft. We were not anxious when a pilot was overdue for there was always a reason, not a problem. Neither I nor any of our pilots ever caused a passenger to wear as much as a band-aid due to our indiscretion. The company is still intact and has suffered nothing more than a minor accident. Most of the pilots are still flying and all are still living, with one exception, and his demise occurred pursuing his own interests.

Don Jonz flew for us only occasionally but I knew Don quite well. He was a very good pilot with a world of experience over much of the world. He was the grooming element for many of the local bush pilots after the regulations required all commercial pilots who carried passengers for hire at night, to have a current instrument rating. He flew for me on several occasions when it was necessary to have another airplane in the air and I didn't have a pilot available. Don never gave me a reason for insisting a flight plan be filed with paper and pencil, but he was adamant about the procedure. Never once did he allow me to file a flight plan by radio nor was I aware he ever broke his own rule, except on his last flight.

307

The enroute weather forecast, for the area through which he would be flying from Anchorage to Juneau, was for turbulence far beyond what would be deemed a comfortable ride. He was flying Nick Begich and Hale Boggs, both members of the U.S. House of Representatives.

On occasions a person must exercise extreme diplomacy when telling customers they just can't fly in the existing or forecasted weather. That is true especially when your customers are congressmen who feel their presence in Juneau by evening is a must which should override all problems or objections encountered. My thinking is a little psychology may have here come into play, especially if I had been the pilot.

In order to not offend my high priced customers, I would have told them the current and forecast weather reports were for an uncomfortable ride and we may not be able to make it at all. However, since the weather was so nice in Anchorage and they were so anxious to go, we could go take a 'look see' and come back to Anchorage if we were to determine the turbulence was too formidable. The idea, of course, is to take them into the turbulence and when their eye teeth begin to rattle *they* will make the decision to return to a safer clime.

After their disappearance, news reports stated Don had filed his flight plan *by radio*, thirteen minutes after take-off at Anchorage. Thirteen minutes puts one right on down the road in that particular airplane. This tells me that when they got out there a fair distance the turbulence was not as bad as had been anticipated so they continued. They never arrived in Juneau, nor did they report passing various stations where they would have normally made position reports. Don was not a timid person, nor was he secretive or reluctant to use his radios to request weather or make pilot reports of the conditions he was encountering, or make position reports along his path of flight.

No trace has ever been found of any wreckage nor has there been any serious clue as to the reason for their disappearance. Actually there is only one logical conclusion I can draw from the known events. They did actually, eventually, hit the turbulence reported. I think they hit it with such abruptness they lost a wing, or both wings, leaving them no time or opportunity to even call on the radio before disappearing into the ocean. I once saw an airplane that lost both wings and the engine simultaneously from one severe overstress. The occurrence was over land, providing enough evidence to make possible a careful scrutiny of the wreckage, and a determination of the cause.

There were reports that a fishing vessel heard Don call on the radio, but that doesn't even sound reasonable to me. Why would he be calling on a maritime frequency, even if he had one, if he could call on an assigned air to ground frequency, which he did have? He wouldn't even have an inkling whether or not anyone was listening, or heard him on a frequency that he otherwise never used.

There are no conclusions to be drawn but there is a good lesson to be learned. Sometimes diplomacy can be insidious also.

The necessity for diversion and recreation was very important, especially in the bush villages. A wise person, especially if he is a hard driver, will make his recreation and diversion totally different from his work. Our choice was snow machining or boating with the family. On a short term, hobby basis, I enjoyed rebuilding old guns and violins. The entire family were avid readers. My wife and girls were all proficient in various forms of needle craft, including knitting. Granny was always knitting something. Stephen kept Granny supplied with ptarmigan.

We held a Federal Firearms License to qualify as a legal dealer for guns and ammunition. I added gunsmithing to the license, with sufficient experience and machinist tools to qualify as a Browning Firearms dealer. It was not only an enjoyable hobby, I made it possible for many people to hunt with a rifle that had previously been relegated to the category of a souvenir.

I bought books on both gunsmithing and violin rebuilding and usually had a gun in buildup and a violin hanging from a beam in my bedroom, curing a fresh coat of varnish.

When the gun was completed, Stephen or one of the girls and I would use that as an excuse to go out to the garbage dump, which was on a high bluff overlooking the Yukon

River, and shoot for a while. When our kids shot in a turkey shoot in the springtime, we were assured of having turkey for dinner.

When a violin was finished to the best of my ability, I would call upon Harold Woods, an accomplished violinist, highly regarded at the Fiddlers Festival, to play for me. I would get across the room and listen and could make small adjustments to the instrument as he played.

Harold would tell people, "That Glenn Gregory can fix a violin better than anybody, and he can't play a note!" He was correct, at least, on the latter part.

The pilots never brought me violins to rebuild but almost every time one would return from one of the villages less often visited they would bring a rifle or pistol to repair. We eventually acquired a good stock of parts to replace those lost or damaged, but I tried to not allow it to be a pressure situation. Even though we were actually selling parts and making machined repairs, I tried to keep it on a hobby basis to reduce stress. I really enjoyed both the violins and the guns.

One fall we had an unusual amount of flying. It came suddenly and was unrelated, making it hard to tell how long the extra demand was going to last. At the time, we also did not have a regular pilot to help me.

The timing was perfect when the doorbell rang and Dr. Morrison, his wife Linda, and Steve Fry entered. After Dr. Morrison introduced me to Steve he proceeded to conduct some business with my wife. She took care of most of the transactions for the store and hunting and fishing licenses while the flying business occupied most of my time. It was after closing time, but we were fairly accommodating to those who needed special favors due to their time schedule preventing them from conducting their business during the regular day.

While my wife provided for the needs of the good doctor and his wife, Steve and I struck up a conversation which revealed he was a flight instructor. He had been instructing for the flight school on Fort Wainwright, a military base near Fairbanks, during the past summer. I asked him if he would be interested in flying a Cherokee Six for a few weeks until I could get caught up on the recently developed work at Lake Minchumina. *WOULD HE??*

I told him to come over in the morning and we would talk about it. The next morning, Saturday, we went out and flew around a little. I was very much impressed with his knowledge and ability. I told him we would make things final Monday morning. We would have to arrange for a check ride with an FAA inspector as they were becoming increasingly jealous of a new area of jurisdiction.

That night there was a party at the local Lions Club building. A typical low fog, peculiar to fall weather, prevailed. A low pressure weather formation was moving through the area making life rather miserable for all comers, except the migrating ducks. My wife and I agreed we had best get to bed early and get some sleep before we were awakened to take care of the Saturday night emergency we had come to expect whenever there was a big party in town simultaneous with bad weather.

I awoke when I heard the Cherokee take-off after midnight. My wife said it sounded like our airplane. She could usually recognize our airplanes as opposed to those like it operated by a competitor. I still don't know how she did it. The next morning, after Sunday School, we heard that Larry Nicholia had shot himself.

Larry was an adopted boy who lived just behind our house with his parents who were always into some sort of trouble, mostly due to over-consumption of alcohol. He was eighteen, and a common fixture around our house for about the last ten years. I was never aware of him drinking, he was very quiet. He was very much disturbed by the trouble so prevalent in his home. He always tried to protect his mother.

At this particular party, on the dance floor, his father was being abusive toward his mother. Larry tried to intercede in a pleasant way, but found his father's full wrath descending upon himself. Larry quietly left the dance floor, saying nothing to anyone.

I am convinced Larry went home and returned with the 30-06 hunting rifle fully intending to, once and forever, put a stop to his father's abuse of his mother.

Anthony Malemute, who had been sitting beside Larry earlier, decided to step outside for a breath of fresh air. He walked out to the bank of the Yukon River, smoking a cigarette, when he heard someone say, "Oh Hell, I got no reason to live anyway!" He started running toward the voice thinking someone planned to jump into the Yukon and perhaps he could deter them. He saw a large flash burn a hole in the darkness simultaneous with a deafening roar. A description of the scene, revealed by flashlight, would be too unpleasant for prudent indulgence. Anthony ran to the nearest telephone to call an ambulance. Larry was not dead!

Dr. Morrison was on call at the hospital. As soon as the nurses had Larry sufficiently cleaned to make an appraisal, a decision was made to take him to Fairbanks where better facilities were available.

Steve was a guest at the Morrison house, so the doctor had Linda awaken him, instead of calling me. They had to fly instruments all the way to town, but Steve was well-qualified to do the job, but it was a rather rude introduction to bush flying.

On the way to town Larry kept trying to feel of his face with his hands. Dr. Morrison assured him he probably would not be able to feel anything in his face as it would be rather numb for some time. He was trying to divert attention away from the fact that he had no face.

Larry was very short in stature. His arms were so short he had to tip his head so far back to get the rifle barrel under his chin and his finger on the trigger that the bullet had missed the brain but effectively removed his entire face, including his eyes. He could still hear....

In Fairbanks, the decision was made to send Larry on to Seattle for better treatment. Larry, however, adamantly refused to allow any surgery or any kind of further treatment.

Upon his return to Tanana, it was determined that effective conversation could be pursued, simply by phrasing everything in the form of questions that could be answered by a positive or negative shake of the head.

Reverend Timothy Sniffen talked with Larry at length and established, unequivocally, it was his wish to not live any longer. All intravenous feeding was stopped and Larry died on a Sunday morning, two weeks after the Lions Club party.

I waited until after Sunday School services to advise the family. Even though the outcome was inevitable, our daughter, Zoanne, was heartbroken. Larry had been so hopelessly confused and she was unable to help when he needed help the most.

It was his habit to come into the store, go to the back, sit at the desk and quietly watch people in the store, or through the back window. He seldom spoke more than a greeting. He never caused any concern. Looking back, it is easy to see little indicators that could have triggered our concern, but we missed them when they did surface. It is sad that he was unable to communicate with someone to avoid the tragedy. Perhaps none of us could have helped, but it would have been nice to try.

All of our pilots were conscientious and willing workers. All were trusted without reservation. Only one indicated an intense dislike for the two o'clock in the morning emergencies. I reminded him that he had chosen his profession and this all went with the pleasant sunshine and smooth flying. His attitude improved since he really understood most patients didn't actually choose to be transported in the middle of the night, in bad weather and turbulence.

The Big Surprise

❋
❋❋

The writing of history is a tedious undertaking. Unless a daily record is kept, events overtake those living right in the midst of exciting change to the extent the full realization of their importance is overlooked and can never be accurately recalled. Keeping a record helps impress more deeply upon the recorder that vast opportunities lie all around him, waiting to be developed. My experiences with keeping daily records, in the form of a journal, have been disappointing, to put it mildly.

We, along with many others, were not totally overwhelmed by the sudden discovery of vast North Slope oil deposits announced by British Petroleum. Having for years been aware of the presence of North Slope oil in huge quantities we were not excited enough to mortgage the farm and buy all the flying equipment available to take advantage of a new source of income. I felt there was some ulterior motive in the announcement, especially since oil companies, historically, try to keep quiet about such discoveries. Harboring our own suspicions about their reasons we kept all our equipment and property debt free.

In the beginning we turned down as many as three charters daily to the North Slope. We had no fueling provisions, no overnight arrangements, but most of all, we would have had to hire pilots who were unfamiliar with North Slope flying, or do it ourselves. We didn't like either option.

It was never my desire to be the world's richest man. We had a good operation giving us much gratification. Our greatest satisfaction was providing a service for people with faces and personalities, rather than some entity recognized mostly by a contract or a signature on a check. We felt secure

315

in the knowledge that taking good care of our customers would support us in return. When most of the North Slope flying came to an abrupt halt we just kept right on doing what we had been doing.

Some people went bankrupt. Some were able to idle their engines until the pipeline construction permit was issued. When the big push to build the pipeline and develop the vast oil fields again took precedence over practically every Alaskan thought, we were influenced considerably, but mostly in the form of what people call "fallout." Many of our "boys" worked on the Slope bringing big money home and buying things previously considered out of their price range. We sold everything from boats to baby shoes.

Earlier mention was made of the fact that we could not extend credit as we couldn't operate without immediate payment for goods sold. We just didn't have the reserve to replace depleted stock. As we developed a system and became better acquainted with the people, we knew who worked steadily, who had a pension check each month and thus were able to carefully extend a small amount of credit to those who proved reliable and regular in their payments. On occasion, when my wife would send out statements, someone, usually one of the older men, would come into the store and loudly proclaim, "You try to cheat me."

My little wife, the very personification of patience and honesty, would sit down with them and methodically go over their account, item by item. We used a cash register with a recording tape so we had a duplicate of every transaction. When she would come to the item in question and explain what it was, the customer would announce, "Oh, yes, now I remember." They would refuse to go over the rest of the statement, the misunderstanding was settled. An outgrowth of that scenario was to bring us the highest compliment of our association with those customers.

One fine summer day I landed in Hughes about a year into the pipeline construction period. Men from all the villages were working up north and returning home regularly for a couple of weeks time off. Occasionally they would return to

The Big Surprise

Fairbanks late in the day, then go straight to their village without leaving the airport at Fairbanks. This would leave them with as high as five or six thousand dollars in checks, but no money to spend. On this day a young man came up to me and gave me about four or five checks and asked me to cash them and bring him back the money. I took them to Fairbanks the next day and happened to have another trip to Hughes that same evening. I gave the money to my wife who held out enough to pay a small account he had in the store and put the rest in an envelope with an itemized explanation of what she had done.

When I arrived at Hughes he was there to meet me. As soon as I had incoming passengers cared for I walked over to him and handed him his money, telling him what the figures on the envelope represented. He just said, "Thanks," tore the envelope open and threw it into a garbage can. Without checking the figures on the envelope or counting the money, he put it into his pocket and went home. I could receive no higher compliment.

The Native Land Claims had finally been settled. The newly organized native corporations were now in possession of money they wanted to put to work helping build the country and provide jobs for the people for years to come. One day Mike Andon, who had been a classmate of our twins, approached me representing the Native organization at Tanana. He asked me about the wisdom of the Tanana organization starting a flying business.

I sat down and explained to him what all was necessary to acquire just the certificate to operate. I also pointed out they would have to advertise to convince the Department of Air Commerce another certificate holder was necessary to handle the business, and frankly it wasn't. Also I would oppose the proposal. To have any kind of an operation at all, even if they could secure the certificate, they would need someone who knew enough about the flying business to be able to recognize bad practices, unsafe equipment, and the most insidious error of all, infractions of rules. If such a person were available, he would need watching himself as he would probably be trying to maneuver into a position to establish his own business. He accepted that, and I am sure it was discussed in

317

their board meetings, in a couple of months he returned and wanted to know if we were perhaps interested in selling our business. I flatly told him, "No."

We had some friends who lived on base at Fort Wainwright. The husband was a military officer in charge of commissary and he did quite a large amount of business with Acord Co. Randy Acord, the owner, salesman, business manager, delivery driver, head of public relations, and anything else one may think of, was a Veteran of WW II. He had flown P-38's and a number of other cold weather test airplanes. After the war, he flew for Wien until his business began to require so much time it was necessary for him to spend full time with the enterprise.

One day during a conversation, my friend asked Randy if he knew me. Randy said he did. He asked him what kind of a pilot I was. Randy said, "Well, he is still alive!" My friend thought it was humorous enough to pass along to me. It put me to thinking.

While the statement was made in jest, it contained many possible appraisals. Here is a fellow who is very cautious, a fellow who is capable, who knows how to endure, who is very lucky, or, as Ernest Gann questioned, how has he escaped Fate as the Hunter? Or, perhaps, here is a person who realizes—it is Too Late Be A Hero.

We had a Cessna 180 I could land almost any place a person would wish. I really liked the airplane. It had a new engine and propeller, was in fair condition and was my hunting and fishing airplane; kept on the certificate just to handle the occasional emergencies requiring skis. The last two years we owned it, it didn't even make us enough money to pay for the liability insurance. It was the airplane I always used in the two o'clock in the morning, snowstorm rescue from an unlighted airport. Of course I had done it many times, but the law of averages eventually catches up to everyone. We reluctantly sold the airplane so we wouldn't have to make decisions to decline to fly foul weather emergencies. It was now a case of, "Sorry, I don't have a ski-equipped airplane." Nobody ever died as a result.

Now that same consideration could apply to the entire operation. We only had two girls left at home and any honest person was compelled to accept the fact that they would soon be following in the footsteps of their sisters. After they had all left home and changed their names, we would not be left with a great deal of pleasure in running the operation. We discussed the offer Mike had made earlier. One day I called Dorothy Jordan, who was a board member along with Mike, and told her we would discuss their offer.

They had, and offered to pay, cash money. With the pipeline work going full blast, us getting older, the slave labor all growing up and getting married—if we didn't accept their proposal, that would go down in the annals of Tanana history as the day when two darned fools met.

The ensuing weeks told me they were not ready to buy a business. They just didn't know how to run one yet. They had the intelligence, money, incentive, and tenacity, but lacked experience. We felt the prudent thing to do was hire a manager, take a vacation, and keep in close telephone contact with the manager. By springtime he would have enough experience to be able to run the operation independently, and they would have someone with experience upon whom they could rely. He would go with the business for one year, they then could follow the dictates of their own conscience.

Early the next spring, after the fur was sold, my father and I drove a truck load of groceries from Salt Lake City to Fairbanks, then barged it on to Tanana, truck and all, for the store. My wife and I later drove another load up, then relieved the managers, Sandy Hamilton and his wife, Stella, who spent the summer in the Arctic, enjoying the most glorious summer in years. Upon their return we went out to our cabin on the Novi River for the month of September. The weather still stayed beautiful. We picked berries by the five-gallon bucket, brought home a nice moose for our winter meat and enjoyed ourselves more than we had been able to for years.

A couple years earlier, having tired of sending Henry Kissinger around the world every year, we decided to invest in some real estate in Utah where Dolly, one of the twins, was now living, and could manage the rentals. We decided to take a look at a different part of the world, before making any final decisions. We saw enough to convince us people should always retire where their hair turns gray.

People would tell me they were so surprised to hear we had sold out. Especially when, for a while, we went to the land of fast foods, traffic jams, and football games. About all I could respond was, "No one was more surprised than I."

The stories told by London, Curwood, and Service would not begin to describe the wonder of this great land. Never could words convey the thrill of watching the breaking of day at four o'clock in the morning in the quiet of the Novi River. Since old age is the most unexpected thing that happens to man, he must be always on guard to reserve some time for being with his loved ones just to enjoy and appreciate his surroundings.

In his book "Heros of the Horizon," Gerry Bruder treats the lives of many older Alaskan pilots and mechanics. Among those are George and Virginia Clayton, Randy Acord, Sig Wien, Don Hulshizer, Jim Hutchison and a number of other well-known pilots and mechanics. During a book signing ceremony held Outside, there were eighteen of those members present. A boy of about eight years of age walked up to Jim Hutchison

Author and his family in 1985. From left to right: Myrna Lee, Lois, Dolores, Vicky, Lolita, Marquita, Author, Lena, Zoanne and Stephen.

and Randy Acord, who were sitting side by side at the time. His question was, "What do you have to do to be a Hero?" Hutch and Randy exchanged glances and it was obvious to Randy that Hutch wasn't going to commit himself so he told the youngster that if he grew up and survived a war, lived about fifty years as a successful participant in the aviation industry, and found himself treated as a character in a book, he would be a candidate for being a hero. Randy said the boy thought that over and walked away quite satisfied.

Well, after winning WW II, establishing a profitable trading business, flying over thirty-five years, much of the time at five thousand feet, after midnight, in a snowstorm, in an effort to perform a mercy mission, maybe it was time to turn things over to a younger generation. After all, perhaps it is "Never Too Late To Be A Hero."

Order Form

To order additional copies of:

Never Too Late To Be A Hero

please send $17.95 plus $3.00
Shipping & Handling,
Washington residents please include 8.2% sales tax.
Make check or money order payable to:

Peanut Butter Publishing
226 2nd Ave W.
Seattle, WA 98119
(206) 281-5965

If you prefer to use VISA or Mastercard, please fill in
your card's number and expiration date. Please circle
appropriate card.

□ □ □ □ □ □ □ □ □ □ □ □ □ □ □ □ □ □

Signature_____

exp. date_____
_____Copies @ $17.95 ea._____
$3.00 Shipping & Handling_____
Washington State residents add 8.2%_____
Total enclosed_____

Name_____
Address_____
City, State, Zip_____

Please list additional copies to be sent to other
addresses on a separate sheet.